Literature for the English classroom

Gweno Williams and Anita Normann (eds.)

Literature for the English classroom

Theory into practice

Second Edition

Copyright © 2021 by
Vigmostad & Bjørke AS
All Rights Reserved

First Edition 2013
Second Edition 2021 / 2. printrun 2022

ISBN: 978-82-450-3500-1

Graphic production: John Grieg, Bergen
Cover design by Fagbokforlaget
Typeset by Bøk Oslo A/S

All chapters have been peer reviewed.

Enquiries about this text can be directed to:
Fagbokforlaget
Kanalveien 51
5068 Bergen
Tel.: 55 38 88 00
email: fagbokforlaget@fagbokforlaget.no
www.fagbokforlaget.no

All rights reserved. No part of this publication may be reproduced, stored in a retrieval system, or transmitted, in any form or by any means, electronic, mechanical, photo-copying, recording, or otherwise, without the prior written permission of the publisher.

Contents

Introduction 9

1
Picturebooks 17
ANNA BIRKETVEIT

Introduction 17
Theoretical background 19
The dual audience 23
Key features 27
Examples of texts and analysis 34
Didactic ideas for the EFL classroom 48
Conclusion 52
References 53
Appendix: Worksheet for picturebook analysis 55

2
Poetry in the English classroom 57
MARTHE SOFIE PANDE-ROLFSEN

Introduction 57
Why poetry? 59
Teacher knowledge and resourcing poetry 63
Ways of reading poetry 68
Writing poetry 75
Conclusion 85
References 86

3
Global Englishes, diverse voices 91
LALITA MURTY AND BECK SINAR

Introduction 91
The status and role of English 94
Diverse classrooms need diverse texts 97
Two sample cases: Texts from the "Outer Circle" 98
Conclusion 111
References 112

4
Fairy tales 119
ANNA BIRKETVEIT

Introduction 119
Theoretical background 120
Key features of the genre 123
Coded content 125
Modern fairy tales 127
Didactic suggestions for the EFL classroom 129
Conclusion: Human footprints in civilisation 137
References 139

5
Novels for teenage readers 141
GWENO WILLIAMS

Introduction 141
Reading in the classroom 143
Teenagers as a distinctive readership 146
Characteristics and stylistic features of teenage fiction 147
Ways of reading in the classroom 160
Further didactic suggestions for class activities 163
Conclusion 165
References 165

6
Reading for everyone 169
LALITA MURTY, BECK SINAR, GWENO WILLIAMS, MARTHE SOFIE PANDE-
ROLFSEN, ANITA NORMANN AND TIM VICARY

Introduction 169
Section 1. Inclusive texts for the classroom 170
Section 2. Texts for differentiation 178

Section 3. Verse novels 182
Section 4. Extensive reading 186
Conclusion 191
References 192

7
Graphic novels in the English classroom 197
HEGE EMMA RIMMEREIDE

What are graphic novels? 198
Motivation 198
Literacy: the relationship between the visual and the verbal texts 199
Key features of graphic novels 200
Narrative storytelling 205
Graphic novels in the classroom 206
Graphic novel adaptations – beneficial for reluctant readers? 212
Classic text adaptations 217
Graphic novels online 224
Concluding remarks 224
Graphic novel suggestions: a resource list 225
References 226

8
Digital approaches to young adult fiction 229
ANITA NORMANN

Introduction 229
Digital and digitised literature 230
Teachers' professional digital competence 235
Action- and production-oriented approaches to working with literature 236
In the classroom 238
Final comments 250
References 251

9
Film in the English classroom 255
ANDY GORDON

Why film? 255
How to study film 256
Didactic rationale 258
Further suggestions 275
Conclusion 277
References 278

10
Drama in the English classroom ... 279
GWENO WILLIAMS

Introduction ... 279
The pedagogic value and demands of drama ... 281
Drama approaches for the primary classroom ... 282
Performing poetry ... 283
Pedagogic case study: "The Owl and the Pussy-cat" ... 284
Further pedagogic example: a Christmas nativity play ... 287
Lower secondary upwards: playscripts and drama adaptations ... 287
Introducing Shakespeare at secondary level ... 289
How to read Shakespeare – key moments or extracts ... 291
Conclusion ... 294
References ... 294

Index ... 297

Introduction

This second edition of *Literature for the English Classroom: Theory into Practice* has been fully revised and updated to align with the new Norwegian LK20 curriculum, including four new or expanded topical chapters. The chapters on writing and reading from Section Two of the first edition remain fully accessible online.

The positive reception of the first edition, edited by Anna Birketveit and Gweno Williams (2013), by students and teachers was very gratifying. This book was envisaged and designed to offer a series of stimulating chapters by expert authors on relevant aspects of teaching literature in the English subject in Norway. It was planned and produced to inspire and support teachers and trainee teachers of English in the classroom. The second edition has the same overall aim as the first: to inspire present and future teachers to draw creatively on a wide range of contemporary authentic English language literature as classroom material to motivate and engage learners.

The range of aspects covered has also been expanded in this second edition, edited by Gweno Williams and Anita Normann. Whilst all chapters have an up-to-date theoretical basis and argument, they also include ample suggestions for didactic approaches and a rich range of up-to-date resources, both paper and digital. The editors hope that this second edition, like the first, can also inspire and interest TEFL teachers and teacher training students across all the Scandinavian countries.

Our aim throughout has been to use literature in the widest sense, meaning authentic texts of many kinds, to bring creativity, energy, motivation and colour into the English classroom. Whilst textbook series can provide a sound learning base, they can rarely offer surprises, excitement or unexpected learning experiences. Here, a rich range of resources and approaches is recommended, which will do just that. As standards of spoken English and comprehension rise steadily in Norway, and the curriculum increasingly emphasises English as a mode of international communication, it is vital that learners have extensive access to engaging authentic contemporary texts of different types, both digital and traditional.

Our deliberately wide focus on global Englishes, encompassing literature from the UK, North America and beyond, offers teachers a multi-cultural and diverse range of materials to choose from. All the high-quality texts recommended in this volume are widely read by native speakers in different English-speaking countries, offering insights into varied English-speaking cultures and environments. Many authors and texts recommended have won prizes for the excellence of the writing or visual presentation. Nothing here is intended "just" for the classroom.

A book which would inspire and support both current and trainee English teachers in their classroom activity was the overarching vision of Anna Birketveit, lead editor of the first edition. As an experienced teacher trainer, Anna was passionate about English lessons in Norway being filled with energy, enthusiasm and excitement. She believed in the value and appeal of authentic books in the classroom, especially what she called the "treasure trove" of picturebooks in English, which she researched intensively during a precious sabbatical study term awarded to her at Cambridge University in the UK. Sadly, Anna died in 2018, just as we had begun to plan the second edition. She is greatly missed, but she was also absolutely committed to collaboration, with the idea that many contributors working together can produce the best results. She would have been delighted that British and Norwegian academics have continued to work together to revise and update the book she originally conceptualised. We hope that this second edition will also help readers to be successful and dynamic teachers who inspire learners, honouring Anna's original vision and her work to bring it about.

Anita Normann joined the editorial team as a valued colleague in 2019 and has been a knowledgeable, purposeful and cheerful tower of strength. Gweno Williams and Anita Normann have researched the new Norwegian school curriculum LK20, new topics for inclusion, and new publications. In this task, we have been supported by an additional six talented chapter authors. Some also contributed to the first edition; some are new. All have considerable successful experience of teaching trainee and in-service teachers as well as international students.

Classroom and curriculum are inextricably linked. Why teachers do what they do, and the ways they work in the classroom, are intrinsically based on the aims of a current curriculum. LK20 presents fewer and more open competence aims than its predecessor, LK06. LK20's aims address three core elements: *Communication*, *Language learning* and *Meeting with English language texts*. This change places greater emphasis on English as a language subject, on understanding and being understood. The advantage is that competent and imaginative English teachers can draw on appealing and interesting literary texts for many purposes, including to develop learners' communicative skills. This edition shares many concrete ideas on how to approach that aim, as well as suggesting a large number and variety of high-quality literary texts in different genres, from primary to upper secondary school levels. Cross-references between chapters indicate where a topic or author is discussed more than once. It is hoped this feature will encourage readers to explore the whole book rather than focusing on a single genre or chapter. Didactic suggestions are provided in every chapter and can be adapted to different grade levels as required.

A new feature of LK20 is that learners are permitted to choose texts based on their own interests. English teachers who are familiar with a variety of texts, genres and modalities will be best prepared to guide learners seeking interesting, self-chosen English texts. Many of the texts and genres suggested in this book represent alternative, relevant, authentic reading material for a range and variety of English language learners of varying proficiency levels. Since teachers in Norwegian schools have both freedom of methodology and freedom to decide which texts to work with in class, external inspiration and ideas can be very important. We hope this book will provide these for both novice and more established English teachers.

An important aspect of the core element *Meeting with English language texts* relates to intercultural competence. LK20 has added *multilingualism* to competence aims in English at all levels, a change which mirrors contemporary society and is closely linked to *multiculturalism*. Authentic texts written by authors who represent diverse Englishes and cultures can contribute powerfully to developing learners' intercultural competence. Diversity and inclusivity have been very important dimensions of our work on the second edition. Diversity principles have influenced the inclusion of a new chapter on Global Englishes, as well as informing the range of authors, texts and didactic activities recommended throughout the volume. Wherever possible, teachers are encouraged to extend their range and use texts originating from beyond Britain and North America in the classroom. Doing so will reflect the wider world, the diversity of English and the cultures and identities it expresses. Indeed, we hope that present and future teachers reading this book will experience a sense of raised awareness about diversity issues in the widest sense, and will also be inspired to use authentic literary texts when focusing on diversity in their English classrooms.

LK20 requires that all teachers, across subjects, continue to support learners in developing the five basic skills, including digital competence. This informs the second new chapter commissioned, which focuses on digital approaches to engaging with literature. Ways of exploiting and integrating digital technology and resources when working with young adult fiction are presented and discussed, with a number of exciting didactic suggestions.

Thus, two central elements of the new English subject curriculum have an additional emphasis in this updated edition, through two brand new chapters. All other chapters have been revised and updated with LK20 competence aims and suggestions for new literary texts and didactic ideas or through a renewed refocusing. A new poetry chapter puts additional emphasis on learners' active engagement and involvement. Chapter 6, "Reading for all", has a larger and more multi-faceted focus on reading for everyone, resulting from collaboration between several of the authors and considerably extending the range of the original "Extensive reading" chapter. Finally, all chapters from the first edition have been updated with the aim of reflecting the core values of LK20, such as diversity, inclusivity, digital competence and learners' active involvement in their own language learning.

The first edition was much commended and enjoyed for its colourful and striking visual illustrations. This feature remains, with new additions.

Chapters

Two chapters from the first edition are now available online. Anniken Telnes Iversen's chapter "Reading novels and short stories" and Barbara Blair's chapter "Reading and writing: Intertwined branches" can be found at www.fagbokforlaget.no/literaturefortheenglishclassroom

The second edition is organised as a single sequence of chapters, as follows:

Chapter 1, "Picturebooks", written by the late Anna Birketveit, with a wonderful selection of colourful illustrations, has minor updating by Gweno Williams for the second edition. The chapter offers a valuable overview of picturebooks as an important genre for readers of all ages, with helpful information about structure, logic and terminology. Ample picturebook examples and didactic suggestions are included.

In chapter 2, "Poetry in the English classroom", Marthe Sofie Pande-Rolfsen discusses creative approaches to both reading and writing poetry. The author's point of departure is that poetry is versatile, in the sense that it can be used to develop learners' basic language skills and their intercultural competence, as well as personal reading experiences and interpretations, in order to build critical and reflective learners for the future. The chapter explores poetry in a variety of ways, with many recommended authors and texts.

Chapter 3, "Global Englishes, diverse voices", written by Lalita Murty and Beck Sinar, addresses important perspectives related to globalisation and diversity. The chapter focuses on how bringing diverse voices and texts responsibly into the EFL classroom provides learners with opportunities to see both themselves and others in a global multilingual and multicultural context.

Chapter 4, "Fairy tales", by the late Anna Birketveit, has been updated by Gweno Williams. The chapter presents fairy tales as a genre, discussing why they are suitable as classroom material for English language learners. It suggests contemporary versions for the classroom, and didactic ideas.

Chapter 5, "Novels for teenage readers", by Gweno Williams, introduces a wide range of recent high-quality texts to engage and interest this important age group, together with didactic suggestions focused on learner independence and autonomy. This chapter also addresses the new LK20 requirement for English to include attention to life skills, health, democracy and citizenship.

Chapter 6, "Reading for everyone", was edited by Gweno Williams with contributions from five of the other authors. It deals with many aspects of reading, including diversity and inclusion, verse novels as a genre, extensive reading and recommended texts for differentiation which can enable reluctant or underconfident readers.

Chapter 7, "Graphic novels in the English classroom", by Hege Emma Rimmereide, presents and discusses graphic novels as a genre. Distinctive features are discussed and didactic ideas for working with graphic novels are presented. Several example texts for various levels are suggested, some of them new for this second edition.

In chapter 8, "Digital approaches to young adult fiction", Anita Normann presents ways of engaging with young adult fiction through digital technology. The chapter suggests approaches for working digitally with texts, or working with digital or digitised texts, within an action- and production-oriented approach to teaching literature.

In chapter 9, "Film in the English classroom", Andy Gordon discusses the interface between film and literature. The chapter's aim is to show teachers ways to facilitate and encourage the move from merely passive watching to being able to analyse, understand and critique. The updated chapter discusses three film adaptations, recommends several more and shares ideas for didactic approaches.

Chapter 10, "Drama in the English classroom", by Gweno Williams, explores the rich ways in which performance, drama and poetry can enable and develop increased oral proficiency, active learning, confidence and learner ownership of material and tasks, including when working on Shakespeare.

Note to readers

We use the term *learners* as a generic term for pupils and learners from all levels in primary and secondary school.

Acknowledgements

Both editors warmly thank all chapter authors for their hard work and commitment to this second edition. The editors also thank Maria Turøy, Andreas Konningen, Pernille Løfblad and Benedicte Lie, who were English students at HiB (now HVL) in 2013, for appearing in the cover photographs.

Gweno Williams has many colleagues to thank, especially from the Norwegian Study Centre at the University of York, where she has been professionally involved for nearly four decades, from guest lecturer to staff member. Professor Erik Tonning, Dr Beck Sinar, and Dr Lalita Murty have all been very supportive and encouraging of recent work on the second edition. Previous NSC Directors Guri Raaen, Kåre Rugesæter and Professor Tom Egan were also very helpful. In Norway, Dr Tale Guldal has been a consistently encouraging professional colleague and friend. It goes without saying that Anita Normann deserves a lion's share of the thanks; she has been a thoughtful, reliable, and conscientious co-editor whom it has been a pleasure to work with.

The final debt of gratitude and appreciation is owed to the late Anna Birketveit, who first envisioned this overall collaborative project and is much missed. We were close friends, as well as colleagues with a shared vision, for more than 20 years.

Anita Normann would like to thank lead editor Gweno Williams as well as Kristin Eliassen, at Fagbokforlaget, for the opportunity to take on the role as co-editor for the second edition. It's been a long but rewarding process. She would also like to express her gratitude to current and former student teachers from the PPU- and *lektor* programmes 8–13 in the Department of Teacher Education at NTNU, who continue to inspire her to further develop didactic approaches for working with young adult fiction in the EFL classroom.

1
Picturebooks

Anna Birketveit

Updated by Gweno Williams

Introduction

Picturebooks are a largely undiscovered treasure trove in EFL despite the fact that they are one of the most exciting and innovative types of authentic texts teachers can use. By telling stories just as much through pictures as through verbal text, they open the door to multiple constructions of meaning, and engage and challenge readers across the boundaries of age and reading skill. They draw on and develop learners' graphic as well as verbal skills and are thus in line with a new, broader understanding of literacy.

    The EFL potential of picturebooks lies in the fact that they have the merits of authentic texts but not their drawbacks. Firstly, by using picturebooks where the decoding of meaning is assisted by numerous pictures, the EFL teacher has access to authentic English without worrying about the learner coming across too many unfamiliar words. Schmitt (2010, p. 32) claims that readers need to know 98–99 % of the words in a text to be able to access its meaning, which clearly posits a challenge for the EFL teacher when using authentic verbal texts. In picturebooks, the pictures are just as important as the verbal text in conveying meaning. As the verbal texts of picturebooks tend to be quite short, readers are not put off by the longer texts usually found in authentic books. Thus, when reading picturebooks the EFL learner is assisted both by the pictures and by texts of manageable length. Moreover, picturebooks truly provide visual support for weak or reluctant readers. The learners have a choice in their meaning-making; they can rely mostly on the pictures or mostly on the verbal text or go back and forth between the two according to where their cognitive strength lies. Thus, picturebooks are excellent material for differentiation.

Secondly, picturebooks are deeply satisfying because they give EFL readers the often underestimated pleasure of reading whole stories. In some Norwegian classrooms there is over-reliance on the material provided by coursebooks (Drew, Oostdam & Toorenburg, 2007), where extracts of stories rather than whole stories are presented as reading material. This can be off-putting and contradict how we make sense of things. The concept of the hermeneutic circle established that we understand the parts in terms of the whole and the whole in terms of the parts, and that we go back and forth between parts and whole in our meaning-making. Rather than motivating the reader, extracts of stories may frustrate the reader in that the narrative desire (Penne, 2010) remains unfulfilled. Thirdly, the language of picturebooks was not made with EFL learners in mind, and tends to be idiomatic, rich, varied and suggestive. They are written for an audience of native speakers, and they are a far cry from the cautious, watered-down and often flat texts of EFL coursebooks.

Another very important asset of picturebooks is that children like them because many are witty and amusing and often defy reader expectations. These books possess unique potential to tell stories through different types of picture-text interaction. When pictures and text act together, the meaning is enhanced, becoming more than the sum of the individual parts. Humour often arises when a neutral verbal text has pictures that exaggerate or even contradict the verbal text. In *Princess Smartypants* by Babette Cole (1996), for instance, the suitor's effort to please the princess by taking her mother shopping evokes laughter when the picture shows him stumbling under heavy shopping bags while the queen herself sails in front looking at baggy undergarments (illustration 1).

Last, but not least, picturebooks are one of the most gratifying subjects to teach as little text and ample illustrations make the texts easily accessible. They are objects of art which can be looked at and enjoyed even without prior learner preparation. Exploring the paratext and story together with learners is very engaging. Picturebooks invite sharing, and it is in their nature to "generate *talk*" (Watson & Styles, 1996, p. 1). The learners can be encouraged to reflect on front and back covers, the title page, fonts, colours, layout, numbers and position of pictures, etc., and suggest what these aspects might add to the meaning. Award-winning authors such as 2009–11 Children's Laureate, Anthony Browne, borrow motifs and techniques from well-known artists. This opens up interesting possibilities for cross-curricular school projects between English and art. How satisfying it is to see the EFL learners integrating different skills and becoming small artists themselves, creating their own picturebooks where they make everything, the pictures as well as the English text, by themselves!

For younger learners, digital literature in the form of *picturebook apps* may be a good way to meet the English language. The aesthetic aspects of an app, related to visual-verbal arrangement, narration and interactive elements, are interrelated in a way which is not possible in a traditional picturebook (Schwebs, 2014). These and other non-linear features may make book apps more available for language learners of all proficiency levels. Many primary school learners in Norway now have their own iPads, with free access to various apps and games.

Theoretical background

Picturebooks are an art form that relies on the interdependence of verbal and visual representation. This is often referred to as iconotext. According to Nikolajeva and Scott (2006: 1), the main function of the pictures is to describe, whereas the main function of the verbal text is to narrate. As opposed to the situation when picturebooks first emerged in the first half of the 1900s, when pictures supported the verbal texts and were thus subordinated to the words (Anstey & Bull, 2004), the pictures today are just as important as the verbal text. According to Lewis (1990), the interplay between words and images and illustrative text makes picturebooks a supergenre. Picturebooks require readers to fill the "gaps" in the texts. According to Iser's reader response theory (1980), the text is a co-construction of the author and the reader. The reader has to take active part in the meaning-making of the text, and each reader brings to the text his or her personal experience on which meaning is constructed. The complexity and multi-layered nature of many modern and postmodern picturebooks make them engaging and excellent material for creating competent readers.

It is useful to distinguish between picturebooks and illustrated books. According to Gregersen (1974), words and pictures are equally important in picturebooks whereas the text can exist independently of the pictures in an illustrated book. Nikolajeva and Scott hold that in an illustrated book "the pictures are subordinated to the words" (2006, p. 8). An example is Roald Dahl's *The Witches* (1983).

A picturebook must have at least one picture on each double spread (opening). If it has fewer, it is categorised as an illustrated book. How much verbal text one finds in a picture book can vary considerably. There are books which apart from the title consist exclusively of pictures, such as Tan, *The Arrival* (2006) (age: 12-adult), and there are picturebooks with quite a lot of verbal text such as Trivizas, *The Three Little Wolves and the Big Bad Pig* (1995) (age: 10–16).

As *The Arrival* consists of pictures only, the readers are freer to construct their own stories, whereas in *The Three Little Wolves and the Big Bad Pig* the story is given by the verbal text and enhanced by the funny pictures. From a language-learning point of view, the verbal text extends and challenges the language skills of learners in a more demanding way than can a book with no words.

Traditionally, picturebooks have been thought of as a children's genre, as expressed in the most commonly used definition of picturebooks:

> A picture book is text, illustrations, total design; an item of manufacture and a commercial product; a social, cultural, historical document; and foremost an experience for a child. As an art form it hinges on the interdependence of pictures and words, on the simultaneous display of two facing pages, and on the drama of the turning page.
>
> *(Bader, 1976: 1)*

Illustration 1. From *Princess Smartypants* (1996) by Babette Cole. © Published by Puffin 2005. Reprinted by permission of Penguin Books Limited.

It is still the case that many picturebooks are for young children, and have little text and few accompanying pictures. Here the goal is often to teach the child something, such as opposites, numbers or the names of clothes or animals. One such book is Carle, *The Very Hungry Caterpillar* (1974), where the little caterpillar literally eats its way through different fruits on different days of the week, emerging as a beautiful butterfly in the end. However, due to social and cultural developments and huge technological improvements, we are now living in a world that increasingly values and relies on the visual. Thus, in the past few decades, picturebooks have undergone considerable development with regard to both content and form, blurring the boundaries between books for children and adults, and making the notion that picturebooks are exclusively for young people difficult to maintain (Anstey & Bull, 2004). Thus humorous picturebooks, for example, where the illustrations

She suggested to Prince Fetlock that he might like to put her pony through its paces.

Illustration 2. From *Princess Smartypants* (1996) by Babette Cole. © Published by Puffin 2005. Reprinted by permission of Penguin Books Limited.

in particular often exaggerate or serve as a counterpoint to the verbal text, will appeal to older children, and some of them to young adults. *Princess Smartypants* is an example of such a text. Regardless of what the princess's suitors try to do to win her heart, as shown through amusing exaggerations in the illustrations, she rejects them all. Her notion of living happily ever after is shown in the last illustration, where she lies on a sunbed with a fizzy drink, surrounded by all her pets (illustration 2). This reversed fairy tale of a modern, mischievous princess questions traditional female roles and looks at the notion of being a princess with irony. This picturebook and others will be discussed in more detail below.

Today, there are picturebooks that one could argue are not for children at all, but rather for young adults and adults. Shaun Tan says about his own picturebooks that "they are not created with children in mind, but rather a general audience. I see each book as an experiment in visual and written narrative, part of an ongoing exploration of this fascinating literary form" (Tan, 2012). *The Wolves in the Walls* (Gaiman, 2004) is a picturebook that is scary both in content and form and is not really intended for children. The story is told through nightmarish descriptions and dramatic images that enhance the story as well as help the reader and EFL learner decode the story.

Picturebooks can include any genre, such as fairy tales, information books, nursery rhymes, pop-up books, comics, newspapers and nonsense. As picturebooks traditionally tend to be based on fairy tales, they have retained a subversive element often expressed in a mismatch or counterpoint between words and pictures. The first British picturebook to truly explore this element was Hutchins, *Rosie's Walk* (1968), which on the surface seems to be a story of a hen walking about the farm calmly and happily and coming back home in time for dinner unaware of any danger. The pictures, however, show the fox chasing her on every picture, culminating in his crashing into a beehive and being chased over the hills. Studying the illustrations, we see that we are dealing with two stories in counterpoint: the hen's and the fox's.

Picturebooks can help stretch and challenge the EFL learner and give valuable and authentic language and culture input. Both reluctant and eager readers will benefit and feel challenged by this genre. Firstly, the many different types of picturebooks make them interesting at many levels in school and for readers across age groups. As Hestenes (2009) points out, picturebooks for young children are often based on fairy tales and repetition, which appeals to children but also functions well for foreign language learning where frequency is seen as a very influential factor in acquiring new vocabulary (Schmitt, 2010). Picturebooks for young children often aim at teaching specific vocabulary such as numbers, the days of the week or the names of fruits. This is also the kind of vocabulary EFL beginners first start learning. Secondly, through extensive reading of authentic picturebooks, pupils can increase their vocabulary and acquire narrative skills as shown in a study by Birketveit and Rimmereide (2012) carried out in an EFL class of Norwegian 11-year-olds.

Authentic picturebooks for older children (9+) usually have more complex texts than traditional Norwegian EFL coursebooks for this age range. For example, one of the picturebook texts discussed later in this chapter, *George and the Dragon* (Wormell, 2003/2002) (illustration 3), actually uses the astonishing number of 19 different adjectives in the course of quite a short (281 words) verbal text. This is a very high number compared to a traditional coursebook text such as "Giant Soup" (*Stairs 6*, 2007) which has 425 words but uses only 9 different adjectives. In the first text there are many low-frequency adjectives that most likely will be new and thus stretch the learner, whereas the coursebook text almost exclusively uses high-frequency adjectives (*big, hot, cold, warm, no good, better*), which the learners are likely to know anyway. Without a doubt, the high lexical density of authentic picturebooks in general provides much more stimulating and challenging language input for the EFL learner than traditional coursebook texts tend to do.

Additionally, picturebooks also meet aims after years 2 and 4 in LK20 regarding encounters with and reading of English-language literature, including picturebooks (Norwegian Directorate for Education and Training, 2019/20). In particular, they provide learners with visual learning material. Moreover, good picturebooks are objects of art and can inspire discussions and reactions to art, and hence be worked with also at lower secondary level. By comparison, see chapter 7 for ways in which graphic novels combine pictures and text.

The dual audience

Traditionally, picturebooks were created with an intended audience of adults reading the books to children. Picturebooks, more than any other narratives for children, tend to address dual audiences. The concept of dual address was established by Wall (1991) and refers to texts that address both the young and the adult reader. There will be meanings constructed both by the child and the adult reader. They understand and notice things differently, but each is an "expert" reader at his or her level. Thus, books that appear simple may actually turn out to be quite complex content-wise, and can thus appeal to more mature EFL learners without seeming too childish. Writer and illustrator Anthony Browne, who was appointed UK Children's Laureate in 2009, writes

He could burn down a forest

Illustration 3. From *George and the Dragon* (2003) by Chris Wormwell. © Published by Jonathan Cape 2002, Red Fox 2003, 2019. Reprinted by permission of Penguin Books Limited.

for dual audiences. His picturebooks have recurring themes and distinctive leitmotifs such as gorillas, brick walls, rainbows and anthropomorphic tree trunks. Moreover, he borrows abundantly from the surrealist painter René Magritte. In *Voices in the Park* (2001), for instance, hats appear as lamp posts and symbols of power throughout the story. The surreal aspects of the story are further underlined by trees which, on closer examination, turn out to be giant fruits or berries, or by trees floating in the air, thus underlining the dog's energy as it races through the park.

with a blast of his fiery breath.

Wash discusses how Browne's picturebooks demand co-authoring from the young reader as well as the adult. In *Voices in the Park*, "(t)he young reader can respond to the visual jokes which the author has scattered throughout the text, but must then puzzle over their contribution to the narrative. The adult reader can enjoy the somewhat humorous references to class in the stereotyped names of the characters, and then reflect on the impact on the global narrative" (1993, p. 17).

There was a very friendly dog in the park and Victoria was having a great time. I wished I was.

Illustration 4. From *Voices in the Park* (2001) by Anthony Browne. © Published by Doubleday. Reprinted by permission of The Random House Group Limited.

Key features
The paratext
The paratexts of picturebooks are particularly interesting to explore from a cross-curricular perspective between the arts and English, where the goal may be having the pupils produce their own picturebooks.

The concept of paratext refers to format, fonts, types of paper (e.g. glossy, neutral) and types of illustrations being used (e.g. drawings, paintings, photography, collage), title page, covers and endpapers. These qualities can be said to be paratextual as they can trigger the reader's expectations and meaning-making. According to Genette (1997) as cited by Mjør (2010), paratexts are visual and iconotextual "fringes" and "thresholds" to a text, and they are usually tightly integrated with the theme of the picturebook. Paratexts are authors', illustrators' and publishers' spaces for securing a successful reception of the book.

The cover is what normally first attracts a reader to a book. It has the potential to create reader expectations and motivation. A particular episode of importance is usually shown on the cover. Whereas the front cover tends to be iconotextual (picture and verbal text together), the back cover often has written information about the story and the author. Taking *Voices in the Park* as an example, the front cover draws the reader into the story through the alley where the girl and the boy gorilla stand at the bottom, the boy handing the girl a flower. This episode is repeated inside the story when they have to part. The surreal aspects of the story reveal themselves already on the cover as the trees of the alley have autumn colours whereas they are surrounded by bright green and summer with two dogs leaping about. The title stands out, especially the word *Voices*. The back cover is a bright green field in the park, and in addition to information and excerpts from reviews, there are pictures featuring an empty bench and the red hat that reoccurs on the title page and end papers as well as being part of the lady gorilla's (the boy's mother) outfit. The hat functions as a motif and symbol of power in the story.

Many endpapers are white, but according to Mjør (2010) there is an increasing tendency to use these empty spaces for paratextual functions or decorations. In Browne's picturebooks, the endpapers often repeat and underline the theme of the story. Thus in *My Dad* (2001) and *My Mum* (2006), the endpapers are the patterns of the father's and the mother's dressing gowns.

The story may start on the title page, where there is often a small picture of the narrative which is repeated inside the book. In *Voices in the Park*, the red hat floating below the title points forward to the climax of the story, where the angry upper-class female gorilla tells the "scruffy mongrel" to get away from her dog and instructs her son to go home and part from his newly found "rough-looking" friend. This is reminiscent of film, where the story often starts before the title and credits. In addition, the title page normally contains the book title, the name of the author and illustrator and perhaps the publisher. This picturebook will be discussed in more detail below.

The formats of picturebooks can relate to story development. Thus, the horizontal format or landscape format is often preferred for portraying movement, whereas vertical or portrait format is usually best suited for portraying single episodes. According to Birkeland and Mjør (2012), the small, square "peek-a-books" signal that they are for toddlers, and horizontal formats are used in books about journeys or development such as *The Very Hungry Caterpillar*.

Fonts can play an important part in picturebooks both on the cover and inside the book. In *Voices in the Park*, where the four characters' voices appear in different fonts, the adult voices have larger, more streamlined print with the working-class male's voice in bold. The children's voices appear in informal-looking print, with the working-class girl's voice in bold. The paper used in picturebooks can be neutral but may also be glossy, thin or thick, or have a special structure.

It seems to be a more or less established picturebook convention that pictures are on the recto (the right-hand page) and the text on the verso (the left-hand page). The verso is also called the home page, and the recto the adventure page. Home is safe but boring, and away is exciting but dangerous.

Pictures can have frames, or they can bleed into the environment. Framed pictures create a sense of detachment, whereas pictures without frames invite the reader into the narrative. Picturebooks often use the presence and absence of frames within the same book to create this dynamic. Unlike film, pictures can have blank spaces, called negative space, around objects and characters. The effect is to direct focus to particular details of the picture and leave out others.

The iconotext and the new literacy

The iconotext in picturebooks is highly innovative and creative, and skilled readers and EFL learners need to be familiar with its conventions and devices to fully appreciate it. Barthes (1977) distinguishes between *anchorage* and *relay*. Images can have multiple meanings and interpretations and *anchorage* occurs when the text is used to support one of these meanings. *Relay* occurs when the text adds meaning, and both text and image work together to elicit meaning. The narrative strategy of picturebooks differs from that of verbal stories in several ways such as in portraying setting and movement; in perspective, plot and characterisation; and in using intertextuality. Chapter 7 also discusses the terms "relay" and "anchorage" in graphic novels.

Setting

According to Nikolajeva and Scott (2006), images are *mimetic*: they communicate by showing, whereas words are *diegetic*: they communicate by telling. Thus, images are best at communicating space, whereas words best communicate time and causality. There are ways of showing time visually as well, such as clocks, calendars and the sun or moon indicating time of day.

The setting can be described by words, by pictures or by both. However, a picture can describe the setting very accurately. In words, the description is selective, and it takes a large number of words to say approximately the same as one picture. As Nikolajeva and Scott point out, "a description is one of the signs of the narrator's presence in the text" (2006, p. 61). Certain things are highlighted for the reader to notice, whereas others are left out. However, with pictures there is no narrator, and therefore pictures are non-manipulative, giving the reader the freedom of interpretation. Like a camera, pictures can give panoramic views, long shots, medium shots and close-ups (illustrations 5 and 6). The sad face of the gorilla in *The Zoo* (Browne, 1994) is as intimate and heart-breaking as any film close-up.

Illustration 5. From *The Zoo* (1994) by Anthony Browne. © Published by Julia MacRae. Reprinted by permission of The Random House Group Limited.

Illustration 6. From *Where the Forest Meets the Sea* (1988) by Jeannie Baker.
© 1987 Jeannie Baker. Reproduced by permission of Walker Books Ltd, London SE11 5HJ www.walker.co.uk.

Movement
Movement is shown through blurs, motion lines, simultaneous succession, and distortion of perspective. Movement is conventionally decoded from left to right, and movement and causality can also be indicated by clever use of verso and recto of double spreads. The situation is often established on the verso, and by looking at the recto the reader can see the change or development of action or plot.

Perspective
One often speaks about *who tells* (narrative voice) and *who sees* (point of view) in a narrative text. Examining perspectives or point of view in picturebooks can be very interesting. The narrative voice is found primarily in the verbal text. Point of view can be reserved for the pictures, and it is fixed as the reader sees the pictures from a certain perspective imposed on him or her by the artist. It cannot be changed. In Monks's *Aaaarrgghh, Spider!* (2004) (illustration 7), the reader shares the spider's upside-down point of view of the family from her place on the ceiling, which is very funny. As is typical in children's literature, there is a first-person narrator. But the pictures do not have a first-person narrator, as that would mean that the narrator would never be seen in the picture but would just be seeing things happening. It is interesting to notice whether the characters are perceived from below, and thus appear powerful, or from above in an inferior position, or neutral, on an equal level with the viewer (reader or one of the characters or both).

Plot and characterisation
According to Nikolajeva and Scott, picturebooks are plot-oriented rather than character-oriented and there is little room for character development. Characters tend to be static. Characterisation is mostly external and accomplished through the pictures. "(P)sychological description, though it can be suggested in pictures, needs the subtleties of words to capture complex emotion and motivation" (2006, p. 83). Picturebooks do not usually have a lot of verbal text, so there is little room to develop complex psychological characters. However, feelings can be revealed through facial expressions, position on the page, tone and colour.

Intertextuality
Intertextuality means verbal or visual representations that refer to other texts or works of art, such as Anthony Browne's reference to René Magritte in *Voices in the Park*. According to Nikolajeva and Scott, "the allusion only

Illustration 7. From *Aaaarrgghh, Spider!* (2004) by Lydia Monks. First published by Egmont UK Ltd, and used with permission from HarperCollins Publishers Limited.

makes sense if the reader is familiar with the hypotext (the text alluded to)" (2006, p. 228). Sometimes intertextual references are culturally dependent. Reversed traditional fairy tales demand intertextual competence. If the original story is unknown, the reader may fail to perceive the irony and humour in stories such as *Princess Smartypants*. To fully appreciate the picturebook *The Incredible Book Eating Boy* by Oliver Jeffers (2009), the reader needs to know the different types of books that exist and the materials they can be made of.

Examples of texts and analysis
Princess Smartypants

This is a funny story with enhancing interaction of pictures and verbal text. It is intertextual throughout, drawing on and challenging the reader's knowledge of traditional fairy tales and stereotypical characters. The first double spread shows Princess Smartypants in front of the TV with all her pets and rubbish lying on the floor. The verbal text reads, "Princess Smartypants did not want to get married. She enjoyed being a Ms." As in a traditional fairy tale, her suitors are given impossible tasks that they cannot accomplish. An example is when Prince Grovel takes the Queen shopping, and the illustration shows him on all fours stumbling under heavy shopping bags while the Queen herself is looking at baggy pink knickers (8th double spread). Only Prince Swashbuckle faces up to the challenge by bringing three elephants along on the Queen's shopping spree. So will he get the Princess as his reward? Not at all. She gives him a magic kiss which turns him into a gigantic toad and sets her free to continue doing exactly as she pleases. Most of the humour lies in the cartoonlike and exaggerated illustrations. The slugs eating her garden, for example, are massive, and Prince Swashbuckle rides blindfolded and with arms crossed "for miles on her motorbike". *Princess Smartypants* is a humorous picturebook which challenges traditional gender patterns.

Voices in the Park

As mentioned above, this picturebook has four narrators, or voices as they are called, thereby presenting different perspectives on the same event. The narrators are all gorillas, but of different social positions. The first voice is a well-off lady who takes their Labrador, Victoria, and her son, Charles, for a walk in the park. The second voice belongs to a working-class, unemployed male gorilla who takes his daughter, Smudge, and their dog to the park. The third voice belongs to Charles, and he is clearly miserable and feels constrained. He envies his dog, who has a lot of fun with another scruffy-looking dog. When a

Albert's always in such a hurry to be let off his lead. He went straight up to this lovely dog and sniffed its bum (he always does that). Of course, the other dog didn't mind, but its owner was really angry, the silly twit.

Illustration 8. From *Voices in the Park* (2001) by Anthony Browne. © Published by Doubleday. Reprinted by permission of The Random House Group Limited.

Illustration 9. From *Voices in the Park* (2001) by Anthony Browne. © Published by Doubleday. Reprinted by permission of The Random House Group Limited.

Illustration 10. From *Voices in the Park* (2001) by Anthony Browne. © Published by Doubleday. Reprinted by permission of The Random House Group Limited.

girl (Smudge) asks him to play, he cheers up. Charles's mother is concerned about social etiquette and behaviour; she finds both dogs and other gorillas in the park frightening and rough and tells Charles to come home with her. The fourth voice belongs to Smudge and presents the events from her point of view. It is clear that Charles's mother seems very unfriendly. In illustration 8 her red hat rises above her head and breaks through the contour of the picture, her eyes are small and threatening, and her mouth shows only the broad lower lip. She is pictured from below in a position of power, and part of the accompanying text underlines the unfriendliness of the lady: "its owner was really angry, the silly twit".

One of the striking features of the book is the change of colours and seasons according to the characters' moods. All the colours change when Charles has fun, and suddenly it is the middle of the summer. When the working-class family walk to the park, it appears to be winter. They walk past a brick wall where Santa Claus is a beggar (illustration 9). His sign says, "Wife and millions of kids to support." Mona Lisa in the painting leaning against the wall appears to be crying. The father feels better on his way home having been cheered up by Smudge, and this time Santa Claus is dancing and so is Mona Lisa (illustration 10). In Smudge's account of what happened in the park the colours are bright, and it appears to be summer throughout, underlining her happy mood.

Where the Forest Meets the Sea

This story has an Australian setting and presents a strong ecological message about the destruction of the natural environment and the Aboriginal way of life. Through beautiful collage illustrations, constructed from natural materials and giving a three-dimensional effect, it shows the journey of a young boy exploring a rain forest in North Queensland together with his father. It looks into the past as well as the future through faded/blurred pictures emerging in the middle of realistic pictures. An example is the last double spread hinting that this untouched spot in the rain forest will be turned into a tourist resort with hotels, sun-beds and swimming pools, all pictured in blurs (illustration 11). The accompanying verbal text underlines the sad prospect through the boy's question: "But will the forest still be here when we come back?" The picturebook won several awards and became the Australian Children's Picture Book of the Year Honour Book in 1988.

The Incredible Book Eating Boy

In 2007, this picturebook became the Irish Children's Book of the Year. Its open-endedness, comic-strip features and metafictive layers make it postmodern. It tells the story of Henry, who literally eats books, but becomes too smart and has to stop. He now turns to reading books, and they are "so good", which shows how Jeffers plays on the sense of the word *good* both as a taste of food and as an intellectual experience. The final joke is the bite on the back cover that shows that Henry now and then falls back into his old habits (illustration 13). The title on the front cover sounds like a circus introduction: "Oliver Jeffers presents The Incredible Book Eating Boy", and the fonts in different sizes, shapes and colours are reminiscent of a circus poster. On some of the letters there is what looks like newspaper print in French. In the bottom left-hand corner is a boy with an enormous mouth devouring a pile of books. Most of the verbal text of the story is in old-fashioned typewriting, but Jeffers plays around with different fonts sometimes in handwriting throughout the story and thus draws attention to individual words. The text can be anywhere and in several places on the page. On closer inspection, the background of the illustrations turns out to be discarded pages and covers of books – often schoolbooks. Notebooks and maps, prints from encyclopedias, maths books, and dictionaries, and so on are partly or wholly visible as background on the pages (illustration 12). This draws attention to books as material artefacts made of different materials. "(I)t is a book about books, which is made of books and paper, it is a source of humour, but it is also thought-provoking and raises questions about the status of books as sources of learning and knowledge as well as potentially ephemeral objects" (Arizipe, 2010, p. 77). Some of the books the boy is eating have recognisable titles, such as *Moby Dick*. Clearly, *The Incredible Book Eating Boy* is a picturebook which appeals most to readers with intertextual competence.

The Wolves in the Walls

This picturebook was written by the British author Neil Gaiman and illustrated by Dave McKean (also British); its intended audience seems to be young adults or adults. Gaiman is the author of several science fiction and fantasy books[1] and also of cartoons – all of which we can find traces of in *The Wolves in the Walls*. Through dramatic images and nightmarish descriptions such as "In the middle of the night when everything was still, she heard clawing and gnawing, nibbling and squabbling. She (Lucy) could hear the wolves in the walls, plotting their wolfish plots, hatching their wolfish

---

1 Chapter 7 discusses Gaiman's novel *Coraline*.

Illustration 11. From *Where the Forest Meets the Sea* (1988) by Jeannie Baker.
© 1987 Jeannie Baker. Reproduced by permission of Walker Books Ltd, London SE11 5HJ www.walker.co.uk.

But will the forest still be here when we come back?

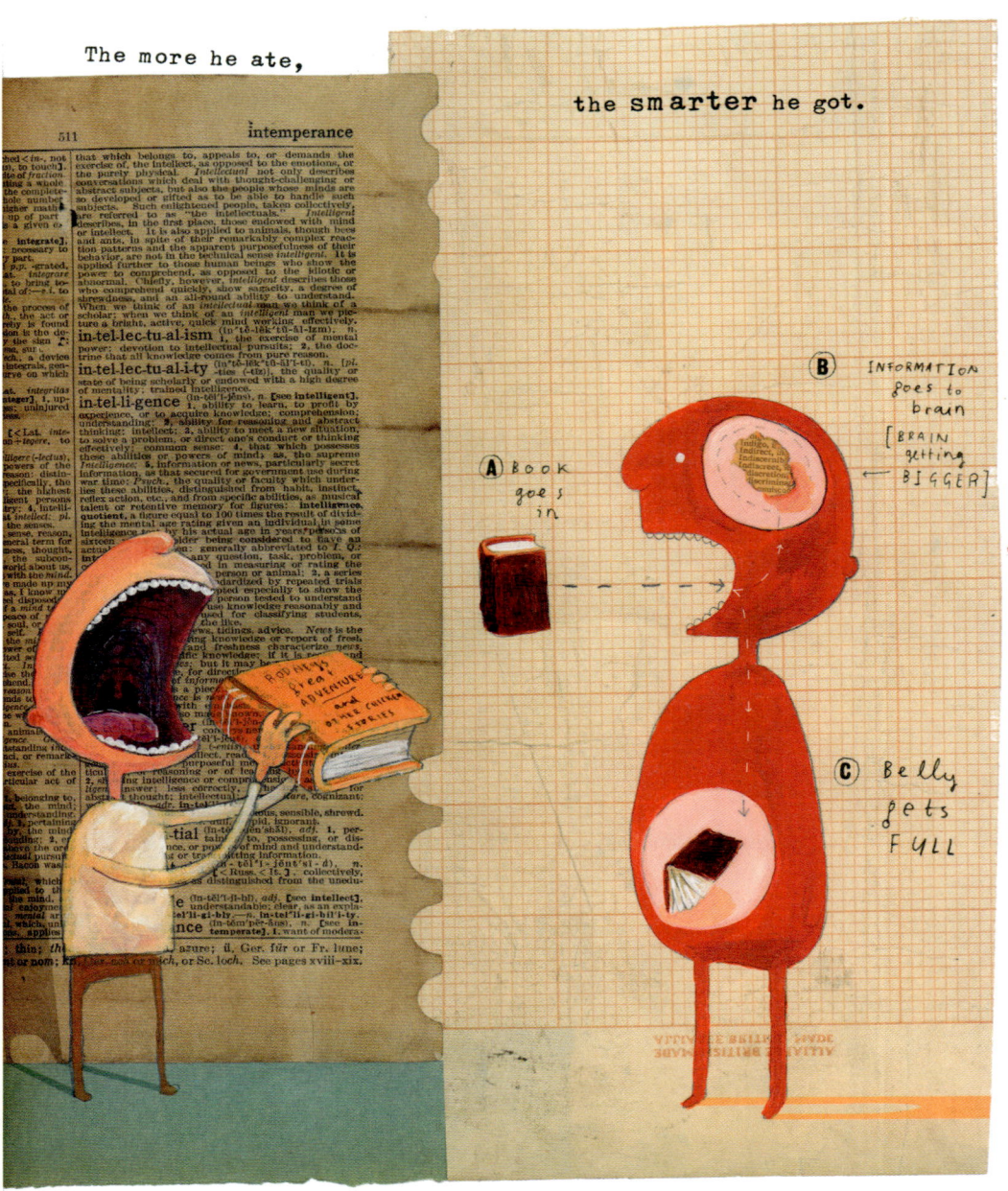

Illustration 12. From *The Incredible Book Eating Boy* (2009) by Oliver Jeffers. Reprinted by permission of HarperCollins Publishers Ltd © 2006 Oliver Jeffers.

Illustration 13. From *The Incredible Book Eating Boy* (2009) by Oliver Jeffers. Reprinted by permission of HarperCollins Publishers Ltd © 2006 Oliver Jeffers.

schemes" (illustration 14), it tells the story of how young Lucy's belief that there are wolves in the walls comes true. The wolves do come out of the walls, and the family have to go and live in a shed in the garden until "the people" come out of the walls and the wolves flee. Gaiman claims he got the idea for the book from his little daughter, who declared that there were wolves in the walls. The book requires an alert reader with visual and verbal reading skills, as the book's images combine photographs, paintings and

Illustration 14. From *The Wolves in the Walls* (2004) by Neil Gaiman.
© Dave McKean 2003, text © Neil Gaiman 2003. Bloomsbury Publishing Plc.

drawings. The fonts have different sizes and shapes, and single words and phrases stand out. The front cover shows Lucy drawing a wolf on the wall and a pair of eyes in a photograph looking out through the eye holes. The title of the book appears to be in Lucy's handwriting. The book has a very strong visual impact, almost like a film, as the images fill entire pages either as single images or as sequences of pictures on the same page. The verbal text is printed on the images.

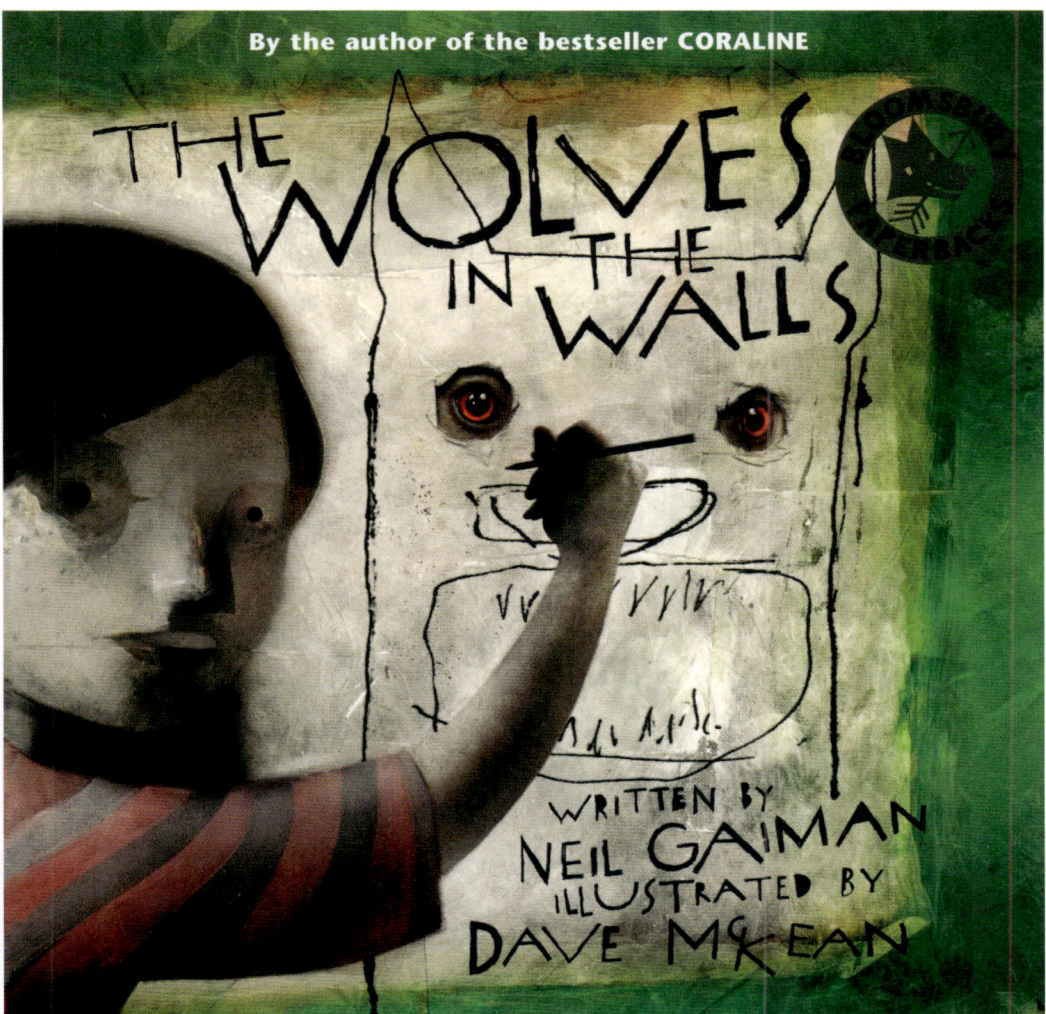

Illustration 15. From *The Wolves in the Walls* (2004) by Neil Gaiman.
© Dave McKean 2003, text © Neil Gaiman 2003. Bloomsbury Publishing Plc.

Multi-cultural examples

A growing number of rich and sensitively written British and American multi-cultural picturebooks are being published, reflecting migration and increasingly diverse societies. The best of these actively feature and celebrate different nationalities, languages, cultures and dress.

For example, *My Two Grannies* (2007) by Floella Benjamin tells the story of Alvina, with one grandmother from England, and one from Trinidad. The two grannies are supposed to look after Alvina when her parents go on holiday. This proves to be no easy task as they each have distinct cultural preferences in terms of food, music, stories and games. It only works when Alvina suggests they take turns looking after her and learn to appreciate each other's differences. The book is bright and colourful; Margaret Chamberlain's illustrations communicate affection. In addition to language learning, it can be used as background material and a source of inspiration when discussing cultural differences and intercultural tolerance. A picturebook like this one can also be linked to the core element "Meeting with English-language texts" in LK20, where it is stated that "English shall help the pupils to develop an intercultural understanding of different ways of living, ways of thinking and communication patterns" (Norwegian Directorate for Education and Training, 2019/29). Sissel Lea Heggernes discusses a number of ways in which picturebooks can be used to foster intercultural learning (Heggernes 2020).

Other British publications include the deceptively simple and universal *My name is not Refugee* (2017) by Kate Milner, endorsed by Amnesty International; *The Colour of Home* (2002) by Mary Hoffman, about leaving Somalia for the UK; and two lively comparative overviews of children's lives globally: *Around the World We Go* (2012) by Margaret Wise Brown and *One Day: Around the world in 24 hours* (2013) by Suma Din. The American picturebook *The Name Jar* (2001) by Yangsook Choi depicts an imaginative, even-handed, child-centred response to the disorientation of moving from Korea to the US. The Australian picturebook *Leaving* (2000) by Katrina Germein is noteworthy both for its striking illustrations by indigenous artist Bronwyn Bancroft, and for its respectful bilingual usage of the Aboriginal language Kriol, ultimately giving all characters from different cultures voice and status.

Illustration 16. From *My Two Grannies* (2007) by Floella Benjamin and Margaret Chamberlain. Frances Lincoln Children's Books, copyright © 2009. Reproduced by permission of Quarto Publishing Plc.

Didactic ideas for the EFL classroom
Teaching potential of picturebooks referred to:

Text	EFL level	Language	Teaching potential: 1. picture-text interaction 2. theme 3. story building 4. cross-curricular
Carle, E. (1974). *The Very Hungry Caterpillar*	beginners/ lower primary	vocabulary: fruits and foods, days of the week, numbers plural and singular of nouns past tense of *eat* and *be*	1. pictures support the verbal text, interactive 2. metamorphosis 3. simple narrative structure 4. natural sciences, arts
Monks, L. (2004). *Aaaarrgghh, Spider!*	lower primary	commands: out you go, look at me, watch me dance/wash, etc action verbs	1. pictures support and enhance the verbal text and highlight perspective 2. pets, family life, belonging, fear 3. ends with a humorous twist 4. natural sciences, arts
Hutchins, P. (2003). *Rosie's Walk*	lower primary	vocabulary about farms prepositions past tense of *go* and *get*	1. counterpoint 2. life on a farm, danger, luck and misfortune 3. different stories and perspectives 4. natural sciences
Browne, A. (2001). *Voices in the Park*	upper primary/ secondary	vocabulary about dog walking and keeping vocabulary about going to the park and playing past tense commands: *sit, come here* dialogue	1. enhance different perspectives and points of view, colours and mood, fonts 2. social class, child–adult 3. home–away pattern 4. arts, physical education
Wormell, C. (2003). *George and the Dragon*	upper primary	vocabulary about dragons, English food and customs, vocabulary of politeness adjectives	1. enhancing, humorous 2. conflict, the weaker getting the upper hand 3. descriptions, fairy tale pattern 4. arts, Norwegian, home economics

Cole, B. (1996). *Princess Smartypants*	upper primary / secondary	vocabulary of accomplishing tasks: *stopping the slugs eating her garden, feeding the pets etc* idioms past tense	1. enhancing, humorous 2. gender roles 3. reversal of traditional fairy tale 4. drama
Trivizas, E. (1995). *The Three Little Wolves and the Big Bad Pig*	upper primary / secondary	idioms, past tense	1. enhancing, humorous 2. danger, the weaker outsmarting the stronger 3. repetition, reversal of traditional fairy tale 4. arts and crafts, drama
Baker, J. (1988). *Where the Forest Meets the Sea*	upper primary	vocabulary of Australian birds and animals vocabulary related to the rain forest plural of nouns present tense	1. collage illustrations, blurred visions of past and future 2. exploring nature with your father, Australian rain forest, Aborigines, ecology and the future 3. description and observation 4. arts, natural science, history, geography
Gaiman, N. (2004). *The Wolves in the Walls*	secondary/ young adults	vocabulary of suspense: *fled, huddled, clawing, gnawing, rustling* vocabulary of house and garden dialogue past tense	1. enhancing use of photography, collage, paintings and drawings 2. nightmares, fear, prediction 3. creating atmosphere and suspense 4. arts, music
Jeffers, O. (2009). *The Incredible Book Eating Boy*	upper primary/ secondary	vocabulary about books past tense, comparison of adjectives	1. postmodern intertextual references 2. the value of books/knowledge 3. humour and fantasy 4. arts
Benjamin, F. (2007). *My Two Grannies*	primary	vocabulary of children's activities and games, food, music, fairy tales vocabulary of politeness suggestions, appreciation dialogue, past tense	1. pictures support and enhance the verbal text 2. multiculturalism and tolerance of cultural difference 3. conflict and solution 4. social sciences, home economics, music

How to use picturebooks in the EFL classroom
Wormell, C. (2003) *George and the Dragon* **(age: 9+).**
This picturebook contains 15 double spreads, mostly filled with fantastic illustrations with a line of verbal text at the bottom of each page. In 281 words, it tells the story of the evil dragon who lived in the castle wall and terrified people, but had one big secret.

A. Have the learners reflect on the iconotext by posing some questions, for example
What do you notice about the pictures?
What do you think the significance of this is?
What do you notice about the verbal text?
What do you think the significance of this is?

(Translated from Bjorvand and Lillevangstu, 2007, p. 111)

B. Have the learners focus on specific language points
A striking feature of the text is the repetition of adjectives to create atmosphere: "Far, far away in the high, high mountains in a deep, deep valley in a dark, dark cave …" but the large number of different and challenging adjectives used is also noticeable, such as *mighty, fiery, monstrous, fierce, draughty, previous, inconvenient, miserable, cosy…* Such a focus on vocabulary aligns well with an LK20 competence aim after year 2, stating that learners will be able to "listen to and explore the English alphabet and pronunciation patterns through play and singing" (Norwegian Directorate for Education and Training, 2019/20). Furthermore, the text teaches collocations, for example "with a sweep of his monstrous wing", "Which was a pity", "the nearest cheese shop was miles and miles away". Below are some teaching ideas focusing on collocation and the use of adjectives.

MATCH THE ADJECTIVES WITH SUITABLE NOUNS

mighty	cave
fiery	owner
monstrous	furnishings
fierce	mouse
draughty	hole
previous	dragon
inconvenient	tail
miserable	wing
cosy	breath

CLOZE TEST
Copy a part of the verbal text and remove some of the adjectives, asking the pupils to fill in suitable adjectives either from a list below the text or freely.

C. Building suspense and creating stories
Ask the pupils to read the story and underline words and phrases that create atmosphere and build suspense. Discuss how these phrases make them feel. Ask the pupils to write the beginning of an exciting story and to comment in pairs or groups on each other's suggestions. Ask them to rewrite their beginnings. Make the pupils aware that each story usually has a conflict of some sort for which the hero or heroine seeks the solution. Ask the pupils to continue their stories by describing a conflict and its solution. Talk about and give the pupils examples of how stories can end. Ask them to finish their stories. Have the pupils illustrate their stories by drawing or painting themselves, cutting out pictures from newspapers or magazines, or using photographs.

Learners making their own picturebooks (age: +/−11)
A cross-curricular project between the arts and English

Making their own picturebooks can be enjoyable for learners at all levels in school and challenge their creative skills as well as enabling them to practise the new literacy of combining visual and verbal skills and understanding. The ideas below have been developed with learners aged 11 and above in mind, but they can be adapted to different levels. At 11 + and above one can expect learners' verbal competence to be good enough to make the picture–verbal text interaction work.

It is important that the learners trust the teacher and dare to tell their stories. Talking about picturebooks and looking at picturebooks should be part of the preparation. The teacher can make learners aware of the different ways pictures and text can interact. The learners can look at how smaller and bigger pictures alternate throughout the picturebook, and talk about what is the significance of this. What are the purposes of long shots and close-ups or illustrations of certain details in the narrative? The learners can be asked to reflect on the use of colour, format and fonts. They can be asked to look at the cover, title pages and endpapers. They can be asked to look at what part of the narrative is told by the pictures and what part by the text. They should be reminded of the different parts of a story such as setting, characters, conflict, climax and resolution, and they could be asked to reflect on what the pictures do best and what the text normally does best. And above all, learners need starting points and ideas for stories. The class can make a picturebook and a narrative together, or they can each make individual ones. These can be well-known fairy tales with a twist, or modern fairy tales. Other ideas could be *A special friend, A dream, Hairy monsters, The friendly dragon, The bad princess, Goodbye Thomas/Sandra, The birthday party, My brother/sister, Spider-man gets lost.*

THE ACTUAL MAKING OF THE OBJECT
1. The learners should make a decision about what kind of format they want the book to have (square, rectangular, or perhaps a circle or a triangle).
2. They need to decide what kind of binding the book will have: sewn, stapled or just folded.
3. They need to decide what kind of material they want to use: paper, fabric, illustrations.
4. They need to decide what the covers, the title page and the end papers will look like.

Some of the classroom activities suggested in chapter 7 may also work well with picturebooks.

Conclusion

As the selection of texts referred to in this chapter shows, picturebooks cover a wide range of different types of texts on a variety of themes, and they carry huge potential in the EFL classroom. The exciting interaction of pictures and verbal text makes them fun and engaging reading material for learners across age groups, and the readers need to draw on their visual as well as their verbal skills in decoding the texts. The texts are usually shorter than other types of authentic materials, and pictures on every double spread enable EFL learners to understand the stories despite the presence of unfamiliar words. As authentic texts, the language of picturebooks is often rich and complex, and picturebooks can challenge and motivate the learners in other ways than traditional coursebooks do. They represent excellent material for extensive reading, and should be a natural part of the teaching material offered to EFL learners. By supplementing the coursebook material with authentic picturebooks, the learners will have an exciting choice of texts to read.

References

Primary texts

Baker, J. (1988[1987]). *Where the Forest Meets the Sea*. Walker Books Ltd.
Benjamin, F. (2007). *My Two Grannies*. Frances Lincoln Children's Books.
Browne, A. (1994[1992]). *The Zoo*. Red Fox.
Browne, A. (2001[1998]). *Voices in the Park*. DK Publishing.
Browne, A. (2001[2000]). *My Dad*. Picture Corgi.
Browne, A. (2006[2005]). *My Mum*. Picture Corgi.
Carle, E. (1974[1969]). *The Very Hungry Caterpillar*. Picture Puffins.
Choi, Y. (2001). *The Name Jar*. Dragonfly Books.
Cole, B. (1996[1986]). *Princess Smartypants*. Puffin.
Dahl, R. (1983). *The Witches*. Puffin.
Din, S. (2013). *One Day: Around the World in 24 Hours*. A&C Black.
Gaiman, N. (2004[2003]). *The Wolves in the Walls*. Bloomsbury Publishing Plc.
Germein, K. (2000). *Leaving*. Roland Harvey Books.
Hoffman, M. (2002). *The Colour of Home*. Frances Lincoln Ltd.
Hutchins, P. (2003[1968]). *Rosie's Walk*. Red Fox.
Jeffers, O. (2009[2006]). *The Incredible Book Eating Boy*. Harper Collins.
Milner, K. (2017). *My name is not Refugee*. Barrington Stoke.
Monks, L. (2004). *Aaaarrgghh, Spider!* Egmont.
Tan, S. (2006). *The Arrival*. Arthur A. Levine Books/Scholastic.
Trivizas, E. (1995[1993]). *The Three Little Wolves and the Big Bad Pig*. Mammoth Reed International Books.
Wormell, C. (2003[2002]). *George and the Dragon*. Red Fox Books.

Secondary texts

Anstey, M., & Bull, G. (2004). The picture book. Modern and postmodern. In P. Hunt (Ed.), *International Companion Encyclopedia of Children's Literature*. Vol 1: 328–339. Routledge.
Arizipe, E. (2010). "All this book is about books". Picturebooks, culture and metaliterary awareness. In T. Colomer, B. Kummerling-Meibauer & C. Silva-Díaz (Eds.), *New Directions in Picturebook Research*, Routledge.
Bader, B. (1976). *American Picturebooks from Noah's Ark to The Beast Within*. Macmillan.
Barthes, R. (1977). The rhetoric of the image. In R. Barthes & S. Heath (Eds.), *Image, Music, Text*. Fontana Press.
Birkeland, T., & Mjør, I. (2012). *Barnelitteratur – sjangrar og teksttypar*. Cappelen Damm AS.
Birketveit, A., & Rimmereide, H.E. (2012). Does reading stories enhance language learning? In A. Hasselgreen, I. Drew & B. Sørheim (Eds.), *The Young Language Learner: Research-based Insights into Teaching and Learning*. Fagbokforlaget.
Bjorvand, A.M., & Lillevangstu, M. (2007). Ord + bilde = sant. Om arbeid med moderne billedbøker. In M. Lillevangstu, E.S. Tønnesen & H. Dahll-Larssøn (Eds.), *Inn i teksten – ut i livet. Nøkler til leseglede og litterær kompetanse*. Fagbokforlaget.
Drew, I., Oostdam, R., & van Toorenburg, H. (2007). Teachers' experiences and perceptions of primary EFL in Norway and the Netherlands: A comparative study. *European Journal of Teacher Education*, 30(3), 319–341.
Genette, G. (1997). *Paratexts. The Thresholds of Interpretations*. Cambridge University Press.

Gregersen, T. (1974). Småbørnsbogen. In S.M. Kristensen & P. Ramløv (Eds.), *Børne- og ungdomsbøker: Problemer og analyser* (pp. 243–271). Gyldendal.

Heggernes, S.L. (2020). Using picturebooks for intercultural learning. In M. Dypedahl & R.E. Lund (Eds.), *Teaching and Learning Interculturally* (pp. 112–129). Cappelen Damm Akademisk.

Hellekjær, G.O. (2005). *The Acid Test. Does Upper Secondary EFL Instruction Effectively Prepare Norwegian Students for the Reading of English Textbooks at Colleges and Universities?* (Doctoral thesis.). University of Oslo.

Hestnes, H. (2009). Picture books in the ESL classroom. *Språk og Språkundervisning, 3*, 4–9.

Iser, W. (1980). The reading process: A phenomenological approach. In J.P. Tompkins (Ed.), *Reader-Response Criticism: From Formalism to Post-Structuralism* (pp. 50–69). Baltimore and Johns Hopkins University Press.

Lewis, D. (1990). The constructedness of texts: Picture books and the metafictive. *Signal, 62*, 130–146.

Mjør, I. (2010). I resepsjonens teneste. Paratekst som meiningsberande element i barnelitteratur. *Barnelitterært forskningstidsskrift* [Nordic Journal of ChildLit Aesthetics] Vol 1. http://www.childlitaesthetics.net/index.php/blft/article/view/5856/6618

Nikolajeva, M. (2006). Word and picture. In C. Butler (Ed.), *Teaching Children's Fiction* (pp. 106–151). Palgrave Macmillan.

Nikolajeva, M., & Scott, C. (2006). *How Picturebooks Work*. Garland Publishing.

Norwegian Directorate for Education and Training. (2019/2020). English subject curriculum (ENG01-04). https://www.udir.no/lk20/eng01-04

Penne, S. (2010). *Litteratur og film i klasserommet. Didaktikk for ungdomstrinnet og videregående skole*. Universitetsforlaget.

Schmitt, N. (2010). *Researching Vocabulary: A Vocabulary Research Manual*. Palgrave Macmillan.

Schwebs, T. (2014). Affordances of an App. *Barnelitterært Forskningstidsskrift, 5*(1), DOI: 10.3402/blft.v5.24169

Thorsen, C., & Unnerud, H.D. (2007). *Stairs 6* (pp. 122–125). Cappelen.

Tan, S. http://www.shauntan.net/books.html

Wall, B. (1991). *The Narrator's Voice. The Dilemma of Children's Fiction*. Macmillan.

Wash, S. (1993). The multi-layered picture book. In P. Pinsent (Ed.), *The Power of the Page. Children's Books and Their Readers*. David Fulton Publishers Ltd.

Watson, V., & Styles, M. (1996). *Talking Pictures. Pictorial Texts and Young Readers*. Hodder & Stoughton.

Further reading

Beckett, S.L. (2012). *Crossover Picturebooks. A Genre for All Ages*. Routledge.

Salisbury, M., & Styles, M. (2012). *Children's Picturebooks: The Art of Visual Storytelling*. Laurence King Publishing Ltd.

Sipe, L.R., & Pantaleo, S. (2008). *Postmodern Picturebooks. Play, Parody, and Self-Referentiality*. Routledge.

Appendix: Worksheet for picturebook analysis

PICTUREBOOK ANALYSIS

Title:

Verbal text:
- central idea, tone, mood
- imagery, exaggerations, puns
- vocabulary, structures, grammar

The object:
- front and back covers
- titlepage and endpapers
- size, format, fonts, colours
- frames or not
- interaction of pictures and verbal text

Setting:
- space
- time
- movement

Perspective:

Plot:

Characterisation:

Intertextuality/symbols:

Themes:

Audience:

2
Poetry in the English classroom

Marthe Sofie Pande-Rolfsen

Introduction

SNAPSHOTS
celebrating Nikki Giovanni

people forget…poetry is not just words on a page…it is…
a snowflake on your tongue…a tattoo on the inside of your arm… a *dashiki* and a *kaftan*…
tripping down the streets of Lincoln Heights…shouting from the hills of Knoxville, Tennessee…

poetry is…barbecue…cotton candy…purple skin beets from Daddy's garden…
blues… the Birdland jazz club…Sunday morning gospel… chasing justice…freedom…

poetry is remembering the things that matter… the ones you love…

when night comes softly…like ripples on a pond

By Chris Colderley[2]

---

2   From Alexander, K., Colderley, C., & Wentworth, M. (2017). *Out of Wonder: Poems Celebrating Poets* (E. Holmes, Illus.). Candlewick Press, p. 9.

As this poem suggests, poetry is more than just words – it is about personal experiences and memories, "snapshots" of life. A poem can also express culturally specific experiences, "a *dashiki* and a *kaftan*", and it offers a space for sharing and remembering, for performance and engagement, as well as for provocation and excitement. Poetry is active, and "like ripples on a pond" it moves us – physically, emotionally and intellectually. Approaching poetry in the classroom should therefore also be active, personal and thought-provoking; it should engage with all the senses and become a gateway for learning about oneself and others.

Unfortunately, poetry teaching practices can often be quite traditional, with a focus on elements such as rhyme scheme, poetic device or looking for main themes (Hestnes, 2012; Coats, 2013). Learners might also be taught there is only one "right" interpretation to a poem's message. Styles (2010) notes that "it is a discouraging truth that technical discussion of poetry puts off not just some readers, but also those who should be inspiring the young – the teachers" (p. xiv). This is further problematised by Coats (2013), who states that teachers (as well as student teachers) often express anxiety connected to reading poetry, not because they do not like reading poetry, but because they are concerned with not *understanding* it (p. 128). This worry is connected to a traditional view of poetry as something elitist or as the "most exalted form of literature" (Pinsent, 2016, p. 89) where only "experts" are able to interpret it (Coats, 2013). Sadly, such views prohibit many teachers from reading and enjoying poetry, as well as including it in their classrooms, and according to Pinsent (2016), there seems to be an "all too prevalent fear of poetry among teachers, which [stands] in the way of quality presentation in the classroom" (p. 89). However, as Coats (2013) explains, if we perceive poetry not as this "high genre", but as part of literature and culture for children, we can examine what poetry means to us, and what poetry *does* to us, rather than what poetry might be about. Poetry teaching should therefore be experiential and performative, as well as flexible, since a poem is not a "static text to be interpreted, but […] a dynamic set of processes within individual human minds and bodies" (Pullinger & Whitley, 2016, p. 315).

"Working with texts in English" is one of the core components of the *English Subject Curriculum*, and learners are expected to engage with literary texts throughout all the different grade levels. The curriculum states that already after year 2 the learners should "learn words and acquire cultural knowledge through English-language literature for children" (Norwegian Directorate for Education and Training, 2019/20). Learners at all levels are expected to listen to, read and talk about texts, and to acquire language and cultural knowledge through texts. For example, after year 4, learners are expected to be able to "read and talk about the content of various types of texts", and after year 7, to "listen to and understand words and expressions in adapted and authentic texts". After year 10 they should be able to "read, interpret and reflect on English-language fiction, including young people's literature", and after VG1, general studies, they should "read, analyse and interpret fictional texts in English" (Norwegian Directorate for Education and Training, 2019/20). Since the *English Subject Curriculum* does not specify any particular genres, it allows both teachers and learners the freedom to choose texts. For the EFL classroom, poetry is both accessible and versatile, and it can serve as authentic texts that represent a variety of voices from different cultures, providing learners with the chance to listen to, read and discuss these texts – reflectively, openly and critically. Learning through and with poetry can thus offer insight into the English-speaking world and develop learner's linguistic, communicative and intercultural competencies, as well as enhance their reading motivation and ability.

This chapter intends to explain some of the main benefits of using poetry in the EFL classroom, before offering several creative, playful and active approaches to show how poetry can engage learners of all ages in different ways. Several examples of activities and strategies for reading and writing poetry will be outlined, alongside a variety of resources and recommendations for teachers and learners to use and explore in and outside of the classroom.

Why poetry?

The value of poetry for the EFL classroom stretches from linguistic benefits to cultural and affective benefits. When asked what they believed to be some of the benefits of using poetry in the EFL classroom, a group of student teachers[3] answered the following:

- Poetry is a good way to experience language
- Poetry shows that language is playful
- Poetry is a way to express thoughts and feelings
- Poetry can raise interest in language and literature
- Poetry can motivate pupils to read

---

3   From MGLU1105 (English 1 (1–7) module 1), spring 2020, at the Norwegian University of Science and Technology (NTNU).

- Poetry can help practise pronunciation
- Poetry can develop deeper understanding of words
- Poetry can be used to improve grammar
- Poetry can be used to learn about other cultures
- By reading poetry, learners can be inspired to write their own poetry
- Poetry is performative
- There is poetry for all levels

And the list could go on. Further attention will be given below to language learning, literary appreciation and performance.

Poetry and language learning

Perhaps the most obvious benefit of working with poetry in the EFL classroom is language learning, whereby poetry can be helpful for practising pronunciation and other prosodic features (such as intonation, pitch, tempo and volume). Bland (2015) states that "[u]sing poems and rhymes with young language learners ensures that pronunciation and prosodic features […] are taken up pleasurably, with singsong ease; and when the rhyme is used as a ritual, it is an expression of the classroom community" (pp. 150–151). Further, she highlights that "[t]hrough salience, repetition and exaggerated prosodic features in performance, the latent structures, lexical patterns and grammatical units within playful language can stimulate the emergence of grammar" (Bland, 2015, p. 149). Poetry can also function as an aid to memory, especially when the poems include rhymes, rhythm and repetition, and it can aid learners' phonemic awareness. Poetry offers learners authentic language that often includes functional chunks, as well as formulaic sequences, which in turn provides important linguistic input in the classroom (Bland, 2015). By introducing poetry at an early age, language is presented as playful, humorous and pleasurable (Coats, 2013).

Furthermore, poetry offers rich and varied language of high quality, which means that "in poetry, simple language can express very complex ideas; thus, although the text may be relatively easy to read, the ideas conveyed can be challenging" (Hestnes, 2012, p. 72). This combination is appropriate when teaching a foreign language, because the language might not present itself as too much of a challenge for the learners, but challenging ideas "can make the reading worthwhile" (Hestnes, 2012, p. 72). This is further emphasised by Simecek and Ellis (2017), who state that "poetry offers a heightened and more complex twofoldness of communicative content than can be found in ordinary language use" (p. 105). One level is understanding the words and sentences within the poem, but another level is understanding how words work together as a complex whole and how these words affect the reader (i.e. how the poem is experienced) (Simecek & Ellis, 2017, pp. 104–105). This is relevant to the language classroom, since language comprehension is a common concern and there is often a need to cater for learners' somewhat limited language proficiency. However, with poetry, it is possible to engage with these two levels of communication, because many poems written with simple, repetitive and seemingly easy vocabulary express complex ideas and offer a space for reflection and engagement.

Poetry as literature and art

Poetry is an important literary genre, and by reading and sharing poetry, teachers can introduce and expose learners to a community of readers and writers of poetry within the English-speaking world. Poems are primarily quite short texts (although there are also many longer narrative poems) and are therefore easy to include in any lesson since they require little time to read. Simecek and Ellis (2017) also argue for the use of poetry *as* poetry, since it can offer a rich aesthetic experience of something "that is active, reflective, and open-ended" (p. 108). Poetry can thus increase learners' interest in both language *and* literature, motivating them to read more, and stimulate a joy of reading. According to Wiland (2019), in order to create a lasting interest in poetry, "the teacher must help to make the student into an autonomous and confident reader, so that [literature] can work *for* the classroom reader, not against her. Only then will literature become a valuable means of personal growth and language development" (p. 275). She further argues that the challenge of teaching literature in the EFL classroom "cannot be ascribed to the students' lack of cognitive curiosity, but to the fact that the student readers are not given time to process their reflections properly and become confident readers" (Wiland, 2019, p. 291). The teacher must therefore make room for learners' own reflections and experiences of the poetry, rather than focus on "rote learning of interpretations conveyed by the teacher" (Wiland, 2019, p. 291). Each individual reader responds differently to a poem, and poetry is therefore affective, as emphasised by Simecek and Ellis (2017).

Furthermore, poetry can make demands and compel the reader to question the world, the people in it, and the culture they live in. According to the *English Subject Curriculum*, texts from the English-speaking world should provide learners with "knowledge and experience of linguistic and cultural diversity" and through reflecting upon and critically evaluating texts "the pupils will develop intercultural competence [...] [and they] shall build the foundation for seeing their own identity and others' identities in a multilingual and multicultural context" (Norwegian Directorate for Education and Training, 2019/20). Fenner (2011) notes that literary texts are not just relevant for acquiring cultural knowledge, but also serve as cultural meetings and promote cultural participation (pp. 41–42). Poetry, as a literary text, represents authentic and personal voices in society, and in order to develop intercultural competence among learners, not only must they learn *about* cultures, but also *through* them (Fenner, 2017, p. 377). This is done when reading authentic texts not merely as "instruments to learn about a cultural topic" or as objects to analyse, but as something to participate *with* through a "creative dialogue" (Fenner, 2017, p. 379). According to Fenner (2017), authentic literary texts are cultural communities through which learners can experience personal growth by learning about themselves and others. Coats (2013) also emphasises how poetry becomes a "communal act as well as a self-referencing one" (p. 134), by which she means that one of the things poetry does is connect us to others, and through this process "poetry enables each of us, no matter what our culture, to move from being bodies in the world to being bodies in language" (p. 134). Poetry therefore represents the kinds of texts teachers need to include in their classrooms, to facilitate learning that is personal, thought-provoking and experiential, as well as social and collaborative.

Poetry is performative

Poetry is first and foremost meant to be heard and read aloud, and through performance, learners practise speaking English in creative and playful ways, giving all learners a voice. Through the process of drama, the learners' ability to communicate in realistic situations can be strengthened and their listening comprehension enhanced (Winston, 2012). Performance is also a way to physically respond to the text, which is particularly important with young learners, but equally relevant for older learners. The relationship between poetry and performance is discussed further in chapter 10.

According to Coats (2013), poetry has "sensual qualities that require the engagement of multimodal ways of processing" (p. 133). Processing poetry requires the whole body: reading with the eyes, listening with the ears, and kinesthetically experiencing the rhythms, the repetitions and the surprises. Moreover, reading poetry does not just invoke embodied experiences, it also produces them, and such experiences "exceed […] linguistic meaning" (Coats, 2013, p. 133). It is thus important to "understand children's poetry as meaningful in its use by children rather than its form or interpretations" (Coats, 2013, p. 133). Furthermore, participating in embodied and performative processes affords other benefits by developing learners' personal resources such as "self-confidence, self-esteem, social skills, communication, emotional resilience, empathy, [and] physical expressiveness" (Winston, 2012, p. 6).

Teacher knowledge and resourcing poetry

When working with poetry, teachers should prepare by also reading poetry for themselves. A good starting point could be to browse through physical poetry anthologies or go on a digital poetry treasure hunt. It is important to remember that each poem needs to be given time and that re-reading is necessary. In her article "Making the Match: Traditional Nursery Rhymes and Teaching English to Modern Children", Prosic-Santovac (2015) argues for and develops specific criteria to help teachers choose poetry for their classrooms. Although the article focuses mainly on nursery rhymes and the younger learners, the criteria are still relevant to poetry for older learners. Prosic-Santovac (2015) highlights content and relevance of the poems, age appropriateness, and whether the material encourages discussion and exploration of values and issues that learners might encounter in their everyday lives. Furthermore, a key criterion is related to the importance of re-examining poems that might reinforce gender-related stereotypes or that are stigmatising towards certain cultures or peoples (Prosic-Santovac, 2015, pp. 32–33). It is therefore important to keep in mind such criteria when choosing poems for the classroom.

In this chapter, recommendations provide a baseline for teachers' own poetry archives, but it is necessary to keep expanding the archive so that it also includes other, less traditionally centred, voices. This is done by being aware and critical of one's own choices, as well as prioritising marginalised, indigenous and diverse poets.

Dipping into poetry anthologies

Finding suitable poems can be tricky if one does not know where to start. Having a poetry anthology offers a perfect point of departure, since someone has already done the work of collecting poems. If anthologies are kept in the classroom, learners can also browse through them. Furthermore, it is possible to collect one's own poems together with those of learners in order to create a class anthology (for example keeping a shared Padlet for poetry or making a physical folder or book where learners submit their favourite poems). Table 1 provides a list of some poetry anthologies that, in my experience, work well for the EFL classroom. Please note that these are just some examples, and that there is a world of poetry out there to be explored and enjoyed.

Table 1. Poetry Anthologies

Title	Editors/Authors	Description
I Like This Poem (1979)	Edited by Kaye Webb	This anthology includes classic poems that have all been chosen by children, and the book is nicely divided into different age levels.
Caribbean Dozen: Poems from Caribbean Poets (1994)	Edited by John Agard and Grace Nichols	A collection that includes a variety of poems by Caribbean poets.
The New Oxford Book of Children's Verse (1996)	Edited by Neil Philip	This anthology provides a solid baseline for both classic and contemporary children's poetry, with poems dating from the 18th century up until today.
100 Best Poems for Children (2002)	Edited by Roger McGough	A lively collection of children's poems that have also been chosen by children themselves.
Rainbow World: Poems from Many Cultures (2003)	Edited by Debjani Chatterjee and Bashabi Fraser	This is an outstanding collection of multi-cultural poetry.
The Rattle Bag (2005) *The School Bag* (2005)	Edited by Seamus Heaney and Ted Hughes	These two extensive anthologies represent a good resource for teachers. They include many classic poems, as well as diverse and contemporary poetry.
Michael Rosen's A to Z: The Best Children's Poetry from Agard to Zephaniah (2009)	Edited by Michael Rosen	Carefully collected poems by poets from A to Z, including lesser-known poets. A good gateway to more contemporary poetry, and the collection is diverse.
Poems to Perform (2013)	Edited by Julia Donaldson	A wonderful place to find poetry well-suited for performance and reading aloud. See chapter 10, on drama, for more about performing literature.
A Poem for Every Night of the Year (2016) *A Poem for Every Day of the Year* (2017)	Edited by Allie Esiri	A rich resource for poetry for every day and night of the year. The book takes into consideration the different seasons, and marks holidays and important days during the year (for example Martin Luther King Day, etc.).
Out of Wonder: Poems Celebrating Poets (2017)	Written by Kwame Alexander, Chris Colderley and Marjory Wentworth. Illustrated by Ekua Holmes.	This is a picturebook with poems written in celebration of other famous poets, it is therefore also rich in images, and it highlights important poets, while at the same time bringing new voices forth. The book also inspires readers to write their own poetry.
Ink Knows No Borders: Poems of the Immigrant and Refugee Experience (2019)	Edited by Patrice Vecchione and Alyssa Raymond	A poetry collection for young adults that addresses the many issues of being immigrants and refugees today.
Fire Front: First Nations Poetry and Power Today (2020)	Edited by Alison Whittaker	This anthology showcases poetry and essays written by First Nations poets in Australia.

Creating a classroom environment for poetry

To former UK Children's Laureate and poet Michael Rosen, poetry is for everyone. He argues for giving space to poetry in classrooms and that teachers should not be too worried about how to teach poetry. The main concern for teachers should be to help learners feel comfortable browsing around poems, to not feel threatened by strange or unusual poetry, and to help them build a repertoire of poems that they know. Teachers should also encourage learners to read poetry, hear it, view it, and make it their own (Rosen, 2011). Teachers should thus try to create a poetry environment in the classroom to generate enthusiasm for poetry. This can be done by activating learners and giving them agency by providing opportunities to perform, read, discuss (openly and thoughtfully), write and play with poetry. See chapter 8 for more ideas on how to take an action- and product-oriented approach to literature.

Poetry wall

When learners write poems, these should be displayed in the classroom as well. Having a physical wall for poetry can create an environment for sharing and reading each other's self-created works, giving learners ownership of their work. The wall will change over time, and it is a nice way to also look back on previously written poems, and to keep adding new ones.

Classic versus contemporary

When working with poetry in the classroom, teachers can include older, more "classic" poetry as well as contemporary poems. The key element to remember is variation. When it comes to classic poetry for the English classroom, some famous names often appear, such as William Shakespeare, W.H. Auden, William Wordsworth, William Blake, Edward Lear,[4] T.S. Eliot, Emily Dickinson, Robert Louis Stevenson, Eleanor Farjeon, Walter de la Mare and Christina Rossetti, to mention a few. Poetry does not have an expiration date, and that is why these poets are still relevant for contemporary classrooms. Poems written 150 years ago can be equally relevant, engaging and thought-provoking today. Some classic poetry also returns in a new modern context, for example "The Witches' Spell" from Shakespeare's *Macbeth*, which also appears in the third Harry Potter film[5] set to music by John Williams. Or T.S. Eliot's poetry collection *Old Possum's Book of Practical Cats* (1939), which

---

4   Visit https://www.nonsenselit.org/ for Lear's nonsense poems. His limericks from *A Book of Nonsense* (1861) are highly recommended.
5   *The Prisoner of Azkaban*.

might be more famous today due to the musical adaptions of these poems by Andrew Lloyd Webber (in the musical, and recent film adaptation, *Cats*).

More contemporary and diverse poetry must be explored by teachers as well. Some suggested names are Kwame Alexander, Benjamin Zephaniah, John Agard, Valerie Bloom, Jackie Kay, Lemn Sissay, Roald Dahl, Michael Rosen, Ken Nesbitt, Naomi Shihab Nye, Nikki Grimes, Jacqueline Woodson, Ted Hughes, Langston Hughes, Maya Angelou, Nikki Giovanni, Brian Patten, Roger McGough and Carol Ann Duffy. These Anglophone poets are recommended because they are diverse voices who take different approaches to poetry. Furthermore, several of these poets have played (and still play) an important role as advocates for children's poetry in education. By reading poetry by these authors and searching for their names on different poetry websites (including the poets' own websites), teachers can find further recommendations for other similar poets. This can lead to an adventure of exploring new and unknown poets and is something both teachers and learners can do: go on an online poetry treasure hunt.

Online poetry treasure hunt: Choosing poems

There is a rich database of poetry online, and going on this adventure, either alone or together with learners, can be exciting and can provide a gateway for new learning experiences, opportunities and ideas. On several poetry websites, it is possible to search for poems by topic (e.g. different subjects, occasions or holidays), by poetic forms (e.g. verse forms such as sonnet or ballad, or technique such as alliteration or simile), by school or literary period (e.g. the Harlem Renaissance or the Black Arts Movement) or by the poets' region. One example of such a treasure hunt is trying the Poem Roulette[6] on the *Poetry in Voice* website. Here one can choose between senior or junior grades, and the roulette has three categories: *poets*, *moods* and *tags*. After choosing one of these, the roulette will randomly select three options (i.e. three different moods, such as "bold", "sarcastic", and "silly"). The number of spins for the roulette is limitless, and when pressing on the poet, mood or tag that appears, the reader is taken to a poem. This is an enjoyable and active exploration of poetry which will lead to new discoveries and reading experiences.

Useful websites

There are many websites offering poetry, scholarly articles and a variety of resources and activities to use in the classroom. Table 2 provides an overview.

---

6   https://www.poetryinvoice.com/roulette/

Table 2. Poetry Websites

Name	Description of resource
The Poetry Archive and the Children's Poetry Archive	The Poetry Archive is an excellent place to search and browse for poetry. It offers poetry from contemporary poets as well as classic poetry (entitled "the mighty dead"). It is possible to search by poem, poet, theme or country/region. The website also offers sound recordings of poets themselves. Links: https://www.poetryarchive.org and https://childrens.poetryarchive.org/
Poetry Foundation	The American Poetry Foundation is an excellent website for teachers, with a range of articles and suggestions for activities, as well as poetry. There is also the option to listen to poems (instead of just reading them). Link: https://www.poetryfoundation.org/
National Poetry Day UK	On this website you can sign up for free resources which change every year for UK National Poetry Day. A great resource for every teacher. On the website you can discover poems as well as ideas for classroom activities and materials available for download. Link: https://nationalpoetryday.co.uk/
Academy of American Poets	This website includes a variety of poetry for children and teens, as well as resources for teacher. The website focuses primarily on American poets and poetry. Link: https://poets.org/
Poetry 4 Kids	American children's poet and former Children's Poet Laureate Ken Nesbitt has a website that includes a variety of poems for children, as well as several ideas for writing poetry. His many guides on how to write poetry are easy to follow and a valuable toolkit for teachers. Link: http://www.poetry4kids.com/
The Red Room Company	The Red Room Company is an Australian organisation that works towards creating, publishing and promoting poetry reflecting a diversity of voices. The website does not include a lot of poetry for the youngest learners, but is nonetheless a highly relevant resource for older learners. Link: https://redroomcompany.org/
Poetry in Voice	This Canadian website is a rich source of poetry, divided into grade levels. Check out their poem roulette. Link: https://www.poetryinvoice.com/poems
Poems on the Underground	An enjoyable website with poems that are displayed on the London Tube. Link: https://poemsontheunderground.org/
World Poetry Day (UN)	Each year World Poetry Day is celebrated globally on March 21. Teachers can consider marking it at their own schools. On the official website there are some resources for teachers available for downloading. Link: https://www.un.org/en/observances/world-poetry-day
Poetry Roundabout	A poetry blog by British poet Liz Brownlee. This is a nice resource for teachers of young learners as it offers ideas and activities for learners up to the age of 12. Link: https://poetryroundabout.com/

The following sections outline some practical examples of how to read and write poetry in the EFL classroom. A section on novels in verse, with more details about this genre, together with a diverse and detailed list of recommendations, can be found in chapter 6.

It is important to note that all examples provided here can be adapted to any grade level, so a specific age level for the activity is not always specified. Each classroom consists of unique learners with diverse backgrounds, and teachers should not limit themselves by considering some activities or some poems as being too "childish" for older learners. In the same way, some activities or some poems should not be considered too "challenging" for younger learners. Teachers should be careful about underestimating learners. Even young learners need to be challenged. Any poem can be revisited at a different stage, to uncover new meanings at a later point in life.

Ways of reading poetry

At any age, poetry is best enjoyed read aloud and this is therefore a valuable way to introduce poetry in the classroom. Historically, most poetry for children came out of the nursery and thus has its foundations in oral traditions. These traditions are an important dimension of poetry, because of "its aural quality and its invocation of the spoken voice" (Styles, 2009, p. 205). Oral approaches to reading poetry will therefore be presented first, emphasising poetry's qualities as a verbal text and its performative elements.

Oral approaches to reading poetry
Choral reading

Reading aloud as a choir is an active way of reading where learners become one collective voice. This way of reading aloud together has several benefits. It warms up everyone's voices (which is important in a language learning classroom). It lowers the "danger" of speaking aloud in class, and it might also help the silent learners feel safer in terms of speaking out loud. In this approach, only one voice is audible – that of the whole class, rather than each individual learner's voice. This can build confidence and a sense of togetherness.

Any poem can be read aloud, but for a choral reading it can be fun to choose a tongue twister to start with (such as, for example, "how much wood would a woodchuck chuck"), because these create a challenge while at the same time providing a playful way to practise pronunciation and experiment with prosodic features, such as volume and tempo.

Here are ways to vary the choral reading:

- **Unison.** Everyone reads the whole text together as a choir.
- **Ask learners to stand up.** There is a big difference in voice projection between sitting down and standing up. This also activates the learners in the process.
- **Stomp the rhythm or clap the beat.** Have all learners do this together, creating a common rhythm.
- **Change the tempo.** This can be done whilst stomping the rhythm or without stomping. Start slowly and then together gradually increase the tempo. It can be fun to try a round where everyone reads as fast as possible or as slowly as possible. The teacher can use hands to "conduct", indicating different tempo (e.g. hands high up = quick, and hands low = slow).
- **Change the volume.** Here, the teacher can conduct by using hands to indicate volume (from low to high). Try to vary the volume (moving between the different volumes, from whispering to shouting).
- **Divide the group.** Have each group read specific sections of the poem. This can also be made into a battle or competition.
- **Call and Response.** The teacher or a learner reads a line which the group then repeats. It is also possible to use a poem such as "Voices of Water" by British poet Tony Mitton, where some learners read the lines and others echo the sounds given in the poem.
- **Cumulative.** One learner begins reading a line, and then line by line new groups of learners chime in until everyone by the end is reading the poem aloud.

Several of these variations can be combined, and different combinations can be tried out for each reading of the same poem. This way the poem is repeated and with each reading learners will be able to appreciate the text more, and perhaps also start to remember it.

IF YOU EVER HAVE TO MEMORIZE A POEM OF TWENTY LINES OR LONGER AND DELIVER IT TO YOUR CLASS, THEN THIS IS A PRETTY GOOD CHOICE

Avocado? Avocado!
Avocado? Avocado!
Avocado? Avocado!
Avocado? Avocado!

Illustration 1. "If you ever have to memorize a poem of twenty lines or longer and deliver it to your class, then this is a good choice" by Chris Harris.[7]

---

[7] From Harris, C. (2017). *I'm Just No Good at Rhyming and Other Nonsense for Mischievous Kids and Immature Grown-Ups* (L. Smith, Illus.). Little Brown and Company, pp. 15–16.

(tiny voice) Avocado? *(deep voice)* **Avocado!**

(tiny voice) Avocado? *(deep voice)* **Avocado!**

(tiny voice) Avocado? *(deep voice)* **Avocado!**

(tiny voice) Avocado? *(deep voice)* **Avocado!**

(fast) Avocado? Avocado!

(slow) A v o c a d o ?   A v o c a d o !

(fast) Avocado? Avocado!

(slow) A v o c a d o ?   A v o c a d o !

(whisper) avocado? *(shout)* **AVOCADO!**

(whisper) avocado? *(shout)* **AVOCADO!**

(whisper) avocado? *(shout)* **AVOCADO!**

(whisper) avocado? *(shout)* **AVOCADO!**

(face left) ¿obɒɔovA   *(face right)* Avocado!
(face left) ¿obɒɔovA   *(face right)* Avocado!
(face left) ¿obɒɔovA   *(face right)* Avocado!
(face forward) Avocado? *(as loudly as possible)*

Poetry performance

The poem in illustration 1 introduces the following section nicely, because it embraces the performance of a poem. As the title states, the poem is to be delivered and it offers a variety of ways to read the text aloud, keeping the language simple. This exemplifies well how a poem does not necessarily need to include complex and challenging language; instead it is about the purpose and the performance. Although the language is repetitive and simple, the performance of the poem itself is far from simple; it is complex and varied, inviting the listeners to consider these two words with care and attention.

Performing poetry "is a powerful way of exploring meaning and deepening understanding, as well as being engaging and enjoyable" (Bearne & Reedy, 2018, p. 255). As Pullinger and Whitley (2016) state, "Even at the establishment of literacy, written and printed poems were generally viewed [...] as material for performance, be it for an exterior audience or an inner self" (pp. 314–315). Thus, a poem needs to be appreciated practically and aesthetically by engaging the whole body. Through a whole-body approach the teacher can consider the verbal, aural, kinaesthetic and visual qualities of poetry and have leaners engage with the texts both physically and intellectually. When it comes to how learners can perform a poem, there are countless possibilities. Below are some suggestions.

Reader's theatre (RT)

This is perhaps the most familiar method used in EFL classrooms to perform poetry. In RT there is always a script, one that can be written by learners or the teacher. The script can be the poem itself or it can be a rewriting of a poem (into a script). Roald Dahl's *Revolting Rhymes* function well for this method, or longer narrative poems (such as "The Raven" by Edgar Allan Poe or "Far over the Misty Mountains" by J.R.R. Tolkien). The number of readers can vary, and it is possible to have a narrator and characters reading their roles aloud. The method requires few to no props, but there is room to be creative and groups can use the props available in the classroom (desks, chairs, etc.), or even make a shadow theatre.

The RT method is well-researched, showing gains in learners' confidence and enthusiasm for language learning, increasing learners' motivation to read (both aloud and in general) (Drew, 2012, p. 296). In addition to these affective benefits, studies have also shown how RT can increase learners' reading comprehension, word recognition and reading speed (Drew, 2012, p. 297). This is a form of repeated reading that can help learners feel safer when performing the text.

Dramatising poetry

In the RT method outlined above, the performance builds on preparing and reading a script. However, there are other ways to include performance by dramatising the text in different ways. Here are some suggestions:

- **Add movements or gestures**. Create a dance to the poem.
- **Read the poem with different voices or different emotions**. This can be particularly effective for poems that include dialogue or question/answer, for example "The Three-Headed Dog" by English poet Clare Bevan, or "The ABC" by Irish poet Spike Milligan.
- **Sing or rap the poem**.
- **Create soundscapes**. Almost any poem lends itself well to being accompanied by sound effects. To make sounds, learners can use their voices or instruments (or even everyday items in the classroom). They can also record their soundscape to be played in the background when the poem is performed. Learners can also find music online (on YouTube, Spotify, etc.) and choose different music genres to accompany the poem (for example one classical and one heavy metal, which will create two unique performances).
- **Hot seating.** This is a drama strategy that can be applied to all kinds of literature. Choosing a character from a poem to hot seat (for example the skeleton in "The Visitor" by English poet Ian Serraillier), learners first prepare questions that they would like to ask, and then one volunteer sits on a chair in front (the "hot seat") and tries to answer "in role" (as the skeleton) the different questions being asked. This strategy works well with poems that include characters and some form of action or event.
- **Poetry in Motion**. Miming the poem or creating freeze frames. Making freeze frames is also a drama strategy that works with any literary text, where learners are asked to distil parts of the text into still images using their bodies. They can be asked to create one or several still images. If they make more than one image, then ask them to consider the transition between the images as well, i.e. that they add a cue (for when to change from one frame to the next). A cue can be a sound (i.e. a word or a clap), or a specific movement (i.e. a wave). This makes the freeze frame performance more dynamic. The freeze frames can also "come alive" for ten seconds, or learners can include specific lines or words from the poem to be recited within each frame.
- **Multimodal poetry**. Have learners find different pictures and photos online that they consider suitable to a poem, or they can create their own images. These pictures can also be put together with music (the soundscape) to create multimodal installations.

Groups can be encouraged to think creatively when preparing for their performance. Learners can, for example, use the room creatively and think about where the audience and they as performers could be. Poems do not always have to be presented in a "traditional" way (i.e. in front of the classroom). See chapter 10 for more ideas on performing literature.

Slam and spoken word poetry

Slam poetry started out as a performance type of poetry that was (and still is) competition-based and has since evolved into its own artistic movement. According to Johnson (2017), the poetry slam "puts dual emphasis on writing and performance, encouraging poets to focus on what they are saying and how they are saying it" (p. 2). Spoken word poetry, on the other hand, has existed longer than slam poetry and also takes place without the competition element (Johnson, 2017). Spoken word and slam are not specific genres in themselves, but within these poetry performance practices there exist a range of styles, tones and modes of address. Further, what makes slam poetry popular, Somers-Willett (2010) notes, "is that it brings verse to be performed in certain ways: expressed with and through particular dialects, formats, gestures and renegade attitudes that underscore its sense of urgency and authenticity" (p. 17).

Slam and spoken word poetry can be quite powerful, and often appeal to adolescents and young adults, perhaps because there is "exceptional emphasis on the role of the author and his or her identity" (Somers-Willett, 2010, p. 17). As Gill (2020) notes, slams are "an inclusive, open space, giving poets from under-represented communities a supportive environment to share their truth, and presenting it in a format so easily accessible and unpretentious, that people who'd never engaged with poetry before are finally able to" (p. vi). The voices of slam and spoken word are often young and belong to diverse people from marginalised and oppressed groups in society (such as, for example, indigenous peoples). Take, for example, the indigenous voices of Alice Eather ("Yúya Karrabúra"/"Fire is Burning", directed by Darius Devas), and the 2018 Australian Poetry Slam Champion Melanie Mununggurr-Williams' ("I run").[8] For further information and resources, visit the *Power Poetry* website,[9] or have a look at the recently published collection *SLAM! You're Gonna Wanna Hear This* (2020), edited by Nikita Gill. This book includes poems by up-and-coming poets, and it is divided into different themes such as "home", "protest" and "acceptance".

---

8 Visit this website for more Australian slam poetry: http://www.australianpoetryslam.com/welcome
9 https://powerpoetry.org/

Poetry as song

Songs are commonly used with younger learners, because there are many familiar chants, rhymes and children's songs which teachers find natural to include in the classroom (see, for example, Wiland, 2016; Munden & Myhre, 2020). However, it is also relevant to continue working with songs with older learners, particularly when working on topics within history, culture and society. An example is "This is America" by the Black American artist Childish Gambino (Glover, 2018). Critical commentary on issues in the US are present in this song, and using it with older learners can be a gateway to discussing matters such as social injustice and racism (for example in relation to the Black Lives Matter movement). The music video is supposed to further provoke the viewer and spark discussions about these issues. Teachers can therefore use the lyrics (the poetry) of this song together with the music video to engage learners in discussing and learning about these events and the social, cultural and historical commentary included.

Writing poetry

How to Write A Poem

Hush.

Grab a pencil
some paper
spunk.

Let loose your heart—
raise your voice.

What if I have many voices?

Let them dance together
twist and turn
like best friends
in a maze
till you find
your way
to that one true word

(or two).

By Kwame Alexander[10]

---

10 From Alexander, K., Colderley, C., & Wentworth, M. (2017). *Out of Wonder: Poems Celebrating Poets* (E. Holmes, Illus.). Candlewick Press, p. 3.

Reading poetry can inspire learners to write their own poems. By reading a variety of different poems, learners can use these as model texts and starting points for their own poems. Bearne and Reedy (2018) note that "Touch, taste, smell and memory are often used as starting points for writing poetry, but poetry is emphatically not always about 'beautiful things and nature'" (p. 259), and can (and perhaps also should) entail more challenging themes and subject matter. In general, the possibilities are endless when it comes to writing poems, and the key is variation, playfulness, fewer rules and more risk-taking. In the following section, a few ideas as to how teachers can approach writing poetry in the classroom will be outlined. Through writing poetry, learners can experience how language is flexible, changeable and malleable, as emphasised by Rosen (2011, p. 22). Language is not a set structure or system, but is constantly changing; through writing poetry, learners can be creative with language. Putting letters, words and sentences together in different ways provides a variety of outcomes, all of which have relevance and carry meaning – and all of which are playful and poetic.

Poetry walk

When writing poetry, it is important to have a starting point: something to write about. Using the space for inspiration is an idea. Going for a walk also engages spatial awareness and it emphasises the active component of writing and of looking and observing. The idea for this activity is taken from the *Poetry Foundation* website (Levin, 2015).

A poetry walk can be a walk inside the classroom, or around the school, perhaps to specific places in the school building (such as the library, the canteen, etc.). The walk can also be done outdoors. The teacher must prepare the walk and the stops, and should aim to have between 10–20 stops (depending on the time frame for the activity and the age of the learners). At each stop, ask learners to write a line inspired by what they see, hear and feel in that space. Half-way through the walk, ask learners to begin connecting their lines to the previous lines. If there are ten stops, then the poem receives ten lines and so forth.

A variation of this activity is to take learners to a specific site (for example a graveyard, a park, a library, etc.), and give them pens and paper. Then divide into groups and ask one group to walk around and write down nouns and the other group to write down adjectives. They should take inspiration from the place they are in (see illustration 2). Then learners get together in pairs (nouns and adjectives) and look through their lists. Taking the list as a start-

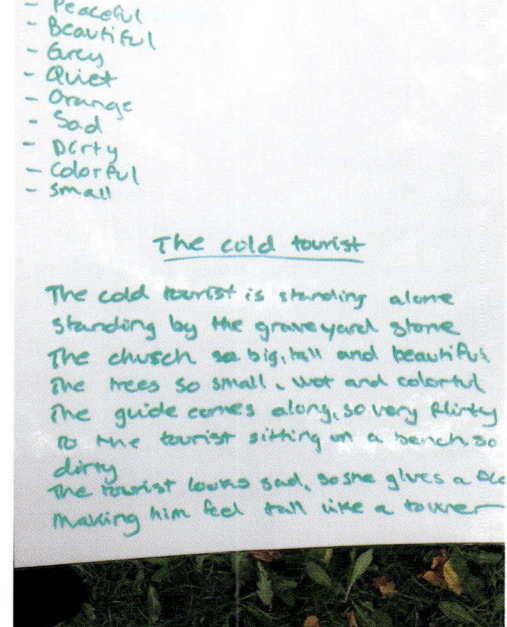

Illustration 2. Poetry Walk

ing point they can write a poem together using these nouns and adjectives. They may now also add other words if they like.

As can be seen in illustration 2, it was raining at the time of this poetry walk (which was nonetheless very successful). It was therefore necessary to provide learners with laminated A3 paper and whiteboard markers. (An easy makeshift whiteboard that functioned well outside, despite the rain.)

Writing frames and prompts

When writing poems, there are several well-known structures to use in order to provide learners with some scaffolding, while at the same time allowing them to be creative. According to Bearne and Reedy (2018), "Giving children a frame can support composition [...]. A simple frame is one which often repeats [...]; offers original poems as stimulus and a kind of frame" (p. 258). They further emphasise that "Over-reliance on frames can be restricting but often they can provide just the nudge a young writer needs to express personal feelings and opinions" (Bearne & Reedy, 2018, p. 258). In the following, a few examples of scaffolded writing activities will be outlined. These activities follow a specific frame or a prompt but are at the same time creative in their own ways.

Biopoem

When working with a specific character (real or fictional), learners can write a biopoem which should include information about the character they have chosen as the subject of the poem. Biopoems usually have ten lines, and each line follows a specific guideline. Visit the *ReadWriteThink* website[11] for a full recipe (with examples) explaining how to write a biopoem.

Acrostic poem

This type of poetry can be about anything. First, a word (or phrase) needs to be chosen as the topic for the poem (this can be any word, thing, name, etc. For example, Summer or Homework). Then this chosen word is written down *vertically*. The first letter in each line begins with the letter in the chosen word. For each line, the learners can include either one word or longer sentences (always beginning with the same letter as the chosen word).

---

11   www.readwritethink.org

Adjective poem

This poem describes an object and it can also help learners become aware of grammatical terms (such as nouns and adjectives). It is possible to use this writing frame in connection to another text (for example a poem, such as "Caged Bird" by Black American poet Maya Angelou. After reading the poem, learners must first highlight or underline nouns in the text, from which they then choose a noun to write a poem about). The guidelines for an adjective poem are as follows:

Line 1: A noun
Line 2: same noun + is/are + adjective 1
Line 3: same noun + is/are + adjective 1 + adjective 2
Line 4: is/are + adjective 1 + adjective 2 + adjective 3
Line 5: adjective 1 + adjective 2 + adjective 3 + adjective 4
Line 6: new noun

Here is an example:

The pencil case
The pencil case is round
The pencil case is round and black
The pencil case is round, black and small
Round, black, small and packed
Ruler

Cinquain

This is a five-line poem (from the French word *cinq*, meaning five) with specific number of syllables in each line. The poem itself does not need to rhyme, and it has an easy structure to follow. Visit Ken Nesbitt's website *Poetry4Kids* to read more about how to write a cinquain (as well as other types of poems, such as a Haiku or a Limerick. Some of his other "How to" instructions include "How to write a funny list poem" and "How to write an 'I can't write a poem' poem").

Found poem

This is a creative task that requires learners to compose their poems with texts they have found. They can find texts in magazines, or the teacher can bring in sentences or other familiar texts (other poems for example) that learners cut out into smaller chunks. Learners can also tear up pages, splitting words

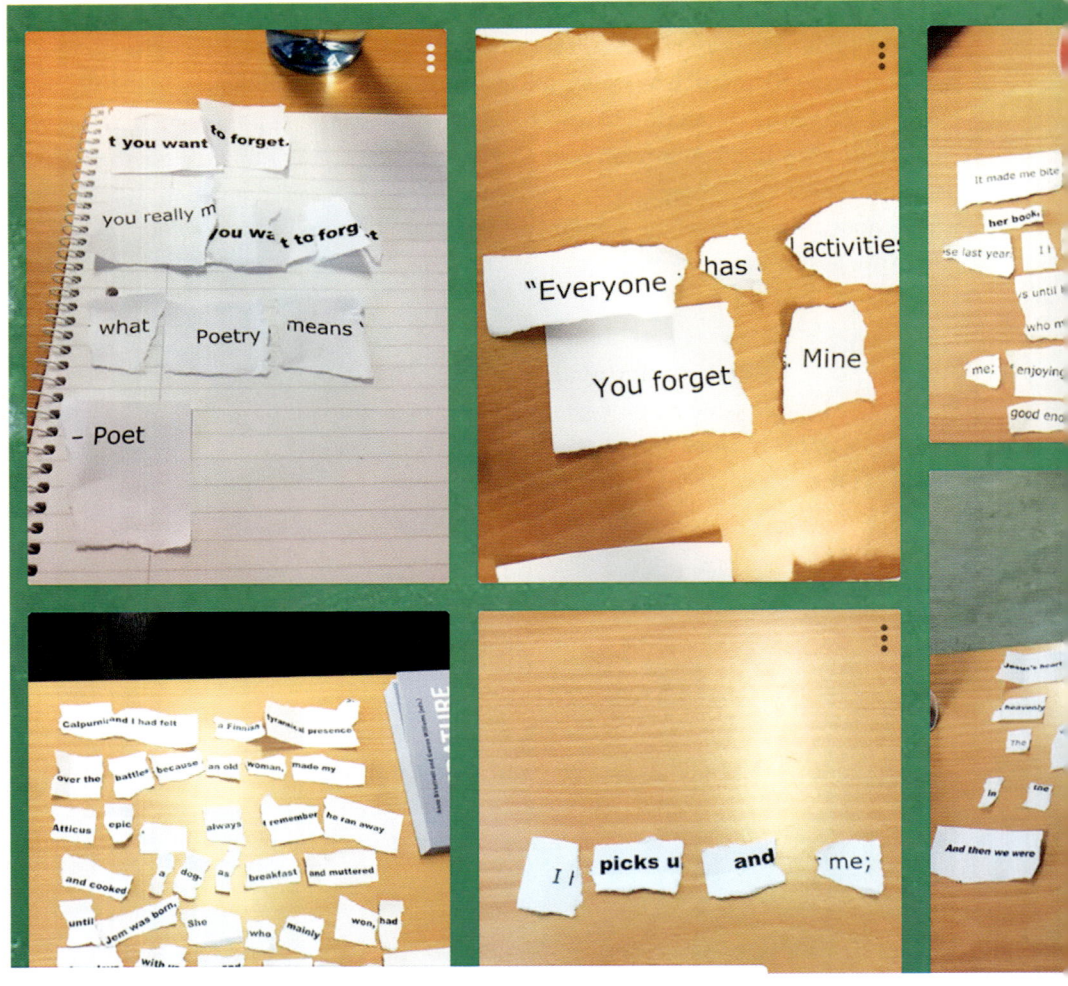

Illustration 3. Found poems

physically. This will give them different words and chunks that they then use to compose a new poem. This composition activity uses already existing texts and can therefore provide all learners with equal opportunities to write a poem. The products do not depend on learners' overall writing skills, but on their ability to choose texts and be creative when putting them together. Learners can also explore meaning and make poems that might challenge views of "correct" sentences (accuracy). This is positive for language learning situations, allowing learners to feel mastery and control of their own writing compositions.

2 Poetry in the English classroom | 81

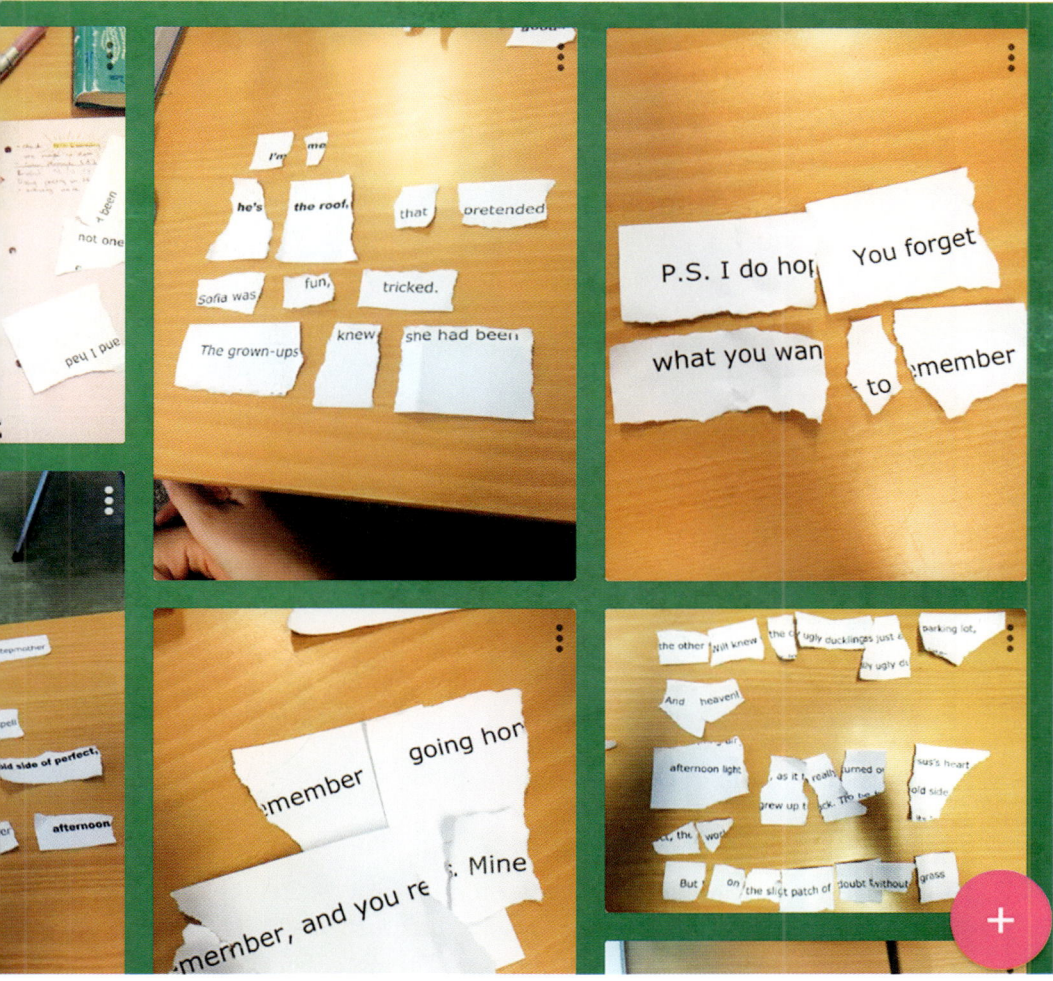

In the example from illustration 3, learners were asked to take a picture of the poems they made and upload it to a shared Padlet.[12] With younger learners, it could be nice to provide them with colourful paper and let them glue their poems on paper to decorate the classroom wall (to create a "poetry wall").

Illustration 4 shows a year 6 learner who has created a bookmark that says: "I don't trust you, i trust This book" [sic].

---

12 Padlet is a digital tool for collaborative writing. Here, the teacher is the only one who needs an account to create "walls" where learners can go in and post their materials. https://padlet.com/

Illustration 4. Bookmark

Concrete or shape poem

The concept is for learners to first choose a shape (of a concrete object), and then write a poem about the object (or something associated with it), using the text to create the actual shape of the poem. The text either outlines or fills in the shape. There are many examples of shape poetry found online or in several of the anthologies recommended earlier in this chapter that the teacher can show learners before they start writing their own. There are also poetry books dedicated solely to concrete poetry, such as *A Poke in the I: A Collection of Concrete Poems* (Janeczko, 2005).

In illustration 5, Håkon, a year 6 learner, has written a shape poem about a milkshake. Each line begins the same way: "Helo, Helo, i am the…",[13] and then describes what the item is and its function. For example, "Helo, Helo, i am the straw. i'm inside the cup to get the drink higher up", and "Helo, Helo, i am the cap i hold the straw back in place and gives it more space". This pat-

---

13   The spelling has been kept as it was written by Håkon in the original.

tern is something Håkon decided on his own when composing his poem, but one can notice how repetition has helped him structure the poem, a strategy that can be emphasised when working with poetry. In this class, the learners were also asked to create a drawing for their poem (without the text); they worked on these both in English and in Arts and Crafts. All learners in the class created a shape poem; the activity works well for differentiation, because there is room to write short and long poems, and the choices made are the learners' own choices – which gives them agency and hopefully also confidence as writers.

Illustration 5. The Milkshake

The room of stars
This activity is from taken from Pie Corbett's (2008) *Jumpstart! Poetry*, a collection which includes a variety of poetry games and activities that can be used in the classroom. Corbett himself is an English educational trainer, a writer and a poet. In this writing activity, learners are divided into two groups: A and B. Those who are A write a list of places. Those who are B write a list of nouns, both concrete (i.e. tables, chocolate, etc.), and abstract (i.e. jealousy, love, etc.). Then the groups are combined: A + B. They share their lists and put them together in the order they were written. This means that some of these places might become very strange, but others become interesting, funny and intriguing. For example, "The Hotel of Hate", "The Bathroom of Stories" or "The Castle of Communication". After asking everyone to share some of their places, learners can then write a poem following one of these two patterns:

In [the room of stars]… or [the room of stars] is where…

Using this model, learners can imagine different things that happen in these places. It is possible to write together in small groups or as a full class. Here is one example from my own student teachers:

The Castle of Communication
In the castle of communication
You hear about a family vacation
And people who snore,
And slam the door
There's also hope,
That help you cope
There's a lot of laughter
That will help you after
It brings you peace –
If you find the keys.

By Marte and Karoline[14]

---

14   From MGLU1105 (English 1 (1–7) module 1), spring 2020, at the Norwegian University of Science and Technology (NTNU).

Transforming Poetry

When writing and playing with poetry, there are many ways to further transform a poem, for example by rewriting it into a new genre, such as a newspaper article, a rap, a retelling or modern retelling, changing the characters, writing the poem from a different perspective, making a storyboard or creating a movie trailer. Learners can also choose a line from the poem and make this their new title for a different poem. Options abound!

Conclusion

As Styles (2009) notes, children's poetry begins "in the nursery", and it is therefore important to emphasise that *all* children have experience and knowledge of "poetic form from almost always [before] they come to school" (Bearne & Reedy, 2018, p. 249). From a young age, children experience rhymes, songs and chants, either on the playground or at home. Poetry is connected to play, to routines and to everyday life, and children experience these types of poems together with adults. The teacher becomes the other important adult in children's lives when they start school and is thus responsible for opening (or keeping open) the door to the mysterious and magical realm of poetry: a place for experience and playfulness, humour and seriousness, wonder and inquiry.

To conclude this chapter, it seems fitting to end with a poem:

The End

When I was One,

I had just begun.

When I was Two,

I was nearly new.

When I was Three,

I was hardly Me.

When I was Four,

I was not much more.

When I was Five,

I was just alive.

But now I am Six, I'm as clever as clever

So I think I'll be six now for ever and ever.

By A. A. Milne[15]

---

15 From Webb, K. (Ed.). (1979). *I Like This Poem*. Puffin Books, p. 82

This poem encapsulates some of the important aspects of poetry that have been highlighted in this chapter. As the title suggests, it is an end to something, as well as an ending to this chapter. However, when the actual reading of the poem does end, it continues "for ever and ever". This poem therefore moves forwards. It is active, and in many ways it symbolises what poetry is and does to us. Firstly, the poem takes us back to childhood, where poetry begins. Then the poem continues for eternity, it lasts forever, and it stays with the reader. In doing so, it unveils a playful yet unknown territory, where there are no right or wrong answers, only what ifs and unanswered questions. It is mysterious and childlike, and highly enjoyable. Poetry moves us, and stays with us – it is not static; it changes with us and offers new insight and meaning at different stages in our lives. Poetry is flexible, performative and playful, and it can engage learners of *all* ages. When teachers take a creative approach to poetry in the EFL classroom, poetry can become a way to experience and practise language, to express thoughts, and to develop understanding and critical awareness of different ideas, perspectives, cultures and experiences.

References
Primary texts

Agard, J., & Nichols, G. (Eds.). (1996). *Caribbean Dozen: Poems from Caribbean Poets.* Walker Books Ltd.

Alexander, K. (2017). How to write a poem. In K. Alexander, C. Colderley & M. Wentworth, *Out of Wonder: Poems Celebrating Poets* (E. Holmes, Illus.) (p. 3). Candlewick Press.

Alexander, K., Colderley, C., & Wentworth, M. (2017). *Out of Wonder: Poems Celebrating Poets* (E. Holmes, Illus.). Candlewick Press.

Angelou, M. (2016). Caged bird. In A. Esiri (Ed.), *A Poem for Every Night of the Year* (pp. 22–23). Macmillan Children's Books.

Australian Poetry Slam. (2018, November 5). Melanie Mununggurr-Williams – Australia Poetry Slam Champion 2018 "I run" [video file]. YouTube. https://www.youtube.com/watch?v=x03nIylz4Hg

Bevan, C. (2013). The Three-Headed Dog. In J. Donaldson (Ed.), *Poems to Perform* (pp. 84–85). Macmillan Children's Books.

Chatterjee, D., & Fraser, B. (Eds.). (2003). *Rainbow World: Poems from Many Cultures.* Hodder Wayland.

Colderley, C. (2017). Snapshots. In K. Alexander, C. Colderley & M. Wentworth, *Out of Wonder: Poems Celebrating Poets* (E. Holmes, Illus.) (p. 9). Candlewick Press.

Dahl, R. (2016). *Revolting Rhymes* (Q. Blake, Illus.). Puffin Books.

Devas, D. [Being Here]. (2019, July 9). The Word – Alice Eather – Poem – Yuya Karrabura [video file]. YouTube. https://www.youtube.com/watch?v=5yla0FMEAmg

Donaldson, J. (Ed.). (2013). *Poems to Perform.* Macmillan Children's Books.

Eliot, T. (1939/2012). *Old Possum's Book of Practical Cats.* Faber & Faber.

Esiri, A. (Ed.). (2016). *A Poem for Every Night of the Year*. Macmillan Children's Books.
Esiri, A. (Ed.). (2017). *A Poem for Every Day of the Year*. Macmillan Children's Books.
Gill, N. (Ed.). (2020). *SLAM! You're Gonna Wanna Hear This*. Palgrave Macmillan.
Glover, D. (2018, May 5). *Childish Gambino – This is America (Official Video)* [video file]. YouTube. https://www.youtube.com/watch?v=VYOjWnS4cMY
Harris, C. (2017). If you ever have to memorize a poem of twenty lines or longer and deliver it to your class, then this is a good choice. In *I'm Just no Good at Rhyming and Other Nonsense for Mischievous Kids and Immature Grown-Ups* (L. Smith, Illus.) (pp. 15–16). Little Brown and Company.
Heaney, S., & Hughes, T. (Eds.). (2005). *The Rattle Bag*. Faber & Faber.
Heaney, S., & Hughes, T. (Eds.). (2005). *The School Bag*. Faber & Faber.
Janeczko, P.B. (Ed.). (2005). *A Poke in the I: A Collection of Concrete Poems* (C. Raschka, Illus.). Candlewick Press.
Lear, E. (1861/2002). *A Book of Nonsense*. Routledge.
McGough, R. (Ed.). (2002). *100 Best Poems for Children* (S. Moxley, Illus.). Puffin Books.
Milligan, S. (1979). The ABC. In K. Webb (Ed.), *I Like This Poem* (pp. 101–102). Puffin Books.
Milne, A. (1979). The End. In K. Webb (Ed.), *I Like This Poem* (p. 82). Puffin Books.
Mitton, T. (2013). Voices of Water. In J. Donaldson (Ed.), *Poems to Perform* (pp. 14–15). Macmillan Children's Books.
Philip, N. (1996). *The New Oxford Book of Children's Verse*. Oxford University Press.
Poe, E.A. (1845). The Raven. Poetry Foundation. https://www.poetryfoundation.org/poems/48860/the-raven
Rosen, M. (Ed.). (2009). *Michael Rosen's A to Z: The Best Children's Poetry from Agard to Zephaniah*. Puffin Books.
Serraillier, I. (2013). The Visitor. In J. Donaldson (Ed.), *Poems to Perform* (pp. 108–109). Macmillan Children's Books.
Shakespeare, W. (1979). The Witches' Spell. In K. Webb (Ed.), *I Like This Poem* (p. 9). Puffin Books.
Tolkien, J.R.R. (1979). Far Over the Misty Mountains. In K. Webb (Ed.), *I Like This Poem* (pp. 135–136). Puffin Books.
Vecchione, P., & Raymond, A. (Eds.). (2019). *Ink Knows No Borders: Poems of the Immigrant and Refugee Experience*. Seven Stories Press.
Webb, K. (Ed.). (1979). *I Like This Poem*. Puffin Books.
Whittaker, A. (Ed.). (2020). *Fire Front: First Nations Poetry and Power Today*. University of Queensland Press.

Websites

Academy of American Poets. (n.d.). *Poets*. https://poets.org/
Australian Poetry Slam (2020, May 19). http://www.australianpoetryslam.com/
Brownlee, L. (2017, July 27). The Poetry Roundabout [blog]. https://poetryroundabout.com/
Chernaik, J., Dharker, I., & Szirtes, G. (Eds.) (n.d.). *Poems on the Underground*. https://poemsontheunderground.org/
National Poetry Day. (n.d.). https://nationalpoetryday.co.uk/
Nesbitt, K. (n.d.). *Poetry4Kids*. http://www.poetry4kids.com/
Nonsenselit. (n.d.). *Nonsenselit: The Edward Lear Home Page*. https://www.nonsenselit.org/

Poetry Foundation. (2020, June). https://www.poetryfoundation.org/
Poetry in Voice. (n.d.). https://www.poetryinvoice.com/poems
Power Poetry. (n.d.). https://powerpoetry.org/
ReadWriteThink. (n.d.). http://www.readwritethink.org/
Red Room Company. (n.d.). *Red Room Poetry: Poetry in Meaningful Ways.* https://redroomcompany.org/
The Children's Poetry Archive. (n.d.). https://childrens.poetryarchive.org/
The Poetry Archive. (n.d.) https://www.poetryarchive.org
United Nations. (n.d.). World Poetry Day 21 March. https://www.un.org/en/observances/world-poetry-day

Secondary texts

Bearne, E., & Reedy, D. (Eds.). (2018). Poetry. In *Teaching Primary English: Subject Knowledge and Classroom Practice* (pp. 248–272). Routledge.
Bland, J. (Ed.). (2015). Grammar templates for the future with poetry for children. In *Teaching English to Young Learners: Critical Issues in Language Teaching with 3–12 Year Olds* (pp. 147–166). Bloomsbury Academic.
Coats, K. (2013). The Meaning of Children's Poetry: A Cognitive Approach. *International Research in Children's Literature, 6*(2), 127–142.
Corbett, P. (2008). *Jumpstart! Poetry.* Routledge.
Drew, I. (2012). Leseteater som metode i fremmedspråksundervisning. *Norsk Pedagogisk Tidsskrift 96*(4), 293–304.
Fenner, A-B. (2011). Litteraturens rolle i utviklingen av interkulturell kompetanse [The role of literature in the development of intercultural competence]. *Communicare, 1,* 40–43.
Fenner, A-B. (2017). Promoting intercultural competence and *Bildung* through foreign language textbooks. In M. Eisenmann & T. Summer (Eds.), *Basic Issues in EFL Teaching and Learning* (3rd ed.) (pp. 371–384). Universitätsverlag Winter.
Gill, N. (Ed.). (2020). *SLAM! You're Gonna Wanna Hear This.* Palgrave Macmillan.
Hestnes, H. (Ed.). (2012). Using poetry in the ESL classroom. In *Språkfag 5: Litteratur* (pp. 71–91). Akademika Forlag.
Johnson, J. (2017). *Killing Poetry: Blackness and the Making of Slam and Spoken Word Communities.* Rutgers University Press.
Levin, H. (2015, December 14). Poetry walk. *Poetry Foundation.* https://www.poetryfoundation.org/articles/70286/poetry-walk
Munden, J., & Myhre, M. (2020). Learning with songs, rhymes and games. In *Twinkle Twinkle: English 1–4* (4th ed., pp. 101–122). Cappelen Damm Akademisk.
Norwegian Directorate for Education and Training. (2019/2020). English subject curriculum (ENG01-04). https://www.udir.no/lk20/eng01-04
Pinsent, P. (2016). *Children's Literature.* Palgrave Macmillan.
Prosic-Santovac, D. (2015). Making the match: Traditional nursery rhymes and teaching English to modern children. *CLELE Journal, 3*(1), 25–48.
Pullinger, D., & Whitley, D. (2016). Beyond measure: The value of the memorised poem. *Changing English, 23*(4), 314–325.
Rosen, M. (2011). Reflections on being children's laureate – and beyond. In M. Lockwood (Ed.), *Bringing Poetry Alive* (pp. 15–25). Sage Publishing.

Simecek, K., & Ellis, V. (2017). The uses of poetry. Renewing an educational understanding of a language art. *The Journal of Aesthetic Education, 51*(1), 98–114.

Somers-Willett, S. (2010). *The Cultural Politics of Slam Poetry: Race, Identity, and the Performance of Popular Verse in America*. University of Michigan Press.

Styles, M. (2009). "From the Garden to the Street": The history of poetry for children. In J. Maybin & N. J. Watson (Eds.), *Children's Literature: Approaches and Territories* (pp. 202–217). Palgrave Macmillan.

Styles, M. (2010). Introduction: Taking the long view – The state of children's poetry today. In D. Whitley, L. Joy & M. Styles (Eds.), *Poetry and Childhood* (pp. xi–xvi). Trentham Books.

Wiland, S.M. (2016). Nursery rhymes and songs. In *Reading and Teaching English Literature* (pp. 158–172). Cappelen Damm Akademisk.

Wiland, S.M. (2019). PhD revisited: Poetry: Prima Vista. Reader-response research on poetry in a foreign language context. In U. Rindal & L.M. Brevik (Eds.), *English Didactics in Norway – 30 years of doctoral research* (pp. 274–294). Universitetsforlaget.

Winston, J. (Ed.). (2012). *Second Language Learning Through Drama: Practical Techniques and Applications*. Routledge.

Further reading suggestions

Corbett, P. (2008). *Jumpstart! Poetry*. Routledge.

Dymoke, S., Lambirth, A., & Wilson, A. (Eds.). (2013). *Making Poetry Matter: International Research on Poetry Pedagogy*. Bloomsbury Academic.

Kleppe, S.L., & Sorby, A. (Eds.). (2018). *Poetry and Pedagogy Across the Lifespan: Disciplines, Classrooms, Contexts*. Palgrave Macmillan.

Lockwood, M. (Ed.). (2011) *Bringing Poetry Alive*. Sage Publishing.

Styles, M. (1998). *From the Garden to the Streets: 300 Years of Children's Poetry*. Continuum.

Whitley, D., Joy, L., & Styles, M. (Eds.). (2010). *Poetry and Childhood*. Trentham books.

Wiland, S.M. (2016). Poetry. In *Reading and Teaching English Literature* (pp. 187–200). Cappelen Damm Akademisk.

3
Global Englishes, diverse voices

Lalita Murty and Beck Sinar

Introduction

Language is at the heart of communication; it is both a *code* and a *social practice*. A code is a system of rules of sounds, vocabulary and grammar. A social practice is concerned with the way the world around is viewed, what sense is made of it and how this understanding is communicated to others. Language is not simply a set of rules to be learnt but something that people "do" in their daily lives to create and understand meaning and to maintain and establish social relationships. As people around the globe are different, so are their social practices of language even where that language is the same; this is especially true with English, which is spoken all around the world.

This chapter encourages teachers and learners to recognise the globalised nature of English and the ways in which today's learners need English to communicate with people globally and locally in real and virtual societies. First, concepts of *Intercultural Competence (IC)* and *Global Englishes* are introduced, which are essential for developing citizenship in democratic systems. Then a range of literary texts is introduced, which teachers can use to develop language awareness and cultural understanding in the classroom. Such texts will be referred to as "diverse texts" reflecting the diversity of language, culture and authors. The focus throughout is on the English classroom in Norway, but ideas expressed apply equally to any English classroom.

Teachers need to help learners understand that different varieties of Englishes, e.g. Indian English or Kenyan English, with their distinct sounds, vocabularies and grammars, are not merely tools of communication but a means of expressing the cultural identities of their speakers. Teachers should use appropriate and relevant texts in their classrooms which originate from beyond Britain, America and Australia,[16] reflecting the wider world, the diversity of Englishes and the cultures and identities these Englishes express.[17]

Encountering texts which use a range of native and non-native varieties of English will help to equip learners with the knowledge and skills needed to meet the following aims of Læreplan for Kunnskapsløftet (2020) (the National Curriculum for Knowledge Promotion), henceforth referred to as LK20. Competence aims for all years include:

1. *Explore* lifestyles and traditions in different societies in the English-speaking world and in Norway and *reflect* over identity and cultural affiliation.
2. Acquire *words, phrases and cultural knowledge* through English-language literature and children's culture.
3. *Explore and describe* lifestyles, mindsets, communication patterns and diversity in the English-speaking world.

(Norwegian Directorate for Education and Training, 2019/20, our emphasis).

"Meeting with English Language Texts", one of the three core elements of the English curriculum (Eng 01-04) in LK20, clearly articulates that by "interpreting and critically evaluating different types of English-language texts, learners will acquire language and knowledge of culture and society. With this, the learners develop intercultural competence so that they can relate to different lifestyles, mindsets and communication patterns. Learners will be given a basis for seeing their own and others' identities in a multilingual and multicultural context." Implied in this core aim is that diverse texts set in different English-speaking countries, and written by authors originating from those countries, provide learners with opportunities to see both themselves (*mirrors*) and others (*windows*) (Bishop 1990; Wissman et al. 2016).

Classrooms in Norway are often multilingual and multicultural, so it is important that teachers use a range of texts. Some texts will signal normality for some learners by mirroring, especially for learners who belong to the culture depicted in the book. At the same time texts will be windows for most, showing the uniqueness of different cultures. For example, a text about children in Somalia read in a classroom in Oslo will mirror the culture of any

---

16 Sometimes known as BANA countries following Holliday (1994). See also discussion in Bland (2020).
17 For further aspects of diversity, such as sexuality and gender identification, please see chapter 6.

Somalian learners. At the same time, it will be a window for non-Somalian learners who will get a glimpse of a different culture.

These windows are also *sliding glass doors* allowing learners to step into the worlds of others, real or imagined, and to hopefully begin to reflect on themselves and their own behaviours as an important aspect of intercultural competence (Martinez, Koss and Johnson 2016). Teachers must remember that interpretation and understanding of texts are affected by cultures, ideas and beliefs. The same texts might make different sense to different learners (see Munden 2019 for a recent study in Norwegian classrooms) so it is important for teachers to guide their learners to develop *critical reading* of texts, even from an early age (Byram et al. 2002).

Intercultural competence is undoubtedly at the heart of LK20,[18] but IC can be a difficult concept to define. Deardorff's (2006) investigation into definitions and approaches to IC found that most scholars define it as the "ability to develop targeted *knowledge*, *skills* and *attitudes* to visible behaviour and communication that are both effective and appropriate in intercultural interactions" as summarised in Figure 1.

Teaching skills and knowledge is often more straightforward than teaching attitudes, but the three are very much connected. Whilst linguistic skills and knowledge of language are important for enabling communication, suc-

Figure 1. Constituent elements of intercultural competence (after Deardorff 2006).

---

18 Please refer to Carlsen, Dypedahl and Hoem Iversen (2020) and Dypedahl and Lund (2020) for a detailed discussion of the concept of IC and its relevance to language teaching, particularly in Norway.

cessful IC needs people to not only develop a knowledge of other cultures, but also to learn to understand themselves. How does one's own culture shape perceptions of oneself, the world and relationships with others? IC shapes attitudes encouraging the development of openness and interest in other cultures, willingness to suspend judgement about other cultures and belief systems, and valuing cultural diversity as a resource (Corapi and Short 2016). What is needed is a "plurivocal approach" that can create a space for diverse voices and for "multiperspectivity" to prevail in the classroom (Dypedahl, 2020, p. 64). A "plurivocal approach" is one where literary texts are an important tool for socialising learners into becoming culturally aware. This enables teachers to make what is "strange" both familiar and known. Texts such as story books and picturebooks can help in developing literary and visual literacy by presenting opportunities to experience a range of perspectives and voices (Heggernes, 2019, 2020, in press).

Dypedahl and Bøhn (2020: 84) assert that "Communicative competence and intercultural competence can also serve as common denominators for the three cross-cultural topics in the LK20, *Health and Life Skills, Democracy and Citizenship, and Sustainable Development*. To be able to manage life, it is an advantage to communicate constructively with other people."

This chapter aims to guide primary and secondary teachers to resources which develop intercultural and communicative competence by helping learners to understand relationships between varieties of English and expression of cultural values and identities. The literary texts suggested will introduce the different ways in which English is used by speakers in different countries to communicate and to express cultural identities. It will be useful to start with a discussion of the concept of global Englishes in the 21st century before showcasing a range of literary texts from different continents along with teaching ideas for the language classroom.

The status and role of English

English is now a *global language* used by *diverse* speakers from different linguistic and cultural backgrounds around the globe for a variety of different purposes (Galloway & Rose 2015; Jenkins 2014; Kirkpatrick 2010). Kachru's (1982, 1985) concentric circles model of English is often used to describe speakers of English, as shown in Figure 2.

Kachru's model depicts the historic situation in which "native speakers" were considered central and superior compared to other users. Unfortunately, this elitist "native speakers are best" attitude still prevails in some

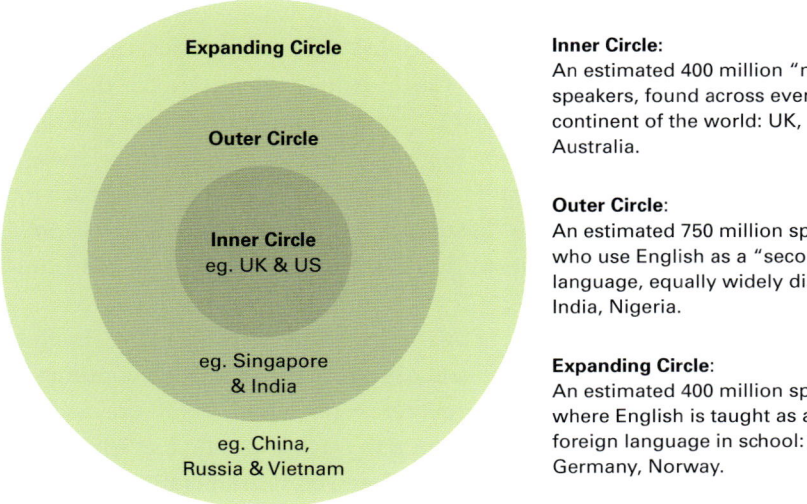

Figure 2. The "Three Circles Model" of global Englishes (after Kachru 1982, 1985).

parts of society and amongst some educators. Kachru strongly critiqued this view. He asserted the validity of diverse Englishes by claiming that non-native varieties of English serve to express cultural identities and to fulfil the communicative needs of speakers just as adequately as native speaker varieties serve the communicative needs of such speakers while also allowing expression of cultural identities.

However, Kachru's model is problematic in today's globalised linguistic marketplace; it assigns status to speakers based on history and geography, rather than how, when and why English is used. The way in which English is used in Norway, for example, is no longer typical of a foreign language but is more like a "second" language (for further discussion of the status and role of English, including in Norway, see Lyngstad 2019; Brevik and Rindal 2020, especially part 1, and the references therein). As global citizens, Norwegian learners will interact with users of many varieties of English and thus need some familiarity with at least some key "outer circle" varieties[19] such as Nigerian English, Indian English or Singapore English. At the same time, they need to be aware that users of these varieties, with their distinct accents

---

19   While the huge sociolinguistic changes of the last two decades have made Kachru's model less relevant, nevertheless, Kachru's labels – inner, outer and expanding circle – are maintained in this chapter. These labels have become a much recognised and frequently used tool in the field to refer to groups of countries that use English for intranational and international purposes.

and lexico-grammatical, discourse and pragmatic features, encode different cultural meanings than those of the so-called "inner circle" varieties of English. Language is an important part of socio-cultural identities. It is therefore more accurate to think about *global Englishes* (plural) rather than one form of English and that hence learning Englishes, particularly global varieties, is as an important way to develop IC. After year 10, in LK20, learners are for instance expected to be able to "listen to and understand words and expressions in variants of English" (Norwegian Directorate for Education and Training, 2019/20).

Despite this global diversity of English today, the voices of "native" English speakers, notably standard British and American English, often continue to dominate English-learning classrooms across the world, to the exclusion of other voices. LK20 does not state the need to teach a specific English accent, such as Generalised American (GA) or Received Pronunciation (RP). Yet attitude surveys in Norway such as Arkelett (2017) and Loftheim (2013) continue to show positive bias towards these varieties and against other so-called "non-standard" varieties, despite these being perfectly intelligible and acceptable varieties of English which mark important aspects of individual, group and national identity (e.g. Indian English).

Unfortunately, "native-speaker" teaching models exclude the majority of today's English speakers and their associated identities and cultures (Byram & Wagner, 2018). They also fail to take into account the variety of ways in which contemporary English is used, and crucially the way in which learners themselves will use English. For most, including those in Norway, the goal is to use *English as a global Lingua Franca* (ELF). That is, as a communication device between speakers from different lingua-cultural backgrounds (Baker, 2017). Teachers should also recognise that their own classrooms are filled with learners from different lingua-cultural backgrounds, so this is a need faced by learners every day.

It is crucial that all learners are therefore given the opportunity to engage with materials that reflect different lingua-cultural backgrounds. They need to become aware of the many forms of English as a global language (knowledge), to build tolerance and understanding for similarities and differences (attitudes) and to develop the skills needed for successful interactions with people from different cultural backgrounds (skills).

Diverse classrooms need diverse texts[20]

The number of immigrants and refugees living in Norway has increased rapidly over recent years (Statistics Norway, 2019). Whilst Norway does not collect statistics on "race" or "ethnicity", statistics are available for learners with an "immigrant background", who appear to account for around 15 %–20 % of learners in compulsory education (Norwegian Directorate for Education and Training, 2016). Pran and Holst (2015) registered 150 first languages in Norwegian schools. The range of abilities, motivations, aspirations, cultures, behaviours and language backgrounds is therefore considerable, which presents challenges and opportunities to and for teachers.

One challenge is to successfully engage all learners and create an inclusive learning environment that will enable everyone to progress. Many approaches can promote inclusivity and engagement (see, for instance, chapters 6 and 8); one key method is to ensure everyone is, and has a chance to be, heard and seen. By using diverse texts, teachers draw upon the intercultural experiences, skills, attitudes and knowledge of learners themselves, encouraging reflective thinking and individual development in keeping with Deardorff (2006) above.

Being seen is an experience which historically has been lacking in many classrooms across the world at all levels of education. In the British and American texts which often dominate English curricula, the disabled, the working class, the LGBTQ+ community and people of colour are very much underrepresented (Booktrust Represents, 2019, Reflecting Realities Project, 2018). See chapters 6 and 8 for more recommendations regarding LGBTQ+ texts.

Langvik (2016) showed that only 36 Norwegian children's books have been published since the 1970s with a "multicultural main character" and Johansen (2019) states that there are "very few" children's books featuring main characters with a "minority background" in Norwegian children's literature, making classroom representation in English language texts even more important.

Not being able to see oneself as the main character, or always being marginalised, stereotyped or made fun of, sends clear signals to learners regarding their value in society and is likely to result in disengagement and disillusionment. Goodman (1982) and Ebe (2010) demonstrate that using culturally rel-

---

20 Some of the ideas and texts discussed in this chapter derive from materials presented by the authors in a 2-year DIKU-funded NOTED collaborative internationalisation project between HVL (Høgskulen på Vestlandet), NSC (The Norwegian Study Centre at the University of York), and two York primary schools (https://www.hvl.no/en/project/616010/). During 2017–2019 the project offered intercultural school and classroom experience in the UK for Norwegian teacher trainees. This is now an option for learners and in-service teachers in the NSC's *York Course* programme, (www.york.ac.uk/nsc/yorkcourse), which includes undergraduate and postgraduate modules (including from the authors) which promote development of intercultural competencies.

evant texts promotes higher reading comprehension and encourages deeper level thinking and learning.

As discussed in chapter 1, books such as *My Two Grannies* (2007) help to promote tolerance and understanding, and ensure everyone is valued; it is both a window and a mirror for different learners. Using different words for food from two different cultures, this book also provides a demonstration of the link between language(s), culture(s) and identity(ies).

It is imperative that teachers and learners are able to select appropriate texts themselves, and for their classrooms and libraries. Teachers (and learners) might ask themselves the following questions (based on rubrics and questions by Adam and Harper 2016, Ebe 2010 and Martinez, Koss and Johnson 2016):[21]

About content: What is the key idea or theme of the text? What is the evidence? Who are the main characters of the text? What is the culture/are the cultures of the main characters? When and where do they live? What are the social characteristics of these characters (age, gender, religion, etc.)? What might learners learn from these characters? How will learners connect with these characters? How did the author organise the text? What do the illustrations show? Do you agree with what the author/illustrator is representing – why/why not?

About language: What role do individual words, phrases, sentences or paragraphs play in the story, e.g. do they tell us something about the identity or cultural beliefs of the characters or about a piece of background knowledge that the people from that culture share?

About the author(s): Who wrote the text? How reliable is the narrator and how do you know? Who is the intended audience?

Teachers should also seek to avoid stereotyping or one-dimensional portrayals of a particular culture in a classroom by presenting multiple texts rather than a single story (Lund 2014, Adichie TED Talk, 2009). Please see also chapter 7.

Two sample cases: Texts from the "Outer Circle"

It is therefore necessary to bring global Englishes into the classroom. Examples of how to do this are provided through case studies of texts representing "outer circle varieties" from (1) the Indian subcontinent and (2) African

---

21   For further details regarding text selection, please see chapter 8.

continent, written by authentic authors born into the culture they are writing about. They are all therefore #ownvoices authors, a concept discussed further in both chapter 2 and chapter 6.

This geographical approach is in keeping with Modernist theories of teaching culture, but teachers can expand such an approach through a postmodernist perspective whereby authentic texts, such as those discussed below, are combined with other texts and shown to represent local or individual views as well as national ones (Kramsch, 2002).

Texts discussed here start with those primarily aimed at young learners and progress to texts for young adults. The main focus is on "literature" in the conventional sense of written texts, but links to film and audio recordings in keeping with the broader sense of text in LK20 are also included in the "Culture Capsules" (p. 101) and table 1 (p. 116). The reference list also provides details of companion websites which include teaching activities. The two case studies can be linked to several competence aims, for instance from after year 7, where learners should be able to "investigate ways of living and traditions in different societies in the English-speaking world and in Norway and reflect on identity and cultural belonging" (Norwegian Directorate for Education and Training, 2019/20).

Of course, more connects than divides human beings, and diverse literature can be used to teach all the language features that "standard" British and American literature can do too – onomatopoeia, alliteration, word formation, grammar, etc. (the code). However, the focus here is on how features such as onomatopoeia help to create cultural meanings in the texts, i.e. help to describe the situations described in the story or show the beliefs and value systems that lie beneath the actions of the characters (the social practice).

Case study 1: The Indian subcontinent

Chitra Soundar is the Indian-born author, now based in the UK, of over 30 colourful and energetic children's books which bring India and a world of imagination to life. *A Jar of Pickles and a Pinch of Justice* won the Eugenie Summerfield Children's Prize in 2018. The "Farmer Falgu" series, all containing bright and bold illustrations by Kanika Nair, currently comprises 4 books. In each story, Farmer Falgu goes on a journey in rural India, facing a number of problems along the way. Throughout the story he finds solutions and meets a range of different characters. These characters, central to the story and the illustrations, are colourful and are shown smiling in the pictures. They are often simply going about their daily lives in rural India, thus providing a window into this way of life and part of the world.

Illlustration 1. From *Farmer Falgu goes on a Trip*. © Karadi Tales Company Pvt. Ltd., (Soundar, 2014, illustrations Nair, 2014).

In this picture from the first book, *Farmer Falgu Goes on a Trip* (2014), Farmer Falgu's (pictured with a red hat) cart is pulled by decorated bullocks (oxen).

There are two possible starting points for a discussion of diversity related to the cart and the bullocks: the type of animal pulling the cart (or more generally modes of transportation) and the fact that the bullocks are decorated with a bindi (red spot). Either could be explored with a "culture capsule", where learners are encouraged to record their thoughts visually with a Venn diagram or visual organiser, as shown on the following page. The example "culture capsule" has been filled out by two learners in the same class: one from the UK and another originally from Myanmar but now resident in the UK (<1 year).

This simple activity, encouraging learners to make observations and compare with their own experiences, could easily be expanded in additional ways. In the example culture capsule, the learner from Myanmar notes that the cart is open. This is likely due to the climate (look also at the clothes) – so what can be learnt about the weather and the role of climate and geography in cultural practices? In these examples, both learners mention colours and decorations – what does this tell us about how a culture views its animals and objects?

Culture Capsules: A way to encourage thought and discussion

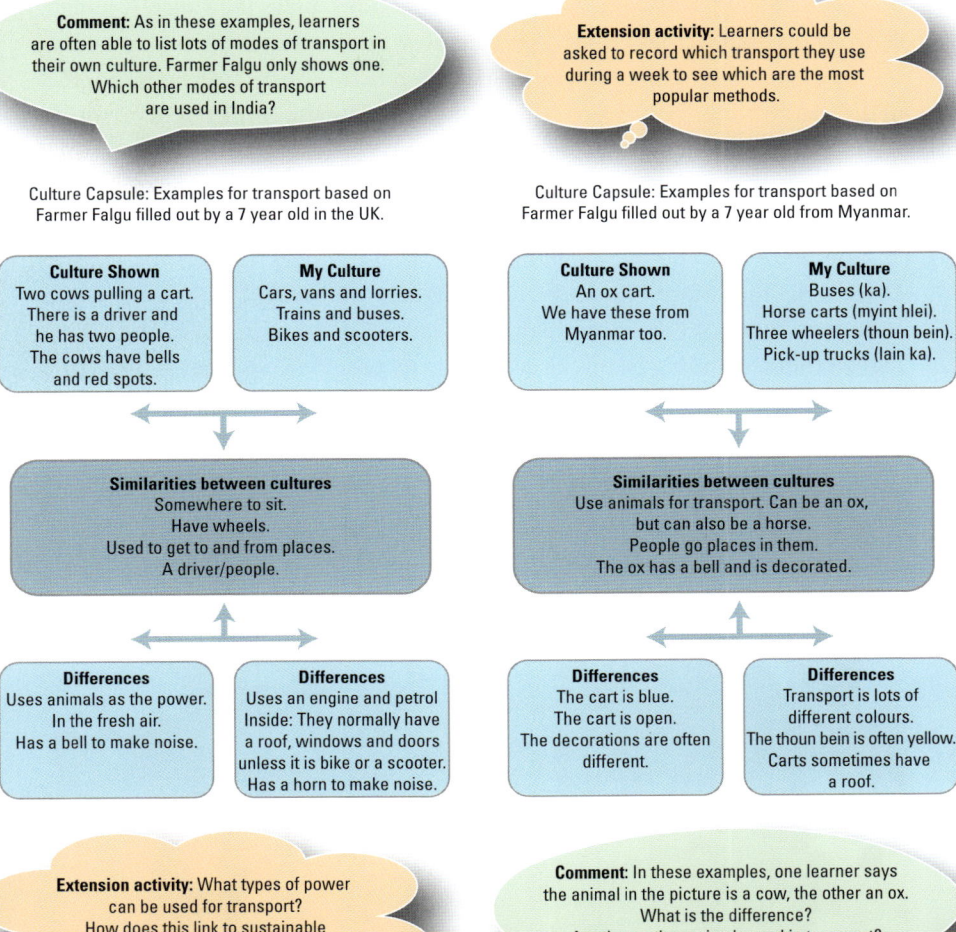

Other topics for a similar "culture capsule" approach might be family roles, body image, time, food, holidays and celebrations, health and hygiene, manners, work, dress, friendships, religion or art, and hence this could work for any text or text type.

The text does not mention the word *bindi*, but if it did, for many learners this would be an unfamiliar word and an unfamiliar concept. Discussion of the word *bindi* could be used to introduce Hinduism and Hindu culture. The

Falgu series, like many texts about different cultures, introduces new cultural concepts and the words used to describe them. For example, the snake charmer, a job not found in all countries/locations, plays *the pungi*. A *pungi* (a word originally from Hindi) is a kind of wind instrument, which may be inferred from the text and/or may be identified in the illustration in the hands of the man with the light green hat. Learners can use the context and pictures to try to infer the meanings, but there is also a glossary at the back of the book, so they are encouraged to use multiple strategies when encountering unfamiliar or new words.

Soundar's latest book, *Shubh Diwali* (2019) introduces learners to the way Diwali, the important Hindu festival of light, is celebrated with family and friends in India. Whilst Hinduism is the largest religion in India, there are many others including Islam (largest minority religion), Sikhism, Christianity, Buddhism, Jainism, Zoroastrianism, Judaism and the Bahá'í Faith.

Illustration 2. From *Golden Domes and Silver Lanterns,* ©2012 Hena Khan. Illustrations by Mehrdokht Amini. Used with Permission from Chronicle Books, LLC. Visit www.ChronicleBooks.com

Pakistani-American Muslim author Hena Khan is the author of more than 10 colourful and lively diverse books aimed at young learners. In *Golden Domes and Silver Lanterns: A Muslim Book of Colors* (2015), a multiple award winning book (Bank Street College of Education Best Children's Books of the Year 2013; Pubwest 2013 Book Design Awards gold winner), the text introduces potentially new vocabulary reflecting the culture(s) and religion of Islam. For example, *minarets* are tall, slender towers on or near a mosque (= a Muslim holy building) from which Muslims are called to pray.

The sensitive illustrations by Mehrdokht Amini combine with Khan's rhyming text to show how everyday colours are given special meaning as learners read about clothing, food and other important elements of Islamic culture such as calligraphy and quotations from the Holy Quran by following a family. All these elements would make good culture capsule topics. Further, the book introduces learners to different languages and scripts, in this case Arabic.

Illustration 3. From Golden Domes and Silver Lanterns, ©2012 Hena Khan. Illustrations by Mehrdokht Amini. Used with Permission from Chronicle Books, LLC. Visit www.ChronicleBooks.com.

Ruskin Bond is an internationally successful Indian author of more than 50 books and poems. He is a John Llewellyn Rhys and Sahitya Academy (Indian Literary Academy) award winner. *The Blue Umbrella* (1992) is a short, humorous novella set in the hills of Garhwal, India, capturing life in a village, with themes of selfishness and materialism, friendship and generosity, all of which could be explored with learners. It was adapted as a successful Hindi film directed by Vishal Bhardwaj (2005), which won the National Film Award for Best Children's Film awarded by the Government of India. Film clips could also be shown in the classroom, for example via YouTube, allowing learners to experience spoken Hindi and see visual representations of parts of the story.[22]

An image from the graphic novel adaptation *The Blue Umbrella – Stories by Ruskin Bond*[23] (Amar Chitra Katha publications, 2012), is seen in illustraton 4. Here, learners could be encouraged to reflect on culture (questions 1–3) and language (questions 4–6).

Illustration 4. From *The Blue Umbrella* (Bond, 2012, Amar Chitra Katha Publications).

---

22 See more about using films in chapter 9.
23 Chapter 7 has a useful discussion on how to use graphic novels in the English classroom and could be used to expand the ideas discussed.

1. Who/What is represented in the illustrations?
2. What is on sale in the shop? Is yoghurt something you would expect to drink or be sold in a glass in your culture?
3. Why is yoghurt being offered? This is a country where it can get very hot and yoghurt is cooling when drunk.
4. What is a "teashop"? Do you have teashops in your culture? How are they similar? How are they different?
5. How are offers and questions constructed? Here the seller says, "Some hot tea for you, Sir? Or a glass of yoghurt perhaps?" What other ways could this offer be made?
6. Why is the address term *Sir* used? What do you learn about the relationship between the speaker and the addressee?
7. What is being offered and what are the associations you have with those items, i.e. how is *hot tea* different to *a cup of tea*? Can you have the opposite of *hot tea*, i.e. *cold tea*? Do you have or know other words for tea?

The questions above can be linked to the competence aim after year 7, where learners are expected to be able to "read and listen to English-language factual texts and literature for children and young people and write and talk about the content" (Norwegian Directorate for Education and Training, 2019/20)

The Bridge Home (2019) is the 4th award-winning novel by Padma Venkatraman, born in India, now living in America. The book has won many awards including WNDB Walter Dean Myers Award for Young Readers, SCBI Golden Kite Award for Middle Grade Fiction, and Paterson Prize for Young People. Two sisters, one of whom has a developmental disability, run away from their abusive father and end up living under an abandoned bridge in the busy city of Chennai where they befriend two homeless boys who live under the bridge. It offers a window into the horrible lives of homeless street children in India, but is also filled with love, beauty, friendship and freedom, and is ultimately a story filled with hope.

Address terms used in this novel give an interesting cultural insight into relationships and kinship terms used in India. When the boys first meet Viji and Rukku on the bridge, they address Viji as *akka*, a kinship word used to refer to an older sister in most South Indian languages. Learners can also observe how various characters are identified in the story, for example, *teashop aunty*. This is also one of many novel compounds in the book: *teashopman; wasteman; beadshop; cookie package* which can all be used to discuss word formation techniques and meaning. A number of audio-visual materials based on *The Bridge Home* are available from the author (https://padlet.com/

venkatraman_padma/6past6aiht5d). Intercultural awareness of the different linguistic and cultural aspects of Indian English can be developed by getting learners to listen to the author read the story. Among the many themes for discussion are: the Indian caste system, Indian weddings and Diwali, disability awareness, social (in)justice, charities. All are well suited to curriculum aims and developing new words and conceptual understanding, as with the texts above. See chapter 6 for more ideas on texts related to diversity.

Case study 2: Africa

English is an official language in many African countries. These include Zimbabwe, Botswana, Namibia, Kenya, Sierra Leone, South Africa, Ghana, the Gambia and Nigeria. This case study focuses on the final three countries.

Dr Tamara Pizzoli, an African American writer living in Italy, has published more than 10 picture books with the aim of bringing wider representation to storytelling. Her first book, *The Ghanaian Goldilocks* (2014), illustrated by Phil Howell, is a modern twist on the classic European fairy tale. Here, Goldilocks is the nickname of a West African boy called Kofi who lives in the Ghanaian city of Accra. Throughout the book a number of West African places are mentioned, which can link to history and geography.

Family, relationships and identity are themes which run strongly throughout. This is evident in the way the characters are named and addressed: both a relationship – *mama, papa, sista, bruh* – and the first name are generally used for adults but not for children. This could be used as a starting point to discuss families and relationships: *Who is in your family? What do you call them?*

Inclusion of *Pombo* (a game) and *kente cloth* (handwoven patterned textiles) provide a mirror for Ghanaian learners, and a window for others. The illustrations, context and explanations in the text are also sliding glass doors. There are many such examples, particularly in the field of food: *Jollof rice, plantain, kenke*.

Further, there is some evidence of linguistic variation in reported dialogue, such as in Sista Francine's: "I told it! The child went in and didn't never come back out, so I called his mama." This shows variation from standard English grammar in the use of negative concord (two negatives: *n't* and *never*) rather than one: *didn't ever*.

Finally, there is occasional evidence of languages other than English used in Ghana. There are two examples of the native language Twi (also known as Akan Kasa, and spoken by around 9 million people in South and Central Ghana): *Mamin* which means "I'm full" and, as shown in illustration 5, *akwaaba* which means "welcome". This is an example of code-switching, which will be

When he opened the front door, he was greeted first by Goldilocks' mother, Mama Abena. Behind her stood all the neighbors and even some friends from across town.

"I understand my son is here?" Mama Abena began.

"Mmmmm-hmmmm" chimed in Sista Francine.

"I told it! The child went in and didn't never come back out, so I called his mama."

Papa Akuffo nodded.

"Well," Mama Abena said, "we figured this was as good a time as any to welcome you and your family to our neighborhood.
Akwaaba! Welcome! And of course I came to get my son."

Papa Akuffo stepped aside and the neighbors filed in carrying an array of wonderful delights. There was jollof rice, plantain, kenke, maasa, kebabs, fufu, fried fish, sweet doughnuts and oh so much more.

The roar of laughter and good conversation soon filled the house completely. Goldilocks tapped his mother gently on her back, his head hung low.

She lifted his chin and silently walked him over to the Osei family.

Illustration 5. From *The Ghanaian Goldilocks* (Pizzoli, 2014, illustrations Howell 2014). The English Schoolhouse.

a feature of speech of many in today's diverse classrooms. Learners might discuss: *Who code-switches? Why do they code-switch? Which languages do they know? When do they use each language and whom do they use it with?* Given that Norwegian adolescents frequently use English, particularly in virtual environments such as social media and gaming, it might also lead to interesting and useful discussions about when, where and why they use English.

Further examples of such multilingualism and code-switching can be found in multi-award-winning American author Miranda Paul's (2015) *One Plastic Bag: Isatou Cessay and the Recycling Women of the Gambia* illustrated by Elizabeth Zunon. Paul has written over 20 fiction and non-fiction books for young and middle-grade learners, often drawing on her experiences living in

Illustration 6. From *One Plastic Bag: Isatou Ceesay and the Recycling Women of the Gambia* (Paul, 2015, Illustrations Zunon 2015). Text © 2015 by Miranda Paul. Illustration © 2015 by Elizabeth Zunon. Reprinted with the permission of Millbrook Press, a division of Lerner Publishing Group, Inc.

Africa. She was recently awarded the CYBILS Award and Green Earth Book award (2020). *One Plastic Bag* is an inspiring and true story of how one African woman began a movement to recycle the plastic bags that were polluting her community. The story is a useful starting point for discussing issues of sustainable development, a key theme in LK20.

This book develops the idea of different languages and scripts by introducing the learner to some Wolof, a language used in the Gambia, Senegal and Mauritania. Unlike in Ghanaian Goldilocks, the grandmother uses whole sentences rather than simply isolated words, as in: *Naka ligeby be?* which means "how is the work?" and the answer is *Ndanka, Ndanka* meaning "slow". In illustration 6, both the grandmother and Isatou are shown using Wolof and English, demonstrating a multilingual community (and world) and how different aspects of culture, language and identity mix.

Mixing of cultures and identities is a theme which runs throughout many of the short stories suitable for young adults in *The Thing Around Your Neck* (2009) by prize-winning Nigerian author Chimamanda Ngozi Adichie. "The American Embassy", one of the stories in this book, won the O. Henry Prize in 2003. Amongst the stories in *The Thing Around Your Neck* are "The Arrangers of Marriage" in which a newly married woman arrives in New York City with her husband and finds she is unable to accept his rejection of their Nigerian identity, and "Tomorrow Is Too Far" where a young woman reveals the devastating secret of her brother's death. In both, learners discover much about Nigerian culture and mixing with the West (in particular America) by following the trials and tribulations of people in their ordinary lives. In "Tomorrow Is Too Far", for example, vivid pictures of an African garden are painted by the author who writes of coconut trees, avocados, cashews and guavas on mango trees. We learn something of the meaning of the surname *Nnabuisi* and gender roles and differences, and learn words such as *nwadiana* ("daughter's son") and *echi eteka* ("tomorrow is too far"). Themes of Adichie's stories include racism, sexism, colonialism, corruption and immigration.

Conclusion

This chapter has argued that English is a global language and that learners need to be equipped with the skills necessary to communicate in this global world. This means recognising that there are many different Englishes and many different cultures associated with them. It is vital that the voices from outside the UK and the US are heard as a way for people to be seen (window), to see themselves (mirror) and to access the worlds of others (sliding doors).

A list of further texts and resources that teachers can use to develop intercultural understanding in their classrooms is provided below. These resources should help learners in deepening their understanding of their own worlds while expanding this understanding to knowledge of other people's worlds.

Using high-quality and diverse texts within the classroom encourages all learners to actively engage, and promotes an inclusive learning environment for the acquisition of language skills. Exposure to diverse texts prepares learners to communicate with speakers of different varieties of English. It also helps learners develop a more positive attitude to the varieties and the people who speak them (Lund, 2020, p. 37). Learners hence have the opportunity to transform relationships – to themselves, to others and to the world around them. By introducing English texts featuring diverse cultural voices "speaking" in diverse Englishes, teachers can help to create a culturally agile citizenship that in turn will promote and uphold the democratic values that underpin Norwegian society. In the words of LK20, "the interdisciplinary theme of democracy and citizenship is about developing learners' understanding that their perception of the world is culturally dependent. By learning English, learners can meet different societies and cultures by communicating with others around the world, regardless of linguistic and cultural background."

This is crucial for efforts to build a more open, tolerant and inclusive society for all, ensuring that everyone's voice is valued (Byram, 2008; Gilles, 2012; Short, Day & Schroeder, 2016). Notions of *them* and *us* can be turned into *we* through everyone developing their *intercultural competences*, a central theme of LK20.

References
Primary texts

Adichie, C.N. (2009). *The Thing Around Your Neck*. Knopf Publishers. https://www.penguinrandomhouse.com/books/881/the-thing-around-your-neck-by-chimamanda-ngozi-adichie/9780307455918/readers-guide/

Bond, R. (1992). *The Blue Umbrella*. Rupa Publications.

Bond, R. (2012). *The Blue Umbrella – Stories by Ruskin Bond*. [Graphic novel]. Amar Chitra Katha publications.

Khan, H. (2015). *Golden Domes and Silver Lanterns: A Muslim Book of Colors*. Chronicle Books. https://cdn.shopify.com/s/files/1/0261/7291/5805/files/hena-khan-books-teacherguide-final.pdf?3431

Paul, M. (2015). *One Plastic Bag: Isatou Ceesay and the Recycling Women of the Gambia*. Millbrook Press. http://mirandapaul.com/for-teachers/

Pizzoli, T. (2014). *The Ghanaian Goldilocks*. The English Schoolhouse. https://www.modernghana.com/news/578679/the-ghanaian-goldilocks.html

Soundar, C. (2014). *Farmer Falgu Goes on a Trip*. Karadi Tales. http://chitrasoundar.com/kids/?cat=5

Soundar, C. (2019). *Shubh Diwali*. Albert Whitman & Co.

Venkatraman, P. (2019). *The Bridge Home*. Nancy Paulsen Books. https://padlet.com/venkatraman_padma/6past6aiht5d

Further recommended texts

There are a number of useful online lists of diverse books, classified by age range:

50 texts to diversify your class reading list available at https://www.tes.com/teaching-resource/50-books-to-diversify-your-class-reading-list-11397499

Once Upon a Garden City: A Selection of Children's and Young Adult Literature from Singapore available at https://www.nac.gov.sg/dam/jcr:097689ef-a460-440a-b877-ed10e375bd6d

Beyond the Secret Garden: BAME writers available at http://booksforkeeps.co.uk/member/karen-sands-o'connor

Children's and Young Adult Books Set in Africa available at https://www.goodreads.com/list/show/12430.Top_Children_s_Y_A_Books_Set_in_Africa

Mirrors, Windows and Sliding Glass Doors: Book List for Sixth Formers and Confident Older Readers available at https://www.englishandmedia.co.uk/blog/mirrors-windows-and-sliding-glass-doors-older-secondary

Young Learners

Fullerton, A. (2013). *Community Soup*. Pajama Press. Canada (Kenya).

Javaherbin, M. (2019). *My Grandma and me*. Candlewick Press, USA (Iran).

Membrino, A. (2019). *I look up to… Malala Yousafzai*. Random House Books for Young Readers. USA (Pakistan/UK).

Middle Grade Learners

Devi, M. (2003). *The Why-Why Girl*. Tulika Publishers (India).

Ravishankar, A. (2005). *Moin and the Monster*. Duckbill Books (India).

Teens and Young Adults

Bhagat, C. (2014). *Half Girlfriend*. Rupa Publications India (India, also a film).

Zoboi, I. (Ed.). (2019). *Black Enough: Stories of Being Young and Black in America*. Balzer and Bray. (USA)

Secondary texts

Adam, H., & Harper, L. (2016). Assessing and selecting culturally diverse literature for the classroom. *Practical Literacy: The Early and Primary Years, 21*(2), 10–14.

Adichie, C. (2009, July). *The Danger of a Single Story* [video] https://www.ted.com/talks/chimamanda_ngozi_adichie_the_danger_of_a_single_story?language=en

Areklett, I.B. (2017). *Norwegian Attitudes towards English Varieties. A sociolinguistic study* [Unpublished MA English Thesis]. University of Bergen. https://pdfs.semanticscholar.org/7949/1de0c1e27b6295b06b4105c26cb94fd674b5.pdf

Baker, W. (2017). *Culture and Identity through English as a Lingua Franca: Rethinking Concepts and Goals in Intercultural Communication.* Mouton de Gruyter.

Bishop, R.S. (1990). "Mirrors, Windows, and Sliding Glass Doors". *Perspectives: Choosing and Using Books for the Classroom.* 6, 3

Bland, J. (2020). Using literature for intercultural language learning in English language education. In M. Dypedahl & R.E. Lund (2020) (Eds.) *Teaching and Learning Interculturally* (pp. 69–89). Cappelen Damm Akademisk.

BookTrust (2019). *BookTrust Represents* [Project]. https://www.booktrust.org.uk/what-we-do/programmes-and-campaigns/booktrust-represents/

Brevik, L.M., & Rindal, U.E. (Eds.) (2020). *Teaching English in Norwegian Classrooms: From Research to Practice.* Universitetsforlaget.

Byram, M. (2008). *From Foreign Language Education to Education for Intercultural Citizenship. Essays and Reflections.* Multilingual Matters.

Byram, M., Gribkova, B., & Starkey, H. (2002). *Developing the Intercultural Dimension in Language Teaching. A Practical Introduction for Teachers.* https://discovery.ucl.ac.uk/id/eprint/1562524/1/Starkey_InterculturalDimensionByram.pdf

Byram, M., & Wagner, M. (2018). Making a difference: Language teaching for intercultural and international dialogue. *Foreign Language Annals, 51*, 140–151.

Carlsen, C., Dypedahl, M., & Hoem Iversen, S. (2020) (Eds.) *Teaching and Learning English.* Cappelen Damm Akademisk.

Centre for Literacy in Primary Education (CLPE), (2018). *Reflecting Realities – Survey of Ethnic Representation within UK Children 2018.* https://clpe.org.uk/RR

Corapi, S., & Short, K.G. (2016). Exploring international and intercultural understanding through global literature. *World of Words.* https://longviewfdn.org/files/2214/4741/8337/Longview_Foundation_compressed.pdf

Deardorff, D. (2006). Identification and assessment of intercultural competence as a student outcome of internationalisation. *Journal of Studies in International Educations, 10*(3), 241–266.

Dypedahl, M. (2020). Culture studies for intercultural learning. In M. Dypedahl, & R.E. Lund (Eds.) *Teaching and Learning Interculturally* (pp. 58–67). Cappelen Damm Akademisk.

Dypedahl, M., & Bøhn, H. (2020). Intercultural Competence and Culture. In C. Carlsen, M. Dypedahl & S. Hoem Iversen, *Teaching and Learning English* (pp. 81–99). Cappelen Damm Akademisk.

Dypedahl, M., & Lund, R.E. (2020) (Eds.) *Teaching and Learning Interculturally.* Cappelen Damm Akademisk.

Ebe, A.E. (2010). Culturally relevant texts and reading assessment for English language learners. *Reading Horizons: A Journal of Literacy and Language Arts, 50*(3), Article 5. https://scholarworks.wmich.edu/reading_horizon/vol50/Iss3/5

Galloway, N., & Rose, H. (2015). *Introducing Global Englishes.* Routledge.

Gilles, C. (2012). Using global literature to build understandings for all students. *WOWS Stories: Connections to the Classroom, 4*(3). https://wowlit.org/on-line-publications/stories/iv3/14/

Goodman, Y.M. (1982). Retellings of literature and the comprehension process. *Theory into Practice: Children's Literature, 21*(4), 301–307.

Heggernes, S.L. (2019). Opening a dialogic space: Intercultural learning through picturebooks. *CLELE Journal, 7*(2). http://clelejournal.org/article-2-intercultural-learning/

Heggernes, S.L. (2020). Using picturebooks for intercultural learning. In M. Dypedahl & R.E. Lund (Eds.) *Teaching and Learning Interculturally* (pp. 112–129). Cappelen Damm Akademisk.

Heggernes, S.L. (in press). Intercultural learning through Peter Sis' The Wall: Teenagers reading a challenging picturebook. In Å.M. Ommundsen, G. Haaland & B. Kümmerling Meibauer (Eds.) *Challenging Picturebooks in Education*. Routledge.

Holliday, A. (1994). The house of TESEP and the communicative approach: The special needs of state English language education. *ELT Journal, 48*, 3–11.

Jenkins, J. (2014). *World Englishes: A Resource Book for Students* (3rd ed.). Routledge.

Johansen, E.B. (2019 September 23). Svært få hovedpersoner med minoritetsbakgrunn i norske barnebøker [Remarkably few main characters with minority backgrounds in Norwegian children's books]. *Aftenposten*. https://www.aftenposten.no/kultur/i/g7jrVL/svaert-faa-hovedpersoner-med-minoritetsbakgrunn-i-norske-barneboeker

Kachru, B. (1982). *The Other Tongue: English Across Cultures*. University of Illinois Press.

Kachru, B. (1985). *The Alchemy of English: The Spread, Functions and Models of Non-Native Englishes*. Pergamon Institute of English.

Kirkpatrick, A. (Ed.). (2010). *The Routledge Handbook of World Englishes*. Routledge.

Kramsch, C. (2002). Culture in language teaching. In H.L. Andersen, K. Lund & K. Risager (Eds.), *Culture in Language Learning* (pp. 11–16). Aarhus University Press.

Langvik, K. (2016). *Picturebooks with Multilingual / Multicultural Main Characters*. https://lesesenteret.uis.no/boker-og-materiell/inspirasjon/lesegledernes-boktips/bildeboker-med-flerspraklig-flerkulturell-hovedperson-article106080-13816.html

Loftheim, H.L. (2013). *The Younger the Yankeer? A Sociolinguistic Study of Norwegian Attitudes to English Varieties*. [Unpublished MA English thesis]. University of Bergen. Repository: https://bora.uib.no/bitstream/handle/1956/7074/106841936.pdf?sequence=1&isAllowed=y

Lund, R.E. (2014). Kulturkunnskap og språkopplæring. In C. Bjørke, M. Dypedahl & G.A. Myklevold (Eds.), *Fremmedspråkdidaktikk* (pp. 168–179). Cappelen Damm Akademisk.

Lyngstad, M.E. (2019). *English Teachers' Choices and Beliefs About Literature in The Norwegian Upper Secondary Classroom* [Unpublished PhD Education thesis]. Inland Norway University of Applied Science. Repository: https://brage.inn.no/inn-xmlui/bitstream/handle/11250/2620522/Lyngstad%2c%20Marit%20Elise.pdf?sequence=5&isAllowed=y

Martinez, M., Koss, M.D., & Johnson, N.J. (2016). Meeting characters in Caldecotts: What does this mean for today's readers? *The Reading Teacher, 70*(1), 19–28.

Munden, J. (2019). Phd Revisited: How students in Eritrea and Norway make sense of literature. In U. Rindal & L.M. Brevik (Eds.), *English Didactics in Norway – 30 Years of Doctoral Research*. Universitetsforlaget.

Norwegian Directorate for Education and Training. (2019/2020). English subject curriculum (ENG01-04). https://www.udir.no/lk20/eng01-04

Norwegian Directorate for Education and Training. (2016). *Kindergartens*. https://www.ssb.no/en/barnehager

Pran, K.R., & Holst, L.S. (2015). *Rom for språk?* https://www.sprakradet.no/globalassets/sprakdagen/2015/ipsos_rapport_rom-for-sprak_2015.pdf

Rosnes, E.V., & Rossland, B.L. (2018). Interculturally competent teachers in the diverse Norwegian educational setting. *Multicultural Education Review, 10*(4), 274–291.

Short, K.G., Day, D., & Schroeder, J. (Eds.). (2016). *Teaching Globally: Reading the World Through Literature*. Stenhouse.

Sims Bishop, R. (1990). Mirrors, windows and sliding glass doors. *Perspective: Choosing and Using Books for the Classroom, 6*(3), ix–xi.

Statistics Norway (2019). *Population Statistics Norway*. https://www.ssb.no/en/befolkning

Wissman, K.M., Naughter Burns, K., O'Leary, J.H., & Tabatabai, S. (2016). *Teaching Global Literature in Elementary Classrooms*. Routledge.

Table 1. Further ideas for teaching potential of the diverse books referred to in the chapter

Text	EFL Level	Language	Culture	Further teaching resources (see also References)
Farmer Falgu goes on a Trip (2014)	Primary	**New Vocabulary** – particularly associated with musical instruments and food **Onomatopoeia** – animals and instrumental noises **Spoken English (Indian)** – https://youtu.be/q25nwE8Jfq4	Appearance – clothes, hair, skin colour and body language Aspects of rural India – including transportation, jobs & behaviour, housing, shops & markets The bell around the bullock's neck can be compared with bells used across the world and in different places/for different purposes	Follow the story and hear Indian singing and music: https://www.youtube.com/watch?v=q25nwE8Jfq4
Golden Domes and Silver Lanterns: A Muslim Book of Colors (2015)	Primary	**New Vocabulary** – particularly associated with religion/Islam, clothes and behaviour **Rhymes** **American English/Spellings** – *colors* not *colours* in the title, for instance	Islamic Religious Practices and objects including clothing and buildings Different languages and scripts (Arabic)	Listen to the author talk about the ideas behind this book (and her next book): https://youtu.be/0nPi0em3_so
One Plastic Bag (2015)	Upper Primary/Lower secondary	**Multilingualism and codeswitching** including a Wolof language glossary. **New Vocabulary**	Learn more about the Gambia and sustainable development and the environment The perspectives of others: some in the village laughed and called them names	http://oneplasticbag.com/teacher-resources/ Actual photos of the women of Njau and a timeline of the events are included in the book, as well as the bright illustrations

3 Global Englishes, diverse voices | 117

Text	EFL Level	Language	Culture	Further teaching resources (see also References)
The Ghanaian Goldilocks (2014)	Upper Primary	**New Vocabulary** – particularly around food, games and clothes. **West African vocabulary, grammar and spelling** i.e. sista for sister. **Codeswitching**/use of multiple languages **Expression of pain**– "ayeeee"	History and geography of West Africa. Clothing, food and traditions, the notion of community and neighbourhood being a family. Discrimination and diversity: Kofi is different from everyone else	*F is for Fufu: An Alphabet Book Based on The Ghanaian Goldilocks* (2014) is a useful companion book for learning vocabulary in an exciting way. Hear and see it here: https://www.youtube.com/watch?v=5rWTttWyK-o
The Blue Umbrella (1992/2012)	Upper Primary/ Lower Secondary	**Collocations**: terraced fields; poor cultivator **Concepts**: sweets = In India usually made of flour, sugar, milk, cottage cheese. Toffee = all soft and hard boiled sweets **Similies**: rods of rain fell like shards of shivered glass **Units of weights, money**: half a kilo milk; rupees, paise	Geography and culture. Description of Monsoon. Himalayas. Winter in India. Agriculture: farm vs field. What is grown in fields? What is grown in farms? Belief systems: bear claw and leopard claw are good luck charms	Lesson plans are available, such as: https://u.osu.edu/literaryglobetrotters/2019/04/22/blog-post-a-lesson-plan-for-indian-cultural-diversity-in-the-blue-umbrella/
Bridge Home (2019)	Secondary/young adults	**Semantics**: Blouse = a short fitting top worn over a skirt of a saree **Code-switching**: pavadai = long skirt would fit **Idioms**: "Inherited from your father"	Belief systems: a better future in the next birth. Contrast between Hindu beliefs and Christian beliefs. Religion in a multi-faith, multicultural society. Diwali	Resources from the author and publisher include lots of teaching ideas: https://padmavenkatraman.com/teacher-resources-for-the-bridge-home-gra19-grabridge-projectlit-justreadit/

Text	EFL Level	Language	Culture	Further teaching resources (see also References)
The Thing Around Your Neck (2009)	Young Adults	**Language attitudes and identity** especially in (The Arrangers of Marriage) **Narrative structure:** The effects of the use of second person narrative to tell the story (Tomorrow Never Comes)	Women, marriage and gender roles in Nigeria, the US and in intercultural relationships. Differing concepts of what it is to be Nigerian in today's society and differing concepts of the "American Dream" and issues around adapting to other cultures.	There are many lesson plans for these stories, including https://www.slideshare.net/heatherdwayne/eng131-lesson-plan-for-adichies-the-thing-around-your-neck https://trackssf.cappelendamm.no/ento/seksjon.html?tid=1935713 https://www.litcharts.com/lit/the-thing-around-your-neck

4
Fairy tales

Anna Birketveit

Updated by Gweno Williams

Introduction

This chapter sets out to highlight the didactic value and the cultural significance of fairy tales.

There are several important reasons why fairy tales are among the most accessible texts a foreign language teacher can use in the classroom. Firstly, the plot and characters are often familiar to learners from their mother tongue, and tales follow a fixed pattern, often with stereotypical characters. This enables learners to guess the meaning of unfamiliar words. It also enables learners at the beginner's level of English to deal with longer and more complex texts than they are usually offered, which is likely to make the learning experience more satisfying. Secondly, another important advantage of using fairy tales is that the vocabulary tends to consist of concrete, everyday language. Usually, actions and situations are repeated three times or more, which reinforces language learning.

Thirdly, fairy tales are part of the oral tradition of storytelling. They are very old – perhaps as old as the beginning of human civilisation. Human beings seem to possess an innate urge to tell stories, to leave something behind, so to speak. Our interest in tales and stories is rooted in an urge to understand time (past, present, future) as something we can talk about and tell stories about. In our stories are ideas about ourselves and about life itself; they provide us with a perspective that helps us understand ourselves.

Stories represent a collective bank of attitudes and opinions shaped during past acts of storytelling but also constantly changing, a little at a time, in the ongoing process of being told to new generations. They are both a collective and an individual means of conveying meaning. An important question is who is telling the tale to whom and why? One closing formula of a fairy tale goes: "This is my story. I've told it, and in your hands I leave it." This underlines the interdependence of the listeners and the storyteller in telling and transforming the story. Karel Čapek, the utopian Czech writer, claimed in the essay "Toward a Theory of Fairy Tale" (1990, pp. 59–60) that: "A real fairy tale, a fairy tale in its true function, is a tale within a circle of listeners."

Giving a simple definition of a fairy tale is a challenge. Basically, the fairy tale follows the U-shaped plot of comedy, where the action goes from a high to a low before the happy ending makes it rise to a high again. What fairy tales all seem to have in common are the element of wonder and the key theme of metamorphosis. American folklorist Stith Thompson (1946: p. 8) defines a fairy tale as a story of a certain length which contains a number of motifs and incidents. It takes place in an unreal world without familiar locations or characters, and it contains magic. In this never-never-land the humble hero kills the opponent, inherits the kingdom and marries the princess. Studies by Propp (1968) and Olrik (1992) identify certain structural functions and laws of the genre which will be discussed below. My definition of a fairy tale includes the presence in a text of these structural patterns as well as the elements of wonder and magic. It should be noted, however, that no fairy tale includes all the functions identified by Propp, whereas many fairy tales incorporate all the laws identified by Olrik. My understanding of the genre is built on the assumption that the presence of some functions and laws together with the element of wonder make a text a fairy tale. The definition is therefore quite broad, and includes both traditional tales and original tales written by a specific author.

Theoretical background
Origins
A distinction is made between fairy tales in oral form and the literary fairy tale in writing. According to American critic Jack Zipes in *When Dreams Came True* (1999, p. 1), thousands of years ago tales were told within tribes and groups to create bonds, explain the unknown and give hope in the face of natural disasters. The literary fairy tale was quite probably based on the oral fairy tale, but patterns, structures and motifs became more fixed and were tailored to address the reading public formed by the aristocracy and the middle classes.

Within the sub-genre of literary fairy tales, a further distinction can be made between fairy tales created by identifiable authors such as Hans Christian Andersen and Oscar Wilde and folk tales told by farmers and servants and modified by collectors such as Perrault and the brothers Grimm.

Most fairy tales are very old. They are part of the Indo-European cultural heritage, and similar stories are found in many countries. The basic plots and themes are similar, but the tale may be culturally embedded. No one knows who first invented them, or why these tales have survived for thousands of years and seem to adhere to a universal pattern. Various theories have been put forward, ranging from fairy tales as representative of archetypes within the human psyche to historical and scientific explanations pointing to the migration of stories from the cradle of origin in Babylonia to Asia Minor and Europe. Perhaps the explanation is closer at hand: the basic theme of metamorphosis in fairy tales mirrors the human motivation for life itself, which involves challenges and seizing the opportunities of life in the hope of a successful outcome.

Many well-known fairy tales can be traced back to two collections of tales: *The Fables of Bidpai* (1st century AD, India) and *A Thousand and One Nights* (10th century, Arabian tales influenced by Persian tales). The major European collections of tales comprise *The Pleasant Nights* by Giovanni Francesco Straparola (1550–1553, Italy), *The Complete Fairy Tales of Charles Perrault* (1697, France) and *Children's and Household Tales* by the Brothers Grimm (1812 & 1815, Germany).

When fairy tales became fashionable among the higher social classes in Europe, economic and political conditions seem to have played a very important role in making them popular. The economic prosperity of the Tudor period in England enabled Shakespeare to write for an audience able to appreciate his works. In plays such as *The Tempest*, *King Lear* and *Macbeth* patterns and motifs of fairy tales can be found (see for example the witches' scene in *Macbeth*, Act I). The heyday of the French fairy tale was during the reign of Louis XIV, a time of economic extravagance, glory and numerous wars. Fairy tales became a useful vehicle in transferring codes of conduct and the new civilité developed at the court of the king. The flowering of the German fairy tale in the 19th century has been ascribed to the decline of the aristocracy and the growth of the middle class, and the desire to educate this class about their German roots. These fairy tales were expressions of Romanticism, and sought a hidden force in human nature ignored by the Church. The messages of these tales tended to reinforce Protestant work-ethic values with an emphasis on industriousness and an optimistic, opportunistic attitude to life. In Norway, Asbjørnsen and Moe's collections of fairy tales from the first part of the 19th century played an important part in the struggle for independence and national identity.

Cultural messages in fairy tales

Before the fairy tale became an accepted literary genre among the ruling class, it existed as an oral form among the lower classes. According to Warner (1994, p. 23), the metaphors "spinning a tale" and "weaving a plot" show the close connection between the work that had to be done and the tellers, who were often older women. Telling tales was a way of passing on experience to the young and teaching them about life.

The famous collectors of fairy tales, Perrault, the Grimms and Asbjørnsen and Moe, transcribed the tales and to some extent altered and edited them to suit the times and their own literary style. However, in 17th-century France, Perrault was outnumbered by at least 20 collectors of fairy tales, many of them women such as Marie-Jeanne L'Héritier and Mme d'Aulnoy. Fairy tales were cultivated in the literary salons run by women and can be interpreted as a way of commenting on a patriarchal society where women had very little influence. In strong contrast to real life, where individuals were subject to marriage arrangements of sense rather than sensibility, the romantic ideal of "tendresse" was cherished. Zipes (1999, p. 13) points out how the name of the genre itself – fairy tale – underlines the female perspective. The term was coined in the 17th-century in France as *conte de fées*. It was a female – a fairy such as the fairy godmother – who held the power of metamorphosis and transformation, not the patriarchal Church.

It is significant that fairy tales were not originally meant for children. The understanding of childhood as a specific period in a human being's life, with special features, did not come into existence until the 19th century. Up to then, children were largely regarded as small adults, to be taught in the same way as adults. As a consequence, children's literature per se did not exist. Significantly, it was from 1830 to 1900, during the rise of the middle classes, that the fairy tale came into its own for children.

Zipes (1999, p. 74) has examined the Grimms' editions of fairy tales from 1812/15, 1819 and 1857 and claims that from 1819 onwards the brothers Grimm began cleansing their tales of their erotic and cruel passages that might be offensive to middle-class minds. They were tailoring them for children, and defined specific roles for male and female protagonists.

Key features of the genre
Patterns in fairy tales
Together with the elements of magic and wonder, the following outline shows the structures and laws present in texts classified as fairy tales. I have included a discussion of the similarities between fairy tales and Bible narratives as this serves to explain the U code, discussed below, as well as pointing to epic laws and structures as fundamental patterns of narratives. It may be argued that in order to survive centuries of oral diffusion, it is perhaps necessary for narratives to adhere to certain fixed patterns and structures. It is also possible to argue that these similarities simply reflect inborn basic patterns of human thought, which Jung called archetypes.

Functions of fairy tales
The Russian structuralist Vladimir Propp (1968) developed an analysis of fairy tales that identified 31 plot actions performed by the dramatis personae in a corpus of Russian fairy tales. The dramatis personae are *the hero* (also "the seeker" or "victim"), *the villain*, *the donor* (from whom the hero gets some magical object), *the magical helper* (the character who helps the hero in the quest), *the dispatcher* (the character who makes the lack known), *the false hero* (the character who takes credit for the hero's actions), *the prince/princess* (the person whom the hero marries), and *the victim* (person harmed by the villain, if not the hero). According to Propp, all folk tales share these stock characters. No fairy tale includes all the functions of all characters listed, but the functions that are present will always occur in a certain specified sequence.

Epic laws of folktales
The Danish researcher Axel Olrik (1992) found that the plots of fairy tales adhere to the following fixed laws.

Opening	Every fairy tale has an introduction such as "Once upon a time" or "One fine summer evening". The initial situation is static and simple. Gradually the characters become more active, and the story more complicated and dramatic.
Unity of plot	Tales have a limited number of characters and motifs. Only actions or events directly relevant to the development of the story are included.
Focus on a leading character	All fairy tales have a hero, usually male, often looking for something.

Two to a scene	There are usually no more than two characters in the same scene. Any third character present is silent.
Contrast	When two characters are present in the same scene, they are described in terms of opposites, for example rich versus poor or good versus evil.
Twins	In many tales, two characters act so alike that they appear as twins, for example the brothers, Per and Paal, found in a large number of Norwegian fairy tales.
Three	Certain numbers form recurring patterns in fairy tales. The number three is the most common. The hero has to perform three tasks, there are three princesses, the hero is given three objects, etc.
Final stress	When an action is repeated three times, the last is always the most important of the three, and the one that brings the story to a solution and a close. This final action is often linked to the youngest of three brothers such as Espen, who manages to perform a task that his elder brothers Per and Paal have failed to accomplish. Similarly, the youngest of three princesses is always the most beautiful.
Closure	Endings of fairy tales also have a common pattern. The story never ends abruptly. It is always brought to a close in a particular way. The listener is told what happened subsequently to the hero and the other characters, after the dramatic events of the story. "They all lived happily ever after" is one such typical ending.

The narrative code of fairy tales and the Bible

Northrop Frye in *The Great Code* (1982, p. 169) declares that the coherence of the Bible's narrative as a whole is created by a "U-shaped plot" typical of comedy. The plot begins with Genesis, the creation of a harmonious family and garden state, is followed by a fall into a long series of alternating historical disasters and triumphs, and concludes with a final ascent back to harmony in the eternal city of Jerusalem at the end of the book of Revelations. This U-shaped pattern also governs dozens of minor plots of fall and rise subsumed in the major story. Moreover, many fairy tales share this U-shaped plot. "Snow White," for example, can be compared to the narrative of "The Prodigal Son" (Luke 15: 11–32). In both of them the main character is initially at home with his or her family before leaving. Away from home both characters succumb to temptation and nearly perish. The career of the prodigal son flourishes when he decides to return home to forgiveness and redemption. Snow White's prospects improve when she is rescued by a prince, whom she marries. They are both, in a sense, reborn into a new and better situation, and their lives follow the U pattern in that they go from a high to a low before rising high again.

Coded content

Fairy tales have, in general, a moralising tone, but on closer examination they often run against the ethics of their time. Conceivably, fairy tales were often a way of voicing the unspoken; their themes contain traces of the lives of the tellers and listeners.

Dealing with the jealousy and wickedness of a stepmother is a theme found in "Snow White" and "Cinderella". Childbirth, one of the most common causes of death before the 20th century, is present in "Bluebird", "Donkeyskin" deals with incest. Cannibalism, rape, marriage and childlessness leading to a second marriage are themes in the version of "Sleeping Beauty" published by Giambattista Basile which Perrault drew on. According to Warner (1994, pp. 220–221), Perrault discarded the theme of rape which was deemed unsuitable for his audience, whereas the Grimms make the heroine undergo no worse hardship than a hundred years' sleep. The rapist has turned into a chivalrous prince who awakens the beauty with a chaste kiss. The tale has now been tailored to address the middle-class audience of the Grimms.

Family life and coping with older brothers and sisters are themes in "Cinderella", the tales about the "Ash Lad" and many others. The messages are clear and optimistic. Be good and you will be rewarded, there is always help to be had, and there is always a happy ending.

According to British feminist critic Marina Warner (1994, p. 35), women's telling of tales and getting together were traditionally looked upon with suspicion. "[G]ossipy gatherings of women together were the focus of much male anxiety about women's tongues in Reformation as well as Catholic Europe." Tales were considered idle gossip and as such dangerous. The ideal woman was silent. The situation and the view of disobedient, rebellious and opinionated women are reflected in tales like "Bluebird" and the Norwegian tale "The Princess Who Had to Have the Last Word".

The rise of the middle class and the interest in children's literature facilitated the publication and distribution of fairy tales created by an author. These tales often follow the pattern and structures of fairy tales, but the characters may be more rounded, the social criticism more explicit, and a happy ending is not guaranteed. Often, in these tales, the audience is invited to feel sorry for the hero or heroine.

Hans Christian Andersen (1805–75) is perhaps the most well-known creator of original fairy tales, including treasures such as "The Ugly Duckling", "The Tin Soldier", "The Emperor's New Clothes", "The Little Match Girl" and many more. The motif of the underdog who has to go through various ordeals to succeed and rise in society is very explicit in his tales. Through middle-class, Protestant work ethic values like hard work, honesty, industriousness, persistence and opportunism, the hero can succeed. Hans Christian Andersen's tales contain autobiographical elements as he himself was of a lower social standing and, like the ugly duckling, achieved transformation and a place among the swans (the rich) through painful ordeals.

Oscar Wilde (1854–1900) gave children and adults beautiful tales like "The Happy Prince" and "The Selfish Giant" interwoven with Christian motifs and references.

Interpreting fairy tales as archetypes

Marie-Louise von Franz, who worked as Jung's assistant, takes a Jungian approach to fairy tales in her book *The Interpretations of Fairy Tales* (1996). Jung believed that our psyche, the Self, comprised both the conscious and the unconscious. He further believed that the Self is innately purposeful and always seeks wholeness and equilibrium. According to Jung, the unconscious serves to compensate the conscious through powerful dreams and images. Psychic energy involves four archetypes, which work together in pairs of conscious and unconscious complementary parts. One of these pairs is the ego and the shadow; the other pair is formed of the persona and the soul image. Jung stressed the emotional side of an archetypal image and warned against repressing it. Fairy tales acknowledge and deal with the emotional, hidden and dark forces in human nature.

According to Franz all fairy tales represent the Self, and deal with the challenges and difficulties presented by nature. Motifs and patterns in fairy tales are abstractions of Jung's archetypes, which Franz defines as a set of universal patterns and elementary thoughts inborn in human nature. "Fairy tales are the purest and simplest expression of collective unconscious psychic processes. In this pure form, the archetypical images afford us the best clues to the understanding of the processes going on in the collective psyche" (1996, p. 1).

In the following I will discuss how the symbols of the king, the queen and the hero function in a fairy tale in relation to the idea that the tale is an expression of the Self. The king may be considered a symbol of the Self, which, in a Jungian sense, is the centre of the self-regulating psyche on which the welfare of the individual depends. In many tales the king is in some sort of trouble and, sick and decaying, lacks the power to sort out his problems. A well may be blocked by a troll or his land will not yield any crops, etc. The queen can be seen as the feminine element accompanying the Self. She represents feelings and irrational attachments relative to this Self. Many fairy tales lack the figure of the queen – the feminine element – and the king is therefore in trouble. Not until the youngest of his sons succeeds in overcoming obstacles and bringing home a princess is a healthy situation restored.

The hero in fairy tales is very often the youngest; this so-called incompetent "Dummling" of the family is the one who puts the family back on their feet. He has what it takes to fight off the evil forces and restore harmony. He possesses "feminine" qualities such as compassion, helpfulness, a social sense and the ability to share. Because of these qualities, he is rewarded and allowed to succeed. According to Franz (1996, p. 62), "the hero is an archetypal figure which presents a model of an ego functioning in accord with the Self". The hero expresses and incarnates the healing qualities of the Self. The hero often descends into the Earth or into a mountain or a well. This symbolises the descent into the unconscious, where feelings reside. In most cultures the Earth is looked upon as a symbol of a mother, something fertile, where things grow. Contact with this "feminine side" is what it takes to restore an unhealthy community. In Jung's terminology, the Ego makes contact with the Shadow and with his female soul-image, and this results in a powerful and healthy Ego.

Modern fairy tales

We never abandon fairy tales. They may take on new forms and use other channels, but the basic pattern of a miraculous transformation and the "happily-ever-after" ending is repeated endlessly. In the 19th century fairy tales were adapted to incorporate Christian and patriarchal messages, and major writers, such as H. C. Andersen and the Grimms produced family tales suitable for socialising children. Qualities such as industriousness, honesty, staying power and achievement were emphasised. Female characters were passive or silenced. According to Zipes (1988, p. 67), by the 19th century

> the fairy tale was no longer a feudal artwork, but had become autonomous. In a free market system, it came to be packaged as a household good, and the family fairy tale as commodity was designed to reinforce patriarchal notions of civilization, whether it was produced by male or female authors.

However, the rise of twentieth century feminism produced many successfully reworked feminist fairy tales. For adult and young adult readers, the most important is likely to be Angela Carter's bold and explicit short story collection *The Bloody Chamber* (1979), filmed by Neil Jordan as *The Company of Wolves* (1984). The increasingly strong and creative tradition in children's books includes Catherine Storr's *Clever Polly and the Stupid Wolf* (1955) series, *The Paper Bag Princess* (1980) by Robert Munsch and modern feminist fairy tales such as Babette Cole's *Princess Smartypants* or *Prince Cinders*, which challenge the gender patterns of fairy tales in amusing ways. Roald Dahl's *Revolting Rhymes* twists well-known fairy tales through funny, subversive rhymes. In *The Stinky Cheese Man*, Jon Scieszka breaks the fairy tale pattern and challenges the paratext of picturebooks.

Fairy tales can emerge in almost any genre, for example operas, songs, poems, advertisements, cartoons, graphic novels, ballets, musicals, dramas or hypertexts on the Internet (Zipes, 2011, p. 8). However, the most significant is film adaptation, given that film has become the dominant vehicle for children's tales. Filmmakers discovered the power of fairy tale material in the 1930s, the period of the Great Depression; Walt Disney set the standard for much of the film industry of the 20th century. According to Zipes (1988) all-male animators developed the story lines. The result is very often that "the ideas, gags, and themes emanated from a kind of boys' locker-room talk. There was often an infantile type of humour in the early Disney films" (p. 71). Some of the films adhere to the patterns of traditional adventure tales. A protagonist quickly gets into trouble and has to fight to overcome this trouble. This, at least, is the case if the protagonist is a male. A female protagonist is not given the power of solving problems. She remains passive, helped by her good looks or inner qualities and an outside helper or hero. Disney thus "depicted clear-cut gender roles that associated women with domesticity and men with action and power" (1988, p. 71). According to Zipes, the art of telling a tale has given way to the consumer industry and technical innovation. It is no longer only about the film, but also about the merchandise and publications sold to accompany the film. Music and sound effects together with stunning new technological solutions make the audience stare, gape, marvel and wonder. Instead of presenting tales that encourage children to make ethical choices, they are addressed as consumers by entertainment makers who both create and satisfy their desires, and make children alike. Zipes shows that the early version of "Puss in Boots" portrays a cat that is cunning as well as independent and wise, and is therefore able to act intelligently on its own. Walt Disney's version is a reduced one. The cat is not intelligent on its own. According to Zipes (1988, p. 38), "Disney continued to frame the discourse of civility within a male frame [...] All of these men bonded ... or collaborated for the same reason: to use cats for their own self-figuration and to rationalize the manner in which power relations are distributed to benefit men in Western society." In *The Enchanted Screen* (2011, pp. 24–25), Zipes claims that Disney sought to establish Utopia in the spectators' minds as a shared vision of a place where those who deserve to rule do so with the blessing of "those who deserve to serve". Through film adaptations, the Disney empire has appropriated almost all of the most well-known fairy tales to the point where the audience thinks that Disney's version is the original. This is the case with, for example, J.M. Barrie's *Peter Pan*. The Disney version of *Peter Pan* (1953) has established the figure of Peter Pan in people's imagination as the green-clad cartoon character that we all know, despite the fact that Barrie's character is different. "[A] lovely boy, clad in skeleton leaves and the juices that ooze out of trees, but the most entrancing thing about him was that he had all his first teeth" (2008, p. 103). Whereas Barrie presents Wendy as intelligent and resourceful and Tinker Bell as an ethereal being, the Disney versions show them as sexual objects and antagonists fighting for Peter's admiration. According to Yeoman (1998, pp. 34–35), Barrie's image of eternal youth has been diminished, "sentimentalised and emptied of mythological and psychological resonance". Discussing more recent films, among others *Mermaid* (2007) and *How to Train Your Dragon* (2010), Zipes sees a shift in fairy-tale filmmaking where children, both as audience and characters, want to play a more active role in narrating and interpreting their lives. He claims that these films "focus on the child as a moral arbiter, who refuses to make compromises with the corrupt ... adult world" (2011, p. 366).

Didactic suggestions for the EFL classroom

As plots are predictable and because many of the same stories exist in Norwegian, fairy tales make it easier for the pupils to compare words in the two languages and to guess meanings. Since actions, situations or objects are repeated several times, the language used tends to be repetitive. In order to learn new words, it is important to repeat the words many times (Munden & Myhre, 2007; Ana & Schmitt, 2010). This makes fairy tales well suited as texts for foreign language learning. In particular, they meet competence aims in LK20 related to language learning and oral communication, such as finding similarities between English and one's native language, understanding the main content of rhymes, songs, fairy tales and stories, and listening to and understanding the meaning of words in context (after year 4).

"The Princess who Had to Have the Last Word": two projects

In this Norwegian fairy tale, the dialogues between the brothers and the Ash Lad are identical except for the new objects the Ash Lad finds while he and his brothers are on their way to the princess. Descriptions follow of how to work with this fairy tale in the classroom as well as outdoors in a cross-curricular project with physical education. The ideas are suitable for lower primary school (8–10-year-olds). English version available at http://www.rootsweb.ancestry.com/~norway/Princess.htm

In the classroom: 4 lessons

Before beginning a new text with learners, the teacher should look for any unfamiliar and important vocabulary. Here, the new vocabulary has been grouped in different word classes.

VOCABULARY

Nouns	Verbs	Adjectives
princess	find (found)	crooked
magpie	say (said)	warm
willow hank	carry	broken
saucer	pick	worn-out
ram	drop	
horn	roast	
mate	twist	
wedge		
shoe sole		
coal		
iron		

Lesson 1

The main task is to create interest and to motivate learners to read the story.

The teacher makes up a lead-in story and brings a rucksack with some (or all) of the items that the Ash Lad found. A dead magpie is obviously impossible to bring, but what about a magpie feather instead? Instead of a willow hank, the teacher could bring a small, soft tree branch.

Example lead-in story

The teacher opens the rucksack and brings out the items, and says to the learners in their *mother tongue*: "Guess what happened to me today. I walked past this marvellous castle made of pure gold and diamonds. First I met two very sad boys with red ears. It looked like somebody had burned their ears. Then I met a very happy boy in rags, but he had a big smile on his face and was jumping up and down for joy. 'All this is mine,' he said, 'and a beautiful princess too.' He threw me this rucksack with all these things in it, and said he no longer needed them, and that maybe they would bring me as much luck as they had brought him. I wondered how a sack with only old rubbish inside could bring him a fortune, and this is the story he told me. Do you want to know what he told me?"

The teacher then reads or tells them the story in English. He or she takes out all the items so the learners can see them while the story is being read. Some teachers may think it best to practise some of the new vocabulary before the actual story is read aloud. By reading (explaining and dramatising a little) and pointing to the items as you read, the teacher can check on what the learners understand without knowing the words beforehand. After checking their understanding, the teacher should hand out and go through the VOCABULARY grid above.

Lesson 2

The main goal is to learn and understand the new vocabulary.

The teacher brings out the items from the rucksack and reviews the words. The learners then work on the new vocabulary in the following ways:

Word search:

By looking horizontally, vertically or diagonally, find the following 8 nouns from the story: *magpie, mate, horn, saucer, wedge, iron, hank, ram*.

B	S	R	H	I	L	W	I	N
L	M	A	G	P	I	E	R	S
A	N	M	A	T	E	D	O	V
K	H	O	R	N	S	G	N	D
R	O	S	A	U	C	E	R	I

Collocation:

Match the nouns and corresponding adjectives.

shoe	warm
saucer	crooked
coal	worn-out
horn	broken

Word match:

Match the English words and their meanings.

English	Meaning in mother tongue
find	bære
say	steke
carry	vri
catch	finne
roast	miste
found	sa
twist	fant
said	fange
drop	si

Bingo:

The learners make a grid of 9 squares (or 16) and write a word from VOCABULARY (Lesson 1) in each square. The teacher puts all the words under vocabulary into a hat and picks up one word at a time and reads it aloud. The learners that have this word tick it. The first learner to have a row of 3 words (or 4) read aloud diagonally, horizontally or vertically wins the game and shouts "BINGO". The teacher checks his or her grid.

Example

princess	found	magpie x
crooked	saucer x	worn-out
shoe x	roast	carry

Variation:
The teacher asks a learner to read the words out of the hat.
The teacher reads the vocabulary in the mother tongue.
The teacher gives a definition of a word or uses the word in a sentence:
"Shoe": Something you have on your feet. I am wearing black shoes today.

Lesson 3

The main goal is to learn the vocabulary in context and to remember the content of the story.

Learners reading the text

The teacher hands out dialogues from the text; learners read in pairs either the roles of the Ash Lad and the brothers or the Ash Lad and the princess.

The Ash Lad (AL) and the brothers (B)
    AL: *"Look what I have found!"*
    B: *"What've you found?"*
    AL: *"I found a dead magpie."*
    B: *"Fie! Drop it! What are you going to do with that?"*
    AL: *"Oh, I've nothing better to do and nothing better to carry, so I'll just take it along with me."*

The learners continue the dialogue until the Ash Lad has found all the remaining objects (the willow hank, the saucer, the two horns, the wedge and the shoe sole). They repeat the same dialogue except for the one word that needs to be changed when the Ash Lad finds a new object.

The Ash Lad (AL) and the princess (P)
    AL: *"Good day."*
    P: *"Good day yourself."*
    AL: *"It's good and warm in here."*
    P: *"It's warmer in the coals."*
    AL: *"I suppose I can roast my magpie there then?"*
    P: *"I'm afraid she'll burst."*
    AL: *"Oh, that'll be no trouble! I'll put this willow hank around it."*
    P: *"It's too wide!"*
    AL: *"I'll drive in a wedge!"*
    P: *"The fat'll run off her!"*
    AL: *"I'll catch it in this!"*
    P: *"You're twisting my words!"*
    AL: *"No! Your words aren't twisted, but this is!"*
    P: *"Well, I have never seen the like!"*
    AL: *"Here's the like of it!"*
    P: *"You're bent on wearing me out, aren't you?"*
    AL: *"No, you're not worn-out, but this is!"*
    P: *"Ehh …"*
    AL: *"Now you're mine! … Yes!!!!"*

One-sided dialogues (More challenging and more fun!)

This also gives variation and reinforcement of vocabulary and structures:

Learners read the dialogues in pairs but each participant can only see his or her part of the dialogue. The teacher cuts the sheet below into two pieces and gives the role of the Ash Lad to learner A and the role of the brothers to learner B. This can also be done with the dialogue between the Ash Lad and the princess.

A	**B**
The Ash Lad (AL) and the brothers (B)	The Ash Lad (AL) and the brothers (B)
AL: "Look what I have found!"	AL: …
B: …	B: "What've you found?"
AL: "I found a dead magpie"	AL: …
B: …	B: "Fie! Drop it! What are you going to do with that?"
AL: "Oh, I've nothing better to do, and nothing better to carry, so I'll just take it along with me."	AL: …

Comprehension:

Give the learners the sheet below and ask them to tick off the following sentences as true or false.

	True	False
The Ash Lad is the youngest of three brothers.		
The Ash Lad finds a dead cat.		
The Ash Lad drops the broken saucer.		
The brothers are burnt on their ears.		
The princess is kind.		
The Ash Lad shows her the magpie.		
The Ash Lad has a wedge.		
The princess has worn-out shoes.		
The Ash Lad can roast his magpie in the coals.		
The Ash Lad wins the princess.		

Lesson 4
Dramatisation:
The teacher asks learners to stand up and dramatise parts of the story as s/he reads or tells it.

Writing:
1. Write five true sentences from the story.
2. Write one of the dialogues from the story as you remember it.

Outdoor learning: double lesson (project developed by Birketveit and Hallås (2011)[24]

In this cross-curricular project between English and physical education "The Princess Who Had to Have the Last Word" is used in star orienteering. Through orienteering the learners must find eight posts in the local environment of the school. At each of the posts they will find one of the objects the Ash Lad found on his way to the princess, in addition to an iron that was used to punish the unsuccessful suitors in the tale. The objects at the posts are: *iron, willow-hank, coal, shoe sole, magpie, broken saucer, horn* and *wedge*. The teacher should use English when interacting with the learners and encourage them to speak English while doing orienteering. The teacher repeats the four geographic directions in English, *north, south, east* and *west*, and teaches the learners expressions such as *can you see the object/post over there? Look, there it is, to the right, to the left, in the middle*, etc. Orienteering in English provides an excellent opportunity to learn vocabulary related to physical education such as *map, compass, run, physical education, local environment, orienteering*, etc. Several LK20 competence aims are relevant to this cross-curricular project: In the core area Communication, after year 4 in the English subject curriculum, this project supports the following aims:

- participate in conversations on the pupil's own and others' needs, feelings, daily life and interests and use conversation rules
- listen to and understand words and expressions in adapted texts

(Norwegian Directorate for Education and Training, 2019/20)

---

24 See chapter 2 for suggestions for poetry outdoor learning activities.

In physical education, the topic is orienteering, and the project meets competence aims after year 4, related to exploring different types of games and movements, as well as making and using maps in their local environment.

Preparatory work
Begin by working with the fairy tale in the classroom. Lessons 1–3 above, offer a good basis for using this text in orienteering. The aim is to learn the names of objects, to learn the names of the four directions – *north, south, east* and *west*, to learn simple structures for giving directions – *to the right, to the left*, and to make learners use English as much as possible when orienteering. *Willow hank* is also a very unusual word in Norwegian; showing learners a small, twisted branch may be necessary to give them a better idea of what it is. Using concrete objects that learners can touch and see will make it easier for them to remember these words. The teacher may also ask learners to bring some of the objects (*shoe sole, saucer, coal*) from home.

Many dialogues in fairy tales are repeated, as are the ones between the Ash Lad (AL) and his brothers (B) each time he finds a new object. If learners master the basic structure of the dialogues and in addition remember the names of objects the Ash Lad finds, they will be able to dramatise or retell parts of the tale.

This project presupposes that the learners have talked about the four directions in other subjects, and that they have talked about what a map is and drawn a simple map of, perhaps, the classroom, the school yard or the sports field. This rhyme provides one way of remembering compass directions in English: *North is up and south is down, right is east and left is west, that's how I remember (it) best.*

The following materials must be provided:

Copies of a simple local map for orienteering where NORTH, SOUTH, EAST and WEST are indicated. The eight objects, each in a plastic bag and hung up at a post within the area of the local map, for example two objects to the north, two objects to the south, etc. Each pupil gets a simple card to mark off each completed task. Each post has a pair of pliers the learners can use to mark their cards.

The outdoor activity
Star orienteering is used. This type of orienteering is well known within physical education (NOF, 2001).

Learners are divided into groups, and each learner has his or her own map. The teacher talks about the map; together learners must find visible objects in the local environment such as a fence, a tree or a building. Then the teacher gives each group an object to find by drawing a circle on their maps of where to find the object. Each learner has a card to mark with each task completed; learners are told to go orienteering together as a group and find the object, to look at it but not take it with them. They mark their cards by using a pair of pliers at the post. Together the group must try to memorise the name of the object, for example *iron*. They must run back to the teacher as a group as quickly as they can and tell the teacher the name of the object or describe it in English. Next, the teacher makes a new circle on group members' maps, and they go orienteering again to find the next post. The activity continues until all the groups have found all eight posts and objects.

After orienteering
The class talk about the activity and whether it was difficult to find the posts and remember the words. This is a good time to repeat the fairy tale or parts of the fairy tale. The teacher may, for example, have written down the dialogue between the Ash Lad and the princess on a big poster, and each group can stand up and read parts of the dialogue. This dialogue is fun to read as the princess and the Ash Lad compete to have the last word.

Another alternative is that each group selects one of the objects to say something about. Alternatively, they can say something about the fairy tale. The most important thing here is that the learners use English orally. The teacher must find a way of organising the activity that makes the learners feel confident.

Another activity is to dramatise the fairy tale as described in Lesson 4 in the teaching programme in the classroom. Various written activities are also good ways of reinforcing vocabulary and structures at this stage (see Lesson 4).

Conclusion: Human footprints in civilisation
As the practical ideas show, fairy tales lend themselves very well to activities both inside and outside the foreign language classroom. In addition, their educational potential and impact are much wider. They are present in all known cultures and with surprisingly similar patterns. Why this is so remains an enigma, but ascribing it to migration only seems a gross oversimplification.

Jungian psychological interpretations generally conclude that fairy tales mirror basic human patterns of thought. From this perspective, fairy tales illustrate the struggle between the conscious and unconscious aspects of the Self or, in other words, the struggle between the light and the dark side of any individual's personality. It is argued that fairy tales can strengthen a child's ego. Through fairy tales vital emotional processes are dealt with and brought to rest in the phrase "they all lived happily ever after".

This chapter has highlighted the international origins and universal aspects of fairy tales. Whilst fairy tale illustration and art are a very large separate topic, it is important to consider the politics of representation in fairy tales, with particular reference to education. Classrooms and school libraries will include many versions of popular fairy tales. In increasingly multicultural Western societies, it is extremely important that teachers ensure that fairy tale characters encountered by learners are not solely depicted as European or as having a limited range of racial or cultural identities. In the interests of inclusivity and individual well-being, versions such as American publisher Simon & Schuster's *Once Upon a World* collection should also be available to learners. With the strapline "Fairy Tales for Everyone, Everywhere", this gorgeously illustrated and visually distinctive series written by Chloe Perkins and Hannah Eliot features an Indian Rapunzel, a Japanese Snow White, a Mexican Cinderella, a Puerto Rican Little Mermaid and a Russian Princess obliged to sleep on a pea. American author Rachel Isadora has also produced a richly illustrated series of well-known fairy tales set entirely in Africa, including *Hansel and Gretel*, *The Twelve Dancing Princesses* and *The Fisherman and his Wife*.

Gender issues are significant in fairy tales; it is important to ask who is telling the tale to whom and why. Since the tellers and many early collectors tended to be women, the tales can be read as veiled criticism of a male patriarchal society. This is a point to bear in mind as Disneyfication of the fairy tale in the 20th century enforced gender-stereotyped behaviour and subjected the child audience to heavy marketing. I have attempted to show that fairy tales are human footprints in our civilisation. If the consumer industry is allowed to devalue and reduce the cultural importance of these footprints, it is indeed a tragic waste of a valuable treasure handed down from one generation to another through thousands of years. Protecting this inheritance, and enabling future generations to trace these footprints, should be a priority for everyone involved in education. Some of the recent developments highlighted above, or for example within the film industry (Zipes, 2011), may give hope that we are moving in the right direction.

References

Ana, P.-S., & Schmitt, N. (2010). Incidental vocabulary acquisition from an authentic novel: *Do Things Fall Apart?*. *Reading in a Foreign Language, 22*(1), 31–55.

Barrie, J.M. ([1904]2008). *Peter Pan*. Collector's Library.

Birketveit, A. (2005). Fairy tales as human footprints. In T. Hansson, R. Kjartansson, A. Larsen & H. Lassen (Eds.), *Tales on the Screen: Narrative Competence in Teacher Education* (pp. 107–120). Syddansk Universitetsforlag.

Birketveit, A., & Hallås, O. (2011). Engelsk i kroppsøving og kroppsøving på engelsk. *Kroppsøving, 4*, 12–17, LFF. Tønsberg.

Capek, K. ([1932]1990). Towards a theory of fairytale. In K. Capek, *Nine Fairy Tales and One More Thrown in for Good Measure* [Trans. D. Hermann] (pp. 59–60). Northwestern University Press.

Carter, A. (1979). *The Bloody Chamber*. Gollancz.

Cole, B. (1992[1987]). *Prince Cinders*. Picture Lions.

Cole, B. (1996[1986]). *Princess Smartypants*. Puffin.

Dahl, R. (1984[1982]). *Revolting Rhymes*. Picture Puffins.

Eliot, H. (2019). *The Little Mermaid* illustrated by Nivea Ortiz. Simon and Schuster.

Franz, M.-L. Von. (1996). *The Interpretation of Fairy Tales*. Shambhala.

Frye, N. (1982). *The Great Code*. Routledge & Kegan Paul Ltd.

Hyde, M., & McGuinness, M. (1999). *Introducing Jung*. Icon Books.

Isadora, R. (1996). *The Steadfast Tin Soldier*. Penguin Putnam.

Isadora, R. (2008). *The Twelve Dancing Princesses*. Putnam Juvenile.

Isadora, R. (2009). *Hansel and Gretel*. Putnam Juvenile.

Muncke, R. (1980). *The Paper Bag Princess*. Annick Press.

Munden, J., & Myhre, A. (2007). *Twinkle, Twinkle*. Høyskoleforlaget.

Norges orienteringsforbund, NOF (2011). *Trygg i naturen med orientering*. Norges orienterings-forbund.

Norwegian Directorate for Education and Training. (2019/2020). English subject curriculum (ENG01-04). https://www.udir.no/lk20/eng01-04

Olrik, A. ([1921]1992). *Principles for Oral Narrative Research* [Trans. K. Wolf & J. Jensen]. Indiana University Press.

Perkins, C. (2016a). *Snow White*. Illustrated by Misa Saburi. Simon and Schuster.

Perkins, C. (2016b). *Cinderella*. Illustrated by Sandra Equihua. Simon and Schuster.

Perkins, C. (2017a). *Rapunzel*. Illustrated by Archana Sreenivasan. Simon and Schuster.

Perkins, C. (2017b). *The Princess and the Pea* illustrated by Dinara Mirtilipova. Simon and Schuster.

Propp, V. ([1928]1968). *The Morphology of the Folktale* [Trans. L. Scott]. University of Texas Press.

Scieszka, J. (1993[1992]) *The Stinky Cheese Man and other Fairly Stupid Tales*. Picture Puffins.

Storr, C. (1955). *Clever Polly and the Stupid Wolf*: Jane Nissen Books.

"The Princess Who Had to Have the Last Word" http://www.rootsweb.ancestry.com/~norway/Princess.htm

Thompson, S. (1946). *The Folktale*. The Dryden Press.

Warner, M. (1994). *From the Beast to the Blonde*. Vintage.

Yeoman, A. (1998). *Now or Neverland: Peter Pan and the Myth of Eternal Youth. A Psychological Perspective on a Cultural Icon*. Inner City Books.

Zipes, J. (1988). *Happily Ever After*. Routledge.
Zipes, J. (1999). *When Dreams Came True*. Routledge.
Zipes, J. (2011). *The Enchanted Screen: The Unknown History of Fairy-Tale Films*. Routledge.

Filmography
DeBlois. D., & Sanders, C. (2010). *How to Train Your Dragon*.
Jackson, W. (1953). *Peter Pan*. Disney.
Jordan, N. (1984) *The Company of Wolves*.
Melikyan, A. (2007). *Mermaid*.

Further reading
Birkeland, T., & Mjør, I. (2012). *Barnelitteratur – sjangrar og teksttypar*. Cappelen Damm AS.
Sundland, E. (1995). *Det var en gang et menneske*. Cappelen Akademisk Forlag.
Solberg, O. (2007). *Inn i eventyret*. Cappelen Akademisk Forlag.
Zipes, J. (2012). *The Irresistible Fairy Tale*. Princeton University Press.

5
Novels for teenage readers

Gweno Williams

Introduction

Contemporary teenage fiction in English is an outstandingly valuable resource for the EFL classroom. This chapter aims to show why and how novels for teenagers can enrich learning and enjoyment in learning, benefitting EFL learners and teachers alike. In competence aims across years, the new Norwegian English curriculum (LK20) requires that learners encounter different types of texts, including self-chosen ones. Authentic novels should be included in this mix for the following reasons:

- To develop reading autonomy and satisfaction by training future readers. Successful readers are both independent learners and self-starters.
- To develop reading confidence and stamina through a sustained, student-led competence activity. Reading simultaneously builds and tests competence.
- Reading thought-provoking fiction readily leads to discussion and writing, which are also identified as basic skills and assessment points.
- To access excellent learning opportunities for developing empathy and respect for others as the reader's character develops and life challenges are encountered. "Those who write for children are trying to arm them for the life ahead with everything we can find that is true" (Rundell, 2019, p. 4).

- To gain pleasure through the habit of reading. So many high quality, well-written texts are available, on a wide range of themes, that every reader can find something to interest them.
- To experience and enjoy creative multi-modal versions of texts, which also offer opportunities for differentiation. Many excellent novels have also been adapted into films (see chapter 9), plays, graphic novels (see chapter 7) or versions for those with reading challenges.
- To access rich opportunities for interdisciplinary work, for example with history, religion, or social studies. LK20 emphasises the importance of cross-curricular co-operation, which is an important element of "in-depth learning" *(dybdelæring)*.

This chapter offers examples of relevant, well-written contemporary fiction to stimulate and enable teenagers to become willing, independent readers with active and empowered responses. It should preferably be read in conjunction with chapter 6, "Reading for everyone", which provides further examples of exciting and varied texts and approaches suitable for teenage readers. Similarly chapter 8, on digital approaches, also offers inspiring YA fiction recommendations.

A variety of didactic approaches are suggested to enable and support teachers in choosing and working with appropriate, compelling stories for teenage readers, including vocational learners, paying attention to different levels of reading ability and stamina. Stamina is defined as the desire and ability to keep going, as in sport, to keep on reading to the end and not give up.

Choosing texts is an important task for EFL teachers as the Norwegian English curriculum does not recommend specific literary works but offers the exciting advantage of flexibility; as new texts or topics become popular, they can readily be incorporated into the teaching syllabus, increasing relevance and intercultural awareness and responding to youth culture and social change. So teachers need to make active, informed choices about texts for the classroom, beyond textbooks. This task is made easier by the numerous excellent publications in English and the rich array of related resources available in a variety of media. "The turn of the millennium has been a golden time for children's book publishing and associated art forms and industries. Arguably, children's books have achieved unprecedented public visibility, sales and popularity" (Maybin & Watson, 2009, p. 1–2). It is hoped that teachers themselves will enjoy reading and engaging with the range of texts suggested here, in order to share and model the pleasures of contemporary teenage fiction to learners. Increasingly, texts are becoming available in digital formats, which hopefully may also help teachers with the challenge of access to enough high-quality literary texts.

Reading in the classroom

Arguably teenagers (11–18-year-olds) should be regarded and treated as a significant distinct readership group, in terms of their transitional character and identity. Terms such as adolescent or young adult (YA)are also used; here, teenager or teen is preferred as retaining the emphasis on transition or "in-betweenness".

The pedagogic task of working with teenagers in English is an ambitious one, beyond just encouraging them to read one or more books in class. The challenge is twofold: to encourage language learning and intellectual development through reading engagement in the present, and to create the lifelong desire to be an autonomous reader of English, positioning the teacher to some extent as reading guide, mentor and role model. The Norwegian government's aim that all learners should remain in secondary or vocational education level to age 19 or later intensifies the importance of exploiting teenagers' potential as lifelong readers. In *The Child That Books Built* (2003) Francis Spufford has written movingly and convincingly of the important influence of his childhood reading on his adult identity.

The ideal is a successful, energised English classroom, where the importance and role of sustained reading in language learning is foregrounded, with a positive impact on learners into the future. At best, English classes can and should inspire all learners with an enduring taste for the imaginative stimulus and satisfaction of reading a range of literature. In the words of children's author Katherine Rundell, "Stories have power" (Rundell 2019, p. 54). Generating and encouraging a passion for reading will help learners to enjoy both the content and the narrative complexities and richness of the texts they meet. For Norwegian learners of English, the habit and skill of also reading in English as a second language will vastly extend the range and variety of reading material available to individuals, both for pleasure and professionally. It will speed up access to new books and media on publication, without waiting for translations, offering quick routes to current material, ideas and global culture. Reading in English will be in addition to reading Norwegian literature, increasing comparative access to literary culture. The goal is lifelong independent reading in English, for continuing refreshed active language competence and towards global awareness and citizenship.

A further recommendation is that, wherever possible, teachers should institute a multi-text classroom for older learners, promoting learner choice of reading material, so a variety of texts are recommended and shared among peers for pleasure and interest. Competence aims after years 7, 10 and VG1 state that learners should also be allowed to read/discuss/reflect on/present self-chosen texts. Such activities will exploit and feed well into teenagers' emerging self-definition, as well as their strong, socially motivated responses to peer influence and alliances. For continuity or comparison purposes, texts selected can be linked by topic, theme, author or genre and might form part of an interdisciplinary project with another subject.

The challenge for teachers of accessing enough English books, and maintaining regular updating, is not underestimated. Importantly, librarians can be powerful allies here, with their responsibility for buying new books, and their available library budgets. A library partnership with the school or local library can bring real benefits for all, particularly when a learner peer review and recommendation element is also incorporated, perhaps through learners creating posters or reader recommendation cards. This will transfer reading authority from teacher to learners in an empowering way. Another approach might be to draw on the increasing number of digital text repositories which are becoming available, such as the excellent and extensive ESL bits[25] or to use e-books, some of which can be downloaded free of charge. See chapter 8 for more about digital and digitised young adult fiction.

Principles for recommending texts and resources

Recommended authors and novels of particular interest and merit are highlighted, with comparable or related texts identified. It is hoped that teachers will encourage learners to read and research further in the works of authors chosen, or on themes studied, to encourage extensive reading beyond the classroom. See chapter 6 on reading, for a discussion of the value of extensive reading.

The main text selection principle is literary quality, which offers reading pleasure and will stand up well to classroom analysis, discussion and activities. Numerous literary prize winning texts are recommended despite some debates about prize overkill since the 1960s (see, for example, Kidd in Maybin & Watson, 2009). Many authors are British, while others are American or diasporic. The majority of suggested texts should appeal to both sexes. Attention is given to gender, race and equality. Most texts mentioned are contem-

---

25 http://esl-bits.net/

porary in their setting, language and cultural references, and explore current issues. Realism is the dominant genre, emphasising relevance to teen readers. Most of the recommended example texts have been tried and tested in recent courses for Norwegian teachers and trainees at the Norwegian Study Centre in York, UK and in Norway.

Brief narrative summaries of recommended texts are provided, without spoilers as far as possible. Endings are usually not revealed, nor are plot secrets disclosed. This is deliberate, to model for readers the engaging and motivating reading experience they will wish to offer learners.

Various critics, including Ann Hewings (in Maybin & Watson, 2009, p. 330) have written about the way that children's literature is rapidly transforming under global and media influences. Many texts discussed here also co-exist in multi-modal versions, e.g. visual, audio, picturebook, performance or other media forms, or have generated prequel, parallel or spin-off texts. These previously unprecedented fluid morphings and dynamic transformations can offer opportunities for the classroom, allowing simultaneous use of different versions of texts for differentiation, to suit learners' varied learning styles and abilities. Hopefully digital and online availability can also increase access to texts suggested in this chapter.

The rich range of fiction being published emphasises the need to remain up to date. English teachers will find online resources and relevant websites invaluable; all listed here are free of charge. Pedagogic strategies are also suggested to involve learners actively in online research and peer text recommendation. For teachers' own research purposes, peer strategies are also likely to be highly effective; establishing in-service reading groups or staff support and information exchanges or liaising closely with librarians can bring many benefits, not least efficiency of shared effort.

Effective teacher strategies for choosing quality texts: prizes and more prizes

Invaluable long-term solutions to choosing and updating classroom texts can be found online, particularly through literary prize web sites. British and American children's literature awards have proliferated hugely in the last 50 or so years. Important British awards include the Guardian Children's Fiction Prize, the CILIP Carnegie Medal, the Kate Greenaway Medal, the Nestlé Smarties Book Prize, the Blue Peter Book Awards and the Waterstones Children's Book Prize, each with a comprehensive website. The premier US award is the Newbery Medal; there are also numerous other North American prizes. Prizes sometimes adapt their names as new sponsors emerge.

As well as annual awards, the UK Children's Laureate website (www.childrenslaureate.org.uk) is a valuable free-of-charge resource. Initiated by Poet Laureate Ted Hughes and children's author Michael Morpurgo in 1999, the Children's Laureate title (with a £15 000 bursary) is awarded every two years to an eminent writer or illustrator of children's books to celebrate outstanding achievement in their field, and to acknowledge the importance of exceptional children's authors in creating the readers of tomorrow. Illustrator Quentin Blake was the first Children's Laureate, followed by authors Anne Fine, Michael Morpurgo, Jacqueline Wilson, poet Michael Rosen, illustrator Anthony Browne, author Julia Donaldson and novelist Malorie Blackman. The website offers creative pedagogic resources for teachers, relevant to different genres according to each Laureate's interests. The USA developed an equivalent scheme in 2008, when the Library of Congress inaugurated its National Ambassador for Young People's Literature title (http://read.gov/cfb/ambassador/). The inaugural Ambassador was Jon Scieszka, followed by novelist Katherine Paterson and poet Walter Dean Myers, who coined the slogan "Reading is not optional."

Another valuable starting point online is to research author websites to fit with chapter 6 usage, which are of increasing quality and well supported by publishers. Such websites can serve a dual purpose, as a useful research and lesson preparation resource for teachers, and as a valuable pedagogic tool and research option for learners, particularly as classrooms become more permeable to technology. They could, for example, be used to generate research or extended writing tasks for learners, including writing reviews for online publication, or sending questions to the author. For both learners and teachers there is the option of inspiring reading engagement by following, and possibly engaging or interacting with, a favourite author. This happens in *Love That Dog* by Sharon Creech (2001) (discussed in chapter 6) when the real American poet Walter Dean Myers responds to an invitation from the fictional protagonist, Jack. These are truly authentic learning experiences with a very clear emphasis on writers as alive and current, publishing an evolving body of exciting work.

Teenagers as a distinctive readership

What exactly is a teenager? What are teenagers' particular strengths? What are their likes and dislikes? What are likely points of pressure or conflict? What kinds of material will engage teenagers and what might alienate or embarrass them? LK20 positions the interdisciplinary topic *Health and Life Skills* within English Studies, emphasising the growth of learners' ability to express themselves in writing and orally as crucial in laying foundations for the healthy expression of feelings, experiences and opinions. Exploring this topic through texts and related classroom activities can help develop new perspectives on different ways of thinking and communicating, and on different comparative ways of living and life situations. Encountering situations that require linguistic and cultural competence and sensitivity can give learners a sense of mastery and contribute to developing a positive self-image and a secure identity. It is notable that the Reading Agency, which sees teenagers' mental health as a significant issue to be mediated and supported through reading, has produced a guide called *Shelf Help*,[26] recommending fiction and other books dealing with mental health topics such as eating disorders, depression or suicide. Equally, some texts recommended in this chapter deal specifically with physical health or illness. Exploring the questions above will help to answer the most important question of all: how can teachers influence and encourage teenagers to engage actively with reading?

For the purposes of this discussion, teenagers can usefully be divided into groups with different reading needs and preferences. Between ages 11–13, some are still pre-pubertal, and on a relatively childlike continuum of interests and responses. They may therefore be potentially embarrassed or bored by texts focused on relationships or sex-related topics. The 13–16 age group can be regarded as true in-betweeners, exploring growth, personal change and identity issues with energy and uncertainty. Ages 16–19 form the "crossover" or semi-adult group, likely to be the most personally confident and mature, as well as the most sophisticated and ambitious readers. Texts for younger age groups are not necessarily simpler in form or content; there is a rich diversity of literary effect and complex creativity in texts recommended for all three age groups. Teachers need to take responsibility for deciding the exact appropriate age range for each text recommended, particularly since the EFL classroom is a mixed ability environment where reading age and interest age may not always closely align for all learners.[27]

Characteristics and stylistic features of teenage fiction

One of the most striking features of teenage fiction is the preponderance of first person narrative voices. Novels written in the first person allow the reader the privilege of identifying with the protagonist and knowing or understanding more than the other characters, as well as communicating

---

26 https://readingagency.org.uk/young-people/ Reading Well
27 See information about Barrington Stoke books in Reading chapter.

the immediacy and intensity of experience and emotions. This offers teenage readers a unique opportunity to view the world through the eyes of others, helping to generate insight and empathy, and relating directly to issues addressed in the Health and Life Sciences curriculum. Teen fiction is often issue-based. Plots frequently concern growing up and life lessons learned, often through painful experience. *Bildungsroman*, or the novel of education and experience, is therefore a particularly key literary form for teenage readers. Sometimes pre-teen narrators are observers of teenagers and adults, trying to make sense of their behaviour. Often teenage characters are engaged in enquiring about and critiquing situations or the world they have inherited; plots centre on a problem, either of their own making or inherited from the indifferent adult world, with a strong imperative towards justice. These texts therefore align closely with LK20's positioning of the interdisciplinary topic *Democracy and Citizenship* within English Studies, with the aim of developing learners' understanding that their perception of the world depends on the cultural context. Studying English allows learners to meet different societies and cultures through communication with others, independently of linguistic and cultural background. Importantly, this can offer different ways of interpreting the world, both to spur curiosity and engagement, and to contribute to preventing prejudice.

In terms of structure and visual layout, teenage fiction is often delightfully experimental, even post-modern. Chapters can be unconventionally organised or deliberately mismatched, with reader expectations about beginnings and endings disrupted. Visually, images, fonts, and intertexts both challenge and generate pleasure, as texts become multi-layered, resisting consolidation or uniformity.

Teenage fiction is sophisticated and unsentimental with regard to closure. Novel endings are often complex, with unexpected or uncertain elements. There are rarely easy solutions to dilemmas and problems encountered; it is much more often a case of exploring, processing and arriving at a compromise or partial solution. Humour is often used successfully to temper sad or serious situations, complicating and moderating the reader's responses.

Recommended texts for grades 5–10

Recommended authors include highly prolific Children's Laureate Michael Morpurgo[28] and American authors Louis Sachar[29] and Jewell Parker Rhodes.

---

28   www.michaelmorpurgo.com
29   http://www.louissachar.com/

The well-established British tradition of children's books featuring anthropomorphised animal protagonists and characters is approached from a new angle by the extremely successful, popular, award-winning novelist Michael Morpurgo. His fiction explores relationships between humans and animals, with a consistent political and cultural agenda of human responsibility for the natural and the animal world. (He founded the charity, *Farms for City Children*,[30] which aims to develop awareness of the interdependence between humans and animals.) The well-understood benefit of fictions with animals as protagonists or key characters is an opportunity for younger readers to explore important and affectionate relationships without being inhibited or embarrassed by human sexual behaviour. Though apparently simple, Morpurgo's novels offer carefully crafted narrative structures which stimulate readers, repay close study and offer effective writing models.

Cool (2002) is a short, easy to read football-themed novel narrated by Robbie, lying in hospital unconscious after a car accident in which he unsuccessfully tried to save the life of his dog, Lucky. Robbie can neither speak nor write, so the reader has uniquely privileged access to his consciousness and voice, interspersed with realistic headline newspaper columns at the beginning of each chapter. This simultaneous dual narrative makes the novel accessible both to under-confident and more mature readers. Learners can follow one or both narrative threads; this surprisingly dramatic and satisfying novel offers verisimilitude and potential writing exercises through the constantly updated newspaper narrative.

Morpurgo's fiction is often fact-based. Another appealing short novel, *This Morning I Met a Whale* (2008), is a tactile, beautifully illustrated, first-person eco-narrative; an audio recording by the author is also available. It has a wonderfully clever and disconcerting narrative structure, in which the title is also the opening line, and which will astonish readers when the line "And that's the end of my story" (Morpurgo, 2008a, p. 43) appears halfway through the novel. The reader then has to consider differences between fact and fiction, genre expectations and multiple meta-narratives. This novel is based on an actual widely reported 2006 event which learners can research; it also offers the opportunity to explore attitudes towards the natural world. The novel can be read from an emotional, intellectual or moral perspective, particularly with its strong focus on intergenerational debt and the responsibilities and empowerment of children. The whale's important message to Michael, the

---

30 https://farmsforcitychildren.org/

narrator, about climate change dangers is: "Only the children will put it right" (Morpurgo, 2008a, p. 42).

Kaspar, Prince of Cats (2008) is another enjoyable, beautifully illustrated novel, following the transatlantic "rags to riches" adventures of a young boy in the early 20th century, interwoven with the story of the eponymous cat. Both experience a series of dramatic adventures, including travelling on the *Titanic*. *The Ghost of Grainne O'Malley* (1996) features a disabled protagonist and asserts the importance of will power and individual choice.

War Horse (1982) is extremely popular, with successful stage (Stafford & Morpurgo, 2007) and film (Spielberg, 2011) adaptations. This moving story of the British working horses taken to the battlefields of the First World War may be more appropriate in subject matter and complexity for slightly older readers, as it asks thought-provoking questions about human beings' right to involve animals in violent conflict. *Private Peaceful* (2003) is a moving and powerful First World War narrative about a teenage soldier sentenced to death for disobeying orders, which uses a very clever double time scheme. It is also adapted into a film and stage play.

American author Louis Sachar's powerful comic novel *Holes* (2000, winner of the Newbery Medal) has generated a film, a teacher's guide and various spin-off publications by the author. *Holes* has a compelling dual time frame and narrative, dealing with racism. Wrongfully convicted of stealing some valuable sports sneakers, which fell from the sky and hit him on the head one day, Stanley Yelnats is sent to a reform summer camp in the Texas desert. The third-person narrative describes Stanley's repetitive experiences at Camp Green Lake, ironically named as the lake has long ago dried up in the scorching desert climate. Camp life is not only tedious, but nonsensical in that the boy inmates' sole task is digging the holes of the title. Stanley realises that there is a mystery around this apparently purposeless task and assumes the role of detective, supported by his ingenious, creative and enterprising fellow campers (all convicted of criminal offences) to understand the mystery and reap the rewards. Stanley's detective role offers intrigue, narrative suspense, danger and satisfaction. In a bizarre comic twist, the mystery turns out to concern onions, among other things.

New York Times best-seller *Ghost Boys* (2018) by American author Jewell Parker Rhodes is a compelling politically aware first person narrative told by Jerome, a twelve year old black boy, who is shot dead on the first page of the novel. Thereafter the book is equally divided into action passages labelled either "Dead" or "Alive" as Jerome moves between the world of the living, which continues forward through the trial of his killer, and the world of the dead, which he discovers to be mysteriously populated by numerous "ghost boys" from the past and present. Jerome and the reader are jointly puzzled by the discovery of this population's existence. The enigma of Jerome and his fellow ghosts' continued presence in a limbo where just a few of the living are aware of them has an explanation both entirely convincing and cautiously optimistic. The novel draws on black history and explores the level of agency that young people might have to change an unfair society. "Only the living can make change" (Parker Rhodes, p. 91). It concludes with useful discussion questions and resources.

The Boy at the Back of the Class (2018) by British Bangladeshi author Onjali Q. Rauf won the Waterstones Children's Book Prize and the Blue Peter Best Story Award. It is an engaging and energetic story of primary school friends who want to help a new refugee schoolmate. Their resourceful and admirable repeated problem-solving attempts are both moving and comic, powerfully exposing some of the ridiculous politics and regulations of the adult world when it comes to individual need and human lives. Ultimately the children feel they must appeal to the highest authority, offering the reader some delightful surprises.

Jessica's Ghost (2015) by Andrew Norriss is endorsed by Amnesty International for its sensitivity about gender difference and the effects of bullying on mental health. Beginning with Francis, a boy who loves to design and make clothes, the novel features a group of friends who have unconventional attitudes towards gender roles. The one thing they have in common is that they are the only individuals who can see the ghost of Jessica, a dead girl central to their friendship group. Neither they nor Jessica understand why she still inhabits the world of the living; like Jerome in *Ghost Boys*, it turns out that Jessica has a responsibility to fulfil. The novel resolves this in a powerfully convincing way. Whilst *Jessica's Ghost* deals with difficult topics such as isolation and teenage suicide, the novel is reassuring about the importance of friendship and the ways in which it can support young people through bullying, grief and mental distress.

The engaging and light-hearted *Planet Omar* series by British Muslim author Zanib Mian offers an excellent bridge from picture books for younger readers, mixing text and visual images in a very readable way. In *Planet Omar: Accidental Trouble Magnet* (2019), *Planet Omar: Unexpected Super Spy* (2020) and *Planet Omar: Incredible Rescue Mission* (2020), Omar and his sister Maryam are ordinary British Muslim children describing a series of comic adventures. The books are narrated by Omar, who comments cheerfully and sometimes quirkily on family, friendship, school and daily life.

1984 Guardian Children's Fiction Award winner *The Sheep-Pig* (1983) by Dick King-Smith, filmed as *Babe* (1995), is a humorous novel with a rural setting, about the serious question of choosing and establishing one's own identity. Babe is an ambitious piglet born on a farm, who wants to become a sheep-dog, and thereby save his own life. (The novel is extremely clear about the future of adult pigs on farms.) The hilarious third-person adventure narrative is accurate and informative about farm life, even including (chapter 11) a diagram of a sheep-dog trial. There is a sequel: *Ace*.

Recommended texts for grades 8–13

Recommended authors include UK Children's Laureates Jacqueline Wilson and Malorie Blackman. David Almond, Benjamin Zephaniah, Berlie Doherty and Mark Haddon also write satisfyingly complex and engaging stories about realistic dilemmas without easy solutions. Many novels recommended are also structurally ingenious, with stimulating meta-fictional elements.

The enormously successful and prolific Jacqueline Wilson mainly creates female protagonists, focusing on the emotions and dilemmas of growing up in an imperfect world. Wilson writes realistically and empathetically about difficult family situations. She creates suspense and uses humour to engage readers with the challenges faced by her teenage characters when the adult world lets them down.

Arguably, Wilson's books appeal more to female readers and are marketed more towards them in terms of titles, content and cover art. Jacqueline Wilson invests heavily in her website[31], which is extremely vivid and colourful, with the author at its heart, looking and speaking directly to the reader in an appealing and inviting manner. Reader interaction is encouraged.

Dustbin Baby (2001) is April's story. The first-person narrative opens on April's 14th birthday, as she sets out to trace the mother who abandoned her as a newborn baby, in a dustbin. Newspaper headlines when she was found abandoned on April 1st, or April Fool's Day, have generated the unkind nickname which forms the book's title. Wilson stresses the ways in which the media can casually but powerfully confer a burdensome negative identity which interferes with self-definition and optimism. The novel is realistic about the feelings of pressure experienced by teenage girls. April's situation is easy for the reader to empathise with, offering a thoughtful perspective on personal agency whilst resisting a fairy-tale ending. Structurally, the novel plays games with readers' expectations by beginning with an "ending" and

---

31 www.jacquelinewilson.co.uk

ending with a new beginning. Written in colloquial language, the chapters are short and focused around the stages of the quest. The novel incorporates a very exciting cliff-hanger when April visits the dustbin where she was found, to find the message "Please call, Baby" (Wilson, 2008, p. 144) and a phone number ...

Wilson's Guardian Children's Fiction Award winning *The Illustrated Mum* (2000) has a stronger fairy-tale structure. Two sisters live with their loving but mentally fragile mother, who is alarmingly addicted to tattoos, hence "illustrated". This novel has a darker tone as mother Marigold's regular compulsion for a new tattoo becomes a recognisable sign of imminent mental breakdown. The plot is structured around these moments of family danger, with different tattoos as the chapter headings. The novel explores very serious social concerns about children as carers and their vulnerabilities in such situations, together with the lengths to which children will go to hide their needs from an apparently unsympathetic adult world. The fairy-tale motif involves the two sisters searching for their different fathers, highlighting inequalities of experience when children are at the whim of the adult world. Domestic and emotional insecurity are major themes and there are no easy answers.

David Almond's lyrical, moving prose engages the reader with the strange and magical. The 1998 Whitbread Children's Book of the Year and 1999 Carnegie Medal winner *Skellig* (1998) is relatively literary in its language and references, for example to 18th-century poet William Blake, but sentences are short and imagery is well-contextualised. Skellig is the mysterious, filthy, dried out, possibly non-human creature found in the abandoned garage of the neglected new house which first-person narrator Michael moves to with his family. Michael's new life is overshadowed by the serious illness of his newborn baby sister; understandably he feels ignored and neglected by his parents. The enigmatic Skellig and friendship with home-schooled Mina come to fill Michael's imagination and life in a semi-mystical series of experiences, involving hope, flying and the richness and incomprehensibility of the natural world. *Skellig* has been adapted into a play, an opera and a film.[32] At times the novel is very funny, exploring family structures, conventional and unconventional education and coming of age. Almond has also published a complementary prequel, in Mina's voice, with experimental fonts. *My Name Is Mina* (2010) suggests that talented Mina may also be dyslexic. Both novels raise questions about education and the constraints of any institution, whilst affirming the power of the human imagination. With

---

32 See chapter 9 for a discussion of *Skellig* the film.

its surprising and stimulating range of typography, fonts and unorthodox reflections by Mina, the novel is also a brilliant source book for classroom creative writing exercises.

Frank Cottrell Boyce's Carnegie Medal winning *Millions* (2004) is 11-year-old Damian's first-person narrative of school and family life, following his mother's death. The novel's recognisable contemporary realistic world includes one crucial difference, as Britain is about to change currency to the Euro. With the heartbreaking logic of a young child, grieving Damian becomes obsessed with saints, to try to make sense of bereavement. He builds a cardboard hermitage by the railway line to hide in and waits for a miracle. A bag of banknotes comes flying through the air and Damian miraculously acquires the millions of pounds of the novel's title. The novel asks profound questions about the value of money, what it can and cannot buy and how it motivates human beings. This fast-paced novel is often comic but also full of danger and excitement as the criminals who originally stole the money trace Damian and want it back. Stylistically, the novel incorporates web references and links as well as examples of handwriting. *Millions* asks serious questions about morality, integrity and honesty, with a thoroughly surprising outcome.

Mark Haddon's crossover novel *The Curious Incident of the Dog in the Night-Time* (2003), awarded both the 2003 Guardian Children's Fiction Prize and the 2003 Whitbread Book of the Year, appeals to both teenagers and adults. The successful stage adaptation set a record by winning 7 Olivier Awards. Christopher, the protagonist and first-person narrator, has Asperger's Syndrome or high-functioning autism. Whilst mathematically brilliant, he is socially and emotionally unsure; the novel shows the world from his point of view, beginning with the opening act of animal cruelty which turns him into a reluctant detective. By turns funny, touching and sad, the deceptively straightforward language of the novel maps and represents Christopher's thought processes as his investigation progresses. Readers quickly learn that the novel is an ongoing meta-fiction; they are in fact reading a detective novel authored by Christopher, who explores and negotiates, as he writes, a balance between an author's preferences and the reader's interests. Christopher's idiosyncratic views and reactions teach the reader about different perceptions and representations of reality; the enjoyably disconcerting meta-text includes diagrams, mathematical equations, images, notices, letters and a range of fonts and styles, raising questions about literacy, numeracy and the authority of the printed text. Cleverly, the novel is simultaneously a relatively straightforward and very sympathetic *Bildungsroman* about growing up, relationships with parents and authority, and future choices.

Berlie Doherty's Carnegie Medal-winning *Dear Nobody* (1991) depicts a young-adult relationship at the point of finishing school and starting out in life towards higher education and the future. Helen and Chris are in love and sleep together, in a very discreetly described scene. The novel's focus is Helen's unanticipated pregnancy and consequent choices as time passes. Family relationships through the generations are explored, with a clear-sighted emphasis on the gender inequalities of the situation. Chris is the first-person narrator, writing emotionally intense sections in relatively simple language. Here, too, the novel is satisfyingly more complex and generically more sophisticated than it first appears, as Chris's narrative is regularly punctuated by letters from Helen to the "Dear Nobody" of the title. "Nobody" is her name for the unimaginable baby, as she reviews and writes about the difficult options before her and the reactions she encounters. The double narrative offers the reader different viewpoints on the moral and ethical dilemma faced by the protagonists, with at least one satisfying and surprising dramatic twist at the end. When editors of this book conducted an informal reading survey among British and Norwegian teenagers, the novel was a clear first choice for a majority of teenagers, regardless of gender. *Dear Nobody* also exists as a playtext (Doherty & O'Neill, 1998).

Boys Don't Cry (2010) by Black British author Malorie Blackman is alternately narrated by two brothers, Adam and Dante, articulating their personal challenges. Eighteen-year-old Dante is astonished when a past, almost forgotten, girlfriend appears at his house with a baby, which she asks him to look after for a moment. He discovers the baby is his, and his ex-girlfriend vanishes, leaving him literally "holding the baby". Dante's unexpected experience of interrupted university plans and new-found parental responsibility is intercut with his brother Adam's exploration of his sexuality and changed life due to a homophobic attack. Both brothers have to re-think their aspirations, their responsibilities and their identities in a challenging novel for older readers. The language is colloquial and straightforward. The first-person alternating voices are clear and compelling; the subject matter of the novel and issues raised are very forthright. In line with the serious subject matter, *Boys Don't Cry* is published with a concluding section of questions for readers, helpline and website information and guidance on the issues explored in the novel. It would be an excellent comparative text to read and discuss with Berlie Doherty's *Dear Nobody*, raising questions about gender and responsibility.

Set in the very near future, Blackman's gripping *Pig Heart Boy* (1997) opens with 13-year-old Cameron dying from heart failure, when he is offered the controversial, pioneering option of a transplanted pig's heart to save his life. Cameron's parents are deeply divided, and the novel explores the secrecy necessary due to the complex ethical aspects of the operation. Cameron, in one of the most astonishing and thought-provoking sections of the novel, asks to meet the pig whose heart he will take. In chapter 6, the reader accompanies Cameron and his parents on a visit to the laboratory as he engages in a powerful internal dialogue about animal and human rights and his own mortality. Cameron has the operation and survives, only to tell his secret to his best friend whose family sell the story to the media. The first-person narrative explores fear, ethics, betrayal and media responsibility, as Cameron is called "Pig Heart Boy" by the press. The novel deals with public reaction, most shockingly expressed when a bucket of pig's blood is thrown at Cameron in the street, and with Cameron's struggle to establish his own personal and moral identity. There is also a BAFTA Award-winning TV adaptation.

Blackman's important thought-provoking *Noughts and Crosses* series is discussed later in the chapter.

Charismatic and unconventional performance poet Benjamin Zephaniah is a self-nominated role model for boys and for reluctant readers; he left school illiterate and did not learn to read and write until his twenties, in prison. Discovering belatedly as an adult that his learning difficulties at school resulted from severe dyslexia, he wrote:

> For those who have struggled like me,
> To read,
> And so be free.
> Sing loud and bang your drum,
> For we shall overcome.
>
> (*Kung Fu Trip*, 2011. n.p.)

Zephaniah's anti-authority stance, his refusal of an OBE honour from the Queen, his anger at social and educational disadvantage and his veganism all inspire interest in teenage readers. He is a prolific poet, with ample humorous, serious and political oral material online, as well as several print publications. Illustrated easy-read biographies include *Black Stars: Benjamin Zephaniah* (Wilkins, 2008) and *Benjamin Zephaniah: My Story* (Zephaniah and Ambrus, 2011), as well as *Kung Fu Trip* (2011), his amusing QuickRead autobiographical account of a martial arts visit to China.[33]

---

33 For QuickReads, see chapter 6, Reading for everyone.

Illustrated print collections of his rhythmic colloquial rap poetry such as *Wicked World* (2000) complement the numerous online and YouTube extracts available.

Three of Zephaniah's teenage novels are recommended: *Face* (1999), *Teacher's Dead* (2007) and *Refugee Boy* (2001), also adapted into a play by Lemm Sissay (2013). Zephaniah deliberately concludes every novel with a poem. Benjamin Zephaniah is explicitly concerned with all forms of prejudice and discrimination; *Face* (also adapted as a powerful playtext) is the story of Martin's life before and after a car accident in which he is severely burned. The novel addresses the dangers of gang and drug culture, and peer pressure. The understated language of the third-person narrative is unsentimental, relating Martin's experiences and feelings in a very matter-of-fact way. Like *Dear Nobody*, *Face* is powerfully concerned with young lives unexpectedly changed, as well as prejudices encountered. The reader is strongly challenged to review his or her own assumptions and reactions. *Teacher's Dead* is based on real knife crime incidents, in particular, tragic cases in London where teachers attempting to stop knife fights at school became victims and died. The schoolboy narrator Jackson Jones witnessed the playground stabbing of his headteacher. He saw the attack clearly but is unsatisfied by the evidence of his own eyes and sets out as a detective to understand the crime and explore alternative explanations. Thoughtful and resourceful, he makes contact, and eventually friends, with the headteacher's widow. Throughout the novel, there is a sense that Jackson's eccentric quest is futile, due to unshakeable eyewitness evidence, yet the novel vindicates his viewpoint and asks unexpected questions about responsibility, guilt and the vulnerability of the perpetrators. Zephaniah offers readers a panorama of problems without easy answers, though the widow's insistence on forgiveness is a powerful element of the conclusion. This first-person narrative begins at the end; chapter 1 is entitled "The Ending", and the novel concludes with Jackson's school report, which turns out not to be about school subjects, but much more about learning from life.

> I have learnt that you can see something happen right in front of you but still you are only seeing part of the picture. Nothing is as it seems. Seeing is not believing. Sometimes, as well as seeing you have to feel, touch, experience, and use your intelligence, and even then you should still question. (Zephaniah, 2007b, pp. 221–222)

Refugee Boy (Zephaniah, 2001) is the story of Alem, half Eritrean and half Ethiopian, whose mixed-race family are dangerously at risk in the civil war. Alem's father brings him to England for an ostensible holiday and leaves secretly, hoping that Alem will gain refugee status and security. The uncertainties and pressures of the refugee experience are powerfully exposed, although Alem himself remains polite and relatively forgiving through a range of increasingly difficult experiences, including separation from family and home. Christine Wilkie-Stibbs offers an extended critique of *Refugee Boy* as an idealised and relatively unrealistic portrayal of youth refugee experience (Wilkie-Stibbs, 2008, p. 33 onwards). However, Alem's patient responses to a series of setbacks and increasingly severe losses underscore the accidental but nonetheless shockingly dehumanising effects of unsympathetic official procedures and rules, as well as media influence. In addition to its strong and very thought-provoking content, *Refugee Boy* engages readers by its structure, using textual repetition to highlight the political dilemmas faced by Alem's family, and playing with closure, so that the novel's ending simultaneously challenges its structure and undercuts expectations of narrative satisfaction. The playtext (Zephaniah & Sissay, 2013) of *Refugee Boy* is faithful to Zephaniah's plot, poetic language and imagery, focused on the stars which shine in the first and last scenes of the play, when Alem finally asserts his identity as himself rather than "Refugee Boy".[34]

The Bone Sparrow (2016) by Australian author Zana Fraillon won numerous awards, including the Amnesty Honour Award, for its thought-provoking depiction of the evolving secret friendship between a refugee boy born behind bars in a displaced persons camp somewhere in Australia and a bereaved girl who wants to rescue him.

Annabel Pitcher's 2011 novel *My Sister Lives on the Mantelpiece*, winner of the Branford Boase Award, begins with the surprising sentence, "My sister Rose lives on the mantelpiece" (2011, p 1). It is the story of family reactions to the death of a sibling in a random terrorist attack. Despite the very serious subject matter, the novel is often funny and intensely moving, focusing through black humour on the difficult topics of loss and grief as well as prejudice and alcohol abuse.

Three further recommended novels are about football, among other topics. Mal Peet's *Keeper* (2003) is a mystery novel set in South America about football and the possible price of success, with a wonderfully atmospheric solution to the mystery. South African author Michael Williams won the 2014

---

34 See chapter 8 for ideas for digital classroom approaches to *Refugee Boy*.

UKLA award for *Now Is the Time for Running* (2012).[35] This novel and the parallel story *Diamond Boy* (2014), set in Southern Africa, explore suffering, disability and the fight for survival in a dangerous world. Black British author Pete Kalu's *The Silent Striker* (2015) also addresses the effects of disability, in this case hearing loss, on talent and life choices. More recommendations for young adult novels can be found in chapter 6, "Reading for everyone", and in chapter 8, "Digital approaches to young adult fiction".

The benefits of novel series

Numerous series for teenage readers have appeared in different genres, in the wake of *Harry Potter* and *Twilight*. These include Malorie Blackman's *Noughts & Crosses*, Rick Riordan's *Percy Jackson*, Zizou Corder's *Lionboy*, Philip Pullman's *Northern Lights*, Suzanne Collins' *The Hunger Games*, M.K. Harris's *The Joshua Chronicles*, Philip Reeve's *Mortal Engines* and *Chaos Walking* by Patrick Ness. Series provide an important opportunity to read independently within a familiar and already negotiated framework. Novel series appeal to confident readers who are already familiar with characters, setting, plotline and style from the first volume, and are hungry for more, enjoying variations on a key concept and a known theme. Whilst teachers are unlikely to have time or opportunity to teach series in class, it will be important to stimulate interest in such texts, to encourage reading opportunities for the most gifted and talented learners.

Malorie Blackman's 5-book series *Noughts & Crosses* is set in a recognisable alternative contemporary reality where the major difference is the reversal of racial hierarchy. It would be an outstanding choice to explore *Democracy and Citizenship* curriculum issues; it has been adapted into a play and a television series. The Crosses, who are black, are the ruling, powerful elite, historically dominant and privileged, whereas the white noughts (without a capital N) are the underclass, second-class citizens serving the Crosses. Noughts and Crosses are restricted to separate lives; the first novel replays *Romeo and Juliet*, exploring how Sephy, a Cross from one of the most powerful families in the country, can have a relationship with Callum, a nought. Its reversal of accepted norms raises issues of racial difference and prejudice in an inescapable manner. The gripping and challenging content of this series makes it very suitable for the most ambitious readers with reading stamina.[36]

---

35 See chapter 8 for ideas for digital classroom approaches to *Now Is the Time for Running*.
36 See chapter 7 for a discussion about the graphic version of *Noughts & Crosses*.

The popular 5-volume *Percy Jackson* series by prolific American author Rick Riordan comprises fast-paced, exciting and fantastic adventures featuring a lively range of male and female teenage characters who turn out to be half human and half gods. These very fast-moving novels are easy to read, with numerous dramatic plot twists and turns. They are based on Greek mythology, so the believable contemporary teenage characters who are in a constant battle to save the world. contrast effectively with their parents, the remote and unpredictable classical gods. There are also two films, graphic novel adaptations of each novel, a game and an off-Broadway musical. The novels originate from the author's concern about his son's challenging learning experiences due to dyslexia and ADHD. There are two follow-up series, *Heroes of Olympus* and *The Trials of Apollo*, and two further related series drawing respectively on ancient Egypt and the Norse gods.

Lionboy (2003) by Zizou Corder is highly recommended as a particular spur to young writers, due to its experimental authorship. The author's name Zizou Corder is invented; the novel is a collaboration between British adult author Louisa Young and her daughter Isabel Adomakoh Young, now a university learners. This exciting and colourful adventure series originated as co-created bedtime stories. Set in a recognisable world, one fantastic difference is that the hero, Charlie Shanti, can speak Cat. In this novel, all cats have a common language, usually neither understood nor noticed by humans. Charlie uses his unique talent to question the cat population of London when his scientist parents are mysteriously kidnapped. His subsequent adventures are thoroughly fast-paced, exciting and full of unexpected drama, including sea voyages, pirates, a circus and encounters with lions. *Lionboy* has also been adapted as a play (Complicité, 2013).

Ways of reading in the classroom
Didactic strategy 1: Reading a single text together, including multiple modes, e.g. film

Organising teaching a novel to a class may seem a daunting task. The best and most natural approach is to simulate the three phases of authentic individual reading experience, whilst incorporating and interspersing tasks based on four key language skills (reading, speaking, writing, listening) in as natural a way as possible. This approach begins with anticipatory discussion, followed by shared initial reading. Learners read the text in sections at their own pace, concluding with discussion and retrospective review.

The pre-reading phase should introduce the initial excitement and anticipation of meeting a new and unknown text, building on the "film trailer" model. Whilst an actual film trailer from an adaptation might sometimes be available, the book's blurb, cover information, author website or peer learner recommendations can all also be used for this purpose, in discussion and writing. What do you expect? What do you anticipate? What interests you at this moment? Generating dialogue and debate in the classroom is one of the most direct routes to active language development and enhancement.

Reading phase 2 should include starting the text at the beginning, reading together for shared pleasure, and discussion and prediction. In a mixed-ability situation it would be unfair to maintain this pace rigidly and prescriptively, as it will inevitably delay and deter the most eager and competent readers. A recommended solution is for the teacher to divide the text into a number of sections, with a signposted programme of lessons and activities for working through the sections. Text sections (which may be organised around chapter groupings) should naturally exploit cliff-hangers and dramatic textual moments or tensions wherever possible. Eager readers should certainly be allowed to read on at their own pace, with the "no spoilers" proviso that they must not communicate information about later sections to their peers. This will maintain the excitement and suspense of the story unfolding, for all. At any point in the study of the sections of the novel, there is the opportunity to interweave the other versions, adaptations and resources available, to compare and contrast for better understanding. In class, learners can work together on topics, themes and language structure from the designated section. These learner tasks do not have to all be the same but can be varied and tailored by the teacher to learner ability and language competence. Such activities promote the concept of re-reading for fuller understanding, and foster ideas of working in depth to explore, discuss, enjoy and revisit the complexities of the text. It will be useful to plan some whole-class staging points, perhaps focused around discussion, to maintain shared pleasure and momentum. Post-reading phase 3, once the whole text has been covered the class should look back over the narrative for discussion and writing tasks which include summing up and reviewing their sense of satisfaction, shared enjoyment and achievement. At this point, learners will discover that reading is not only linear; analysis and discussion will ideally move backwards and forwards through the text, giving insight into narrative structures and author choices. Ideally, studying a novel together should be a circular, iterative process, where the concluding activities incorporate the responsibility of review and recommendation to other learners, just as enthusiastic readers naturally make recommendations to each other. Ideally, learner reviews should be published, whether on paper, online, or as posters, as authentic writing tasks directed at a real audience.

Didactic strategy 2: the theme-based multi-text classroom, reading complementary texts together

An alternative approach, highly recommended, either for older learners or to enable differentiation, is to orchestrate the simultaneous reading of several complementary texts or versions in one classroom. Whilst more complicated to organise and manage, this has the benefit of echoing real reading experience by allowing learner choice of reading text, which can feel democratically desirable to teenagers. It readily creates possibilities for comparative discussion and understanding, for example of different literary genres or of issues and themes. This approach can also spontaneously stimulate additional reading through peer influence, as learners become inspired to read each other's texts. It also allows tactfully for different reading and learning abilities and preferences, without infringing on learner dignity. It can be particularly effective in involving boys and reluctant readers. Another argument relates to research stating that vocational learners are commonly considered poorer readers than learners in general study programmes (Brevik, Olsen & Hellekjær, 2016). Being allowed to choose their own texts can therefore be particularly relevant for vocational learners, and is also stated as a competence aim after VG1.

Below are a few text examples.

Michael Morpurgo's *Kaspar, Prince of Cats* (2008) could be used with Factfile *Titanic* by Tim Vicary (2009) together with selected relevant online historical research, as well as scenes from the film *Titanic*. The common narrative strand is the well-known story of the Titanic.

Any of Benjamin Zephaniah's novels, including *Face* (2008), *Refugee Boy* (2007) and *Teacher's Dead* (2007), fit well together with QuickRead *Kung Fu Trip* (2011) and an easy-read biography such as *Benjamin Zephaniah: My Story* (Zephaniah and Ambrus, 2011) or *Black Stars: Benjamin Zephaniah* (Wilkins, 2008) together with poetry performances from YouTube and/or a volume such as *Wicked World* (Zephaniah, 2000). This offers a very interesting mix of genres.

Face by Zephaniah pairs well with *Wonder* by R. J. Palacio.[37]

---

37 See chapter 3 for more about *Wonder*.

If *Refugee Boy* (2007) is selected then the theme of migration could be explored with Shaun Tan's wordless *The Arrival* (2006) and Zana Fraillon's *The Bone Sparrow*. If *Teacher's Dead* (2007) is selected then QuickRead *Hello Mum* (2010) by Bernardine Evaristo also deals with knife crime, as does Jason Reynolds's verse novel *Long Way Down*.[38]

Further didactic suggestions for class activities
Independent student learning can also be incorporated into these activities.

1. Key questions
The following topics are fruitful starting points either for text selection or for text groupings in the multi-text classroom. They can be used to generate either discussion, or writing activities, or both, on many of the recommended texts. They also align very well with the interdisciplinary curriculum topics of *Health and Life Skills* and *Democracy and Citizenship*.

Identity: Who am I? What name do I choose? Can the outside world determine my identity? Can the media name me? Who can I become? What level of agency do I have? Identity covers themes of self-determination, role, personal choices, moving beyond the family framework, social position, future options.

Responsibility: to self, to others, to disadvantaged others, in inter-species relationships, for the natural world, in dealing with intergenerational debt, when adults have already damaged or spoiled the world.

Relationships: with peers, with bullies, with the adult world and with future selves. Teenagers are on the cusp of adulthood, changing, growing, adapting. The theme of relationships includes important questions of authority and power, and what to do when adults fail.

Challenges/Mysteries/Secrets: In leaving childhood behind, teenagers often discover previously hidden knowledge, for instance that the world is not straightforward and that there are no easy answers to some issues and questions. Many texts feature secrets, and the difficulties resulting from their discovery.

---

38 See chapter 6 for more about *Long Way Down*.

2. Equality, diversity and prejudice

A number of contrasting texts deal explicitly with disability, including learning difficulties such as dyslexia. Several texts deal with racial identity and migration; others deal powerfully with disadvantage, exploring levels of will power and agency required to move forward. Learners can be encouraged to research and debate these topics, using examples from the text as case studies and exploring issues of restitution, inclusion and social attitudes. These topics are particularly appropriate for cross-curricular teaching. Learners could also focus on some of the Amnesty International or Reading Agency *Shelf Help* recommendations.

3. Ethical debates

Taking different characters' roles and points of view, without assigning blame, learners can discuss some of the complex and multi-faceted ethical issues raised. This is likely to be a popular and effective activity due to teenagers' heightened sense of justice and empathy. It might include researching issues, putting together a case, using a trial format and hot-seating witnesses, with polling at the end.

4. Media influence

Look at real media headlines, and those in texts studied. What is the relationship between fact and fiction? Are the media neutral? How do the media label individuals, or simplify complex issues? How do the media do damage? How are sound bites turned into stories? What about the influence of social media? Writing and research possibilities include finding sources for stories in the media, writing an alternative version and writing what happened next. (One important difference between media and fiction can be empathy; first-person narratives allow readers to relate to inner feelings.)

5. Reading Day/Festival

Peer activities are crucial for this age group; the importance of learners promoting texts to each other cannot be overstated. Organise an inclusive, enjoyable Book Festival or Reading Event or Book Day where learners research and recommend books to each other or to other year groups. It is really valuable for everyone when older learners read to younger ones, or recommend favourite books. Posters, published or online reviews, pitching for particular books, prizes and voting for the winner can all be included.

Conclusion

In conclusion, the Norwegian English curriculum gives teachers the privilege and responsibility of choosing the best, most stimulating, most relevant books to inspire their learners. Introducing young readers to quality, variety and choice at the earliest opportunity will give them agency and create an appetite for continuing extensive reading, including for more demanding novels and for new texts not yet published. This chapter has emphasised stimulating the teenage imagination through reading, so that they know themselves to be citizens of a world of books.

References
Primary texts
Almond, D. (1998). *Skellig*. Hodder Children's Books.
Almond, D. (2010). *My Name Is Mina*. Hodder Children's Books.
Blackman, M. (1997). *Pig Heart Boy*. Corgi Books.
Blackman, M. (2001). *Noughts & Crosses*. Corgi Books.
Blackman, M. (2010). *Boys Don't Cry*. Corgi Books.
Collins, S. (2008). *The Hunger Games*. Scholastic Children's Books.
Corder, Z. (2003). *Lionboy*. Puffin Books.
Cotterell Boyce, F. (2004). *Millions*. Macmillan Children's Books.
Doherty, B. (1991). *Dear Nobody*. Collins.
Fraillon, Z. (2016). *The Bone Sparrow*. Hachette Children's Group.
Haddon, M. (2003). *The Curious Incident of the Dog in the Night-Time*. Vintage.
Kalu, P. (2015). *The Silent Striker*. Hope Road.
King-Smith, D. (1983). *The Sheep-Pig*. Puffin Books.
King-Smith, D. (1991). *Ace*. Puffin.
Mian, Z. (2019). *Planet Omar: Accidental Trouble Magnet*. Hachette Children's Group.
Mian, Z. (2020a). *Planet Omar: Unexpected Super Spy*. Hachette Children's Group.
Mian, Z. (2020b). *Planet Omar: Incredible Rescue Mission*. Hachette Children's Group.
Morpurgo, M. (1982). *War Horse*. Egmont.
Morpurgo, M. (1996). *The Ghost of Grainne O'Malley*. Scholastic Children's Books.
Morpurgo, M. (2002). *Cool!* Collins.
Morpurgo, M. (2003). *Private Peaceful*. Harper Collins.
Morpurgo, M. (2008a). *This Morning I Met A Whale*. Walker Books.
Morpurgo, M. (2008b). *Kaspar, Prince of Cats*. HarperCollins Children's Books.
Ness, P. (2008). *Chaos Walking*. Walker Books.
Norriss, A. (2015). *Jessica's Ghost*. David Fickling Books.
Peet, M. (2003). *Keeper*. Walker Books.
Pitcher, A. (2011). *My Sister Lives on the Mantelpiece*. Orion Children's Books.
Pullman, P. (2011). *Northern Lights*. Scholastic.
Rauf, O. (2018). *The Boy at the Back of the Class*. Penguin Random House.
Reeve, P. (2001). *Mortal Engines*. Scholastic Children's Books.

Riordan, R. (2005). *Percy Jackson and the Lightning Thief*. Puffin.
Riordan, R. (2010). *Heroes of Olympus*. Penguin.
Riordan, R. (2016). *The Trials of Apollo*. Penguin.
Rowling, J.K. (1997). *Harry Potter and the Philosopher's Stone*. Bloomsbury.
Sachar, L. (2000). *Holes*. Bloomsbury.
Williams, M. (2012). *Now Is the Time for Running*. Tamarind.
Williams, M. (2014). *Diamond Boy*. Tamarind.
Wilson, J. (2000). *The Illustrated Mum*. Corgi Books.
Wilson, J. (2001). *Dustbin Baby*. Corgi Books.
Zephaniah, B. (2000). *Wicked World*. Puffin Books.
Zephaniah, B. (2007a). *Refugee Boy*. Bloomsbury.
Zephaniah, B. (2007b). *Teacher's Dead*. Bloomsbury.
Zephaniah, B. (2008). *Face*. Bloomsbury.
Zephaniah, B. (2011). *Kung Fu Trip*. Bloomsbury.

Films and plays

Boyle, D. (Director). (2004). *Millions* [Motion picture]. UK: Pathé Distribution.
Columbus, C. (Director). (2011). *Percy Jackson and the Lightning Thief* [Motion picture]. USA: 20th Century Fox.
Complicite UK. (2013). *Current Productions: Lionboy*.
Cooke, D. (Director), Blackman, M. (Writer). (2008). *Oxford Playscripts: Noughts & Crosses*. Oxford, UK: Oxford University Press.
Davis, A. (Director)., & Sachar, L. (Screenplay). (2003). *Holes*. [Motion picture]. USA: Buena Vista Pictures.
Doherty, B. (Writer), & O'Neill, R. (Script editor). (1998). *Dear Nobody*. [Play]. London, UK: Collins.
Haddon, M. (Writer), & Stephens, S. (Script editor). (2012). *The Curious Incident of the Dog in the Night-Time*. [Play]. London, UK: Bloomsbury Methuen Drama.
Jankel, A. (Director), Brignull, I. (Screenplay). (2009). *Skellig: The Owl Man* [Motion picture]. UK: Sky Television.
May, J. (Director). (2008). *Dustbin Baby*. [Motion picture]. UK: Kindle Entertainment.
Noonan, C. (Director). (1995). *Babe*. [Motion picture]. USA: Universal Pictures.
Ross, G. (Director). (2012). *The Hunger Games*. [Motion picture]. USA: Lionsgate.
Spielberg, S. (Director). (2011). *War Horse*. [Motion picture]. UK: Walt Disney Studios Home Entertainment.
Stafford, N. (Script writer), Morpurgo, M. (Original Author). (2007). *War Horse* [Play]. London, UK: Faber & Faber.
Zephaniah, B. (Writer), & Sissay, L. (Script editor). (2013). *Refugee Boy*. [Play]. London, UK: Bloomsbury Methuen Drama.

Secondary texts

Broad, L. (2008). *Read & Respond: Activities Based on Holes by Louis Sachar*. Scholastic.
Cogan Thacker, D., & Webb, J. (2002). *Introducing Children's Literature: From Romanticism to Postmodernism*. Routledge.

Grandin, T., & Panek, R. (2013). *The Autistic Brain: Thinking Across the Spectrum*. Houghton Mifflin Harcourt.
Grenby, M.O. (2008). *Children's Literature*. Edinburgh University Press.
Hahn, D., & Flynn, L. (Eds.). (2006). *The Ultimate Teen Book Guide*. (2nd ed.). A & C Black Publishers.
Hunt, P. (Ed.). (1992). *Literature for Children: Contemporary Criticism*. Routledge.
Manlove, C. (2003). *From Alice To Harry Potter: Children's Fantasy in England*. Cybereditions Corporation.
Maybin, J., & Watson N.J. (Eds). (2009). *Children's Literature: Approaches and Territories*. Palgrave Macmillan.
Montgomery, H., & Watson N.J. (2009). *Children's Literature: Classic Texts and Contemporary Trends*. Palgrave Macmillan.
Reynolds, K. (1994). *Children's Literature in the 1890s and 1990s*. Palgrave Macmillan.
Reynolds K. (Ed.). (2005). *Modern Children's Literature: An Introduction*. Palgrave Macmillan.
Rundell, K. (2019). *Why you should read children's books, even though you are so old and wise*. Bloomsbury.
Spufford, F. (2003). *The Child That Books Built*. Faber & Faber.
Tucker, N., & Eccleshare, J. (2003). *The Rough Guide to Books for Teenagers*. Rough Guides.
Wilkie-Stibbs, C. (2008). *The Outside Child In and Out of the Book*. Routledge.
Wilkins, V. (2008). *Black Stars: Benjamin Zephaniah*. Tamarind Books.
Zephaniah, B., & Ambrus, V. (2011). *Benjamin Zephaniah: My Story*. Collins Big Cat.

Further reading suggestions

British Children's Laureate: www.childrenslaureate.org.uk
National Ambassador for Young People's Literature scheme: http://read.gov/cfb/ambassador/

6
Reading for everyone

Lalita Murty, Beck Sinar, Gweno Williams, Marthe Sofie Pande-Rolfsen, Anita Normann and Tim Vicary

Introduction

Important aspects of reading, one of the five basic skills emphasised in the new national curriculum LK20, are the focus of this multi-authored chapter. The English subject curriculum (LK20) states that "reading in English means understanding and reflecting on the content of various types of texts on paper and on screen, and contributing to reading pleasure and language acquisition" (Norwegian Directorate for Education and Training, 2019/29). This chapter seeks to help teachers address some of the most common challenges related to reading.

The overarching theme of the chapter is reading for all. LK20 emphasises, e.g. after VG1 for both general and vocational English, that learners should be able to "read, discuss and reflect on the content and language features and literary devices in various types of texts, including self-chosen texts" (Norwegian Directorate for Education and Training, 2019/20). The text types and titles suggested in this chapter will hopefully help the professional English teacher find, select and suggest varied reading material for all groups of learners, with consequent benefits for learner motivation and classroom management.

Lalita Murty and Beck Sinar recommend important inclusive approaches and texts to acknowledge diversity and build empathy which are key initiatives for modern global citizenship and upholding democratic values. Gweno Williams, who is also the overall editor of this chapter, suggests exciting, well-designed texts and resources that can support differentiation and help to make every child a reader, including reluctant readers and those who lack reading confidence or stamina. Marthe Sofie Pande-Rolfsen and Anita Normann extend the diversity of genres and texts further by recommending verse novels, some of the most contemporary texts available, with particular accessibility for less confident readers. In conclusion, Tim Vicary, author of books for young readers and adults, including award-winning graded readers, adopts an informal conversational tone to recommend the benefits of extensive reading in the classroom.

Section 1. Inclusive texts for the classroom
Lalita Murty and Beck Sinar

> Inclusive education allows learners of all backgrounds to learn and grow side by side, to the benefit of all.
>
> UNESCO

A successful education system is an *inclusive education system* in which all learners, regardless of ethnicity, race, age, language, gender, sexuality, ability or socio-economic status, have opportunities to develop, grow, and achieve their potential.[39] *Equality* and *inclusion* are central features of Norwegian educational policy (Læreplan for Kunnskapsløftet (2020), henceforward referred to as LK20), reflecting the wider egalitarian values of Norwegian society (Lien, Lidén & Vike, 2001). The core values of LK20 encourage acknowledging and appreciating diversity, developing self-insight and identity, and promoting respect and tolerance, summarised as inclusivity. This section encourages teachers and learners to read *inclusive and diverse texts* across a range of genres as a way of engaging with the lives of "others", with regard, in particular, to gender and sexual identities, diverse abilities and socio-economic status. This links to LK20's key themes of *democracy* and *citizenship*. Suggested texts are by British, Australian and American authors; they also provide opportunities for inter-cultural learning about diversity and inclusion in Britain, Australia and America today. For an extended discussion of linguistic and cultural diversity, and further discussion of the value of being seen and seeing others, please see chapter 3, "Global Englishes, diverse voices".

Inclusive practice, which challenges traditional constructs of "normality", needs teachers and learners to be aware of, to accept, and to understand

---

39 Booth and Ainscow (2002) provide a straightforward and comprehensive "index for inclusion" which can be used in addition to resources mentioned in this section to develop learning and participation in education for all learners.

the differences and diversities that learners bring into today's heterogeneous classrooms (Booth & Ainscow, 2011; Kricke & Neubert, 2017). UNESCO-IBE (2016, p. 109, our emphasis below) suggests eight indicators to help teachers review their classrooms:

1. Teaching is planned with *all learners* in mind
2. Lessons encourage the *participation of all learners*
3. Learners are *actively involved* in their own learning
4. Learners are encouraged to *support one another's* learning
5. *Support* is provided when learners experience difficulties
6. Classroom discipline is based on *mutual respect* and healthy living
7. Learners feel that they have *somebody to speak to* when they are worried or upset
8. Assessment contributes to the achievement of *all learners*

These key measures of an inclusive education are framed by Banks and Mac-Gee Banks (2010) as multicultural education, with 5 key dimensions that are inclusive and effective (Figure 1).

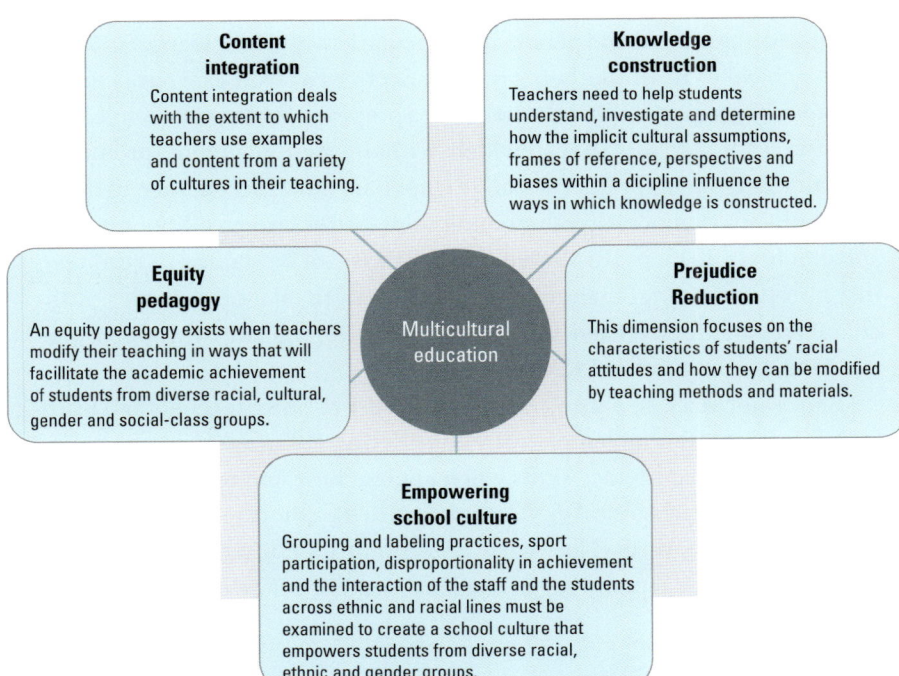

Figure 1. Multicultural Education (Banks & MacGee Banks, 2010, p.23).

Content Integration and *Knowledge Construction* are particularly important in relation to classroom texts as they relate to *the selection of appropriate materials* and making strategic use of these teaching materials in *developing awareness and understanding*. In fulfilling the aims of LK20, this framework can be adopted by carefully selecting and critically evaluating texts that are both *diverse* in genre, e.g. poetry, fact, fiction, and *inclusive* in content, showcasing different lives, perspectives, values and ideas in the cause of fair representation (especially for #ownvoices[40] authors).

Using high-quality, diverse and inclusive texts is also one way to consider and promote LK20's key themes of *democracy* and *citizenship*. Such texts offer both challenges and opportunities for ethical and moral growth. Kricke and Neubert (2017) discuss the relationship between inclusive education and democratic societies. They demonstrate that inclusive education and schooling are necessary for promoting inclusion in society and for challenging discrimination and marginalisation. Diverse and inclusive texts give teachers and learners a chance to engage with sometimes difficult themes, and to learn about themselves and their own attitudes, perceptions and beliefs, as well as those of others. This can be potentially challenging as materials may be culturally sensitive, and discussions have the potential to get heated, emotional and personal, particularly with older learners. Teachers may have to re-think their own perspectives as well as what is taught and how. They may ultimately feel under-prepared for this challenge. One solution is for teachers to read widely without pre-judgement, promoting the same activity and values for all learners. In short: acceptance of difference enlivens democratic values and builds better citizens. Koopman and Hakemulder (2015, p. 101) argue that learners can be trained to read texts in a non-judgemental manner that helps them to take on the roles of the characters and follow their lives, thereby developing empathy and understanding, key features of LK20.

Banks and MacGee Banks' (2010) framework requires teachers and learners to (further) develop empathy by considering differing perspectives and developing critical literacy skills when approaching and reading texts. The development of such *critical thinking* is found in the competence aims for English from year 7 onwards (Norwegian Directorate for Education and Training, 2019/29), but can actually begin much earlier. The following questions can

---

40 #ownvoices is a recent campaign and recognition of the value of hearing stories from people who are writing about or from their own experiences.

be used to promote critical literacy in the classroom (see also Roche (2014) and Janks (2014) for further suggestions and classroom based examples):[41]

1. Who is the author?
2. Who are the intended readers, and what is the evidence?
3. Who is represented? For example: What kinds of family roles and relationships are shown in the book? How are people of different ages, abilities or sexualities shown? *Who is missing?*
4. Can the readers relate to the events depicted in the story? Can they put themselves in the events depicted and imagine how they will respond?
5. Do the people who feature in the text speak and behave like the readers and their families?
6. What point of view, values, information, attitudes or opinions are expressed overtly? Which are implied?
7. How does the author make the readers feel about _____?
8. Do the readers agree with the author's point of view about _____?
9. How might different readers interpret the text differently?
10. Are the images needed? Why or why not? How do they influence interpretation of the text?

These questions encourage reflection and help to challenge existing conventional biases. For example, recent analyses of textbooks across a range of subjects from Norway (Steinland, 2015, Røthing, 2017) and around the globe (Thornbury, 2013, Sleeter & Grant, 2011) show that many depict characters who are cis-gender,[42] white, able-bodied, from economically stable households and with heterosexual love interests. On the few occasions where "others" are represented, these characters are typically marginalised, sanitised or depicted in self-contained, issue-based study units (Seburn, 2017). Recognising the ideologies underpinning such textbooks requires consideration of how the reader is being "positioned", other possible positions and perspectives, and possible unconscious bias of the text authors and illustrators. This can be addressed by trying to reframe the textbook content from a different position (repositioning) or by including other texts with differing perspectives. For example, Amnesty International UK annually publishes a list of

---

41 For further questions, including application to a text, see chapter 3.
42 The prefix *cis-* means "on the same side as" so *cis-gender* means someone whose gender identity matches their birth sex. Conversely, *transgender* means to move across gender and hence refers to someone whose gender identity is not the same as their physical birth sex.

recommended and endorsed ethical children's books on topics covered in this chapter.[43]

EmpathyLab[44] is an exciting and valuable not-for-profit online resource offering rich literature recommendations and free resources on empathy for teachers and families. Empathy is defined as being able to imagine and share someone else's feelings; annual free-of-charge EmpathyLab booklists of up to 50 children's books promoting empathy with others form a terrific resource for teachers.

The 2020 EmpathyLab book judging panel say: "Scientific research shows that reading builds empathy. So, let's use stories to help the rising generation develop superb empathy skills, and build a better world. It's our best hope for the future." Annual Empathy Day is now celebrated in June, with a wide range of available resources (including free short stories online) and activities focusing on how to use books to learn to step into someone else's shoes.

In using a range of diverse and inclusive texts, the point is to create an open dialogue across difference. Rather than analysing or debating an "issue" the purpose is to understand, respect and empathise with differing perspectives and lives. Starting in year 4, in LK20 English, there is a requirement to "participate in conversations on the pupil's own and others' needs, feelings, daily life and interests and use conversation rules" and "talk about some aspects of different ways of living, traditions and customs in the English-speaking world and in Norway" (Norwegian Directorate for Education and Training, 2019/20). Hence it can never be too early to promote an inclusive and diverse range of texts. Below are some suggestions for useful texts for a diverse and inclusive classroom which can build empathy, an important part of modern global citizenship and democratic values:

Gender and sexual identity including LGBTQ+[45]

Binary notions of gender, biology and sexual orientation exclude large swathes of human diversity; learners should be encouraged to recognise that these exist on a spectrum. Young learners should be able to recognise that families vary, whereas older learners should begin to consider aspects of gender and sexual identity/ies.

---

43 https://www.amnesty.org.uk/amnesty-endorsed-books-2019
44 https://www.empathylab.uk/about)
45 LGBTQ+ is an initialism for lesbian, gay, bisexual, transgender and queer or questioning. These terms are used to describe a person's sexual orientation or gender identity.

Young Learners

The Family Book by American author Todd Parr (2003) is bright and colourful and shows the diversity of modern families, including same sex, adoptive, step and single parent families. It won the 2004 Oppenheim Toy Gold Award, building on the successful multi-award winning *Earth Book* by the same author.

Harriet Gets Carried Away by American author Jessica Sima (2018) is an entertaining book featuring the adventures of a young girl who just happens to have two dads in an interracial marriage.

Dress Like a Girl by American author Patricia Toht (2019) is a delightful picture book which examines gender stereotyping through fashion.

Young Adults

Boy Meets Boy by 2004 ALA award winning American author David Leviathan (2003) is a short novel centred on issues of friendship, love, trust and relationships with strong gay male characters.

The Art of Being Normal by Waterstones Children's Book Prize winning British author Lisa Williamson (2001) is an emotional book about friendship, and a family featuring two transgender teens.

All Out: The No-Longer Secret Stories of Queer Teens Throughout the Ages by #ownvoices American editor Saundra Mitchell (2018) includes short stories by 17 authors across the queer spectrum. The range is diverse across cultures, time periods and identities.

Proud by #ownvoices British editor Juno Dawson (2019) comprises 12 poems and short stories written by LGBTQ+ authors. These are contemporary, short and upbeat and likely to appeal to reluctant readers. *Proud* won Visionary Honours Book of the Year 2020.[46]

Diverse Abilities

A disability or functional impairment may be cognitive, developmental, intellectual, mental, physical, sensory or some combination. Here texts should show people of diverse abilities in their everyday lives.

---

46 See chapter 8 for didactic, digital suggestions for classroom work for *Proud*.

Young Learners

Andy and His Yellow Frisbee by American author Mary Thompson (1996) is a story about Andy, a boy with autism. A sibling's perspective is also provided.

El Deafo by #ownvoices American author Cece Bell (2014) is a funny and perceptive graphic novel memoir about growing up hearing impaired. Its main focus is growing up and all the embarrassing moments along the way. *El Deafo* won both the Newbery Medal Honor and the Eisner Award.

Dan and Diesel, by British author Charlotte Hudson (2006) is a moving picture book filled with information and emotion. It only becomes clear to the reader at the end that Dan is blind and that his best friend Diesel is also his guide dog.

Young Adults

Wonder by multi-award-winning American author R.J. Palacio (2012) features 10-year-old August Pullman, who has severe congenital facial abnormalities. The book starts from his point of view but also shows the perspectives of his classmates, sister, her boyfriend and others. *Wonder* has won more than 35 international and national awards. A complementary volume, *Auggie & Me: Three Wonder Stories* (2014), adds more points of view, including that of the bully.

Marcelo in the Real World by American author Francisco X. Stork (2009) won the Schneider Family Best Book for Teens award. This novel features Marcelo, who is a very high-functioning autistic character, and compares well with *The Curious Incident of the Dog in the Night-Time* by Mark Haddon.

Diamond Eyes by Australian author A.A. Bell (2010) is the first in a series of books about Mira Chambers, who is blind but has the ability to see things others cannot – including secrets. *Diamond Eyes* won the 2011 Norma K. Hemming Award.

Socio-economic status (or social class)

Most discussions of inclusion concern sexuality and ability, but few mention social class. Norwegian culture strives for equality, which makes discussion and acknowledgement of social class differences culturally sensitive (Skarpenes & Saklind, 2010; Dahlgren & Ljunggren, 2010). However, despite its wealth, Norway is not a classless society and poverty does exist.

Working-class voices and experiences are poorly represented in literature and education; it is widely known that lower-class learners often feel excluded and perform poorly in schools (Reay, 2017; Gilbert, 2018). This is particularly true for males, who are often the most reluctant readers (Brozo et al., 2014).

Young Learners
Demolition Dad by #ownvoices British author and musical artist Phil Earle (2015) is an entertaining book which shows a very loving working-class father-son relationship and the lengths people go to for the ones they love. It won a 2017 CBBC book award. It would pair well with Roald Dahl's *Danny the Champion of the World*.

Last Stop on Market Street by American Matt de la Peña (2015) won the 2016 Newbery Medal. It sensitively considers material wealth as the boy asks his grandma why they don't own a car like others or why they get off the bus in the dirty part of town. Each answer is encouraging, showing the beauty in their "different" way of life.

Still a Family: A Story about Homelessness by American author Brenda Reeves Sturgis (2017) is a story about a homeless family who are divided by life in different shelters, but remain a family. Reeves Sturgis won Roxyanne Young's Smart Writers in 2007 and the MeeGenius Author Challenge in 2014.

Young Adults[47]
Rhythm and Poetry by #ownvoices British hip-hop artist, poet and author Karl Nova (2018) won CLiPPA 2018. The poems reflect on Nova's journey from childhood to adulthood in working-class Britain through the lens of hip-hop culture. To bring oral language into the classroom, learners can watch and hear Nova perform:

https://vimeo.com/265488966
https://karlnovaworld.wordpress.com/
https://clpe.org.uk/poetryline/interviews/nova-karl

Me Mam. Me Dad. Me. by British author Malcolm Duffy (2018) is a dramatic coming-of-age novel set in working-class Newcastle and Edinburgh. It tackles domestic violence head-on. The book won the Sheffield Book award and Redbridge Child book award in 2019.

---

47 Thank you to Dr Megan Roughley of the Norwegian Study Centre, York, for recommending the books in this section during the past few years.

Liccle Bit by #ownvoices British author Alex Wheatle (2015) is the first in the Crongton Series of books, recently adapted for the stage. The novel is short, features drugs, gangs and colloquial language, and is likely to appeal to reluctant readers due to the fast pace of the storyline and strong characters. It has potential for teaching about race relations and variation of language in the UK as well as reflecting the lives of low-income families in inner cities. A 10-minute dramatisation (2019) is also available online.[48]

Diverse and inclusive texts[49] can be a springboard for learners to develop a sense of fairness, tolerance and respect for difference through encounters with imaginary worlds and the characters that inhabit them. Such texts play a critical role in promoting the joys of language and narrative while drawing the learner's attention to ways in which prejudices and biases can be overcome through coming to understand "otherness".

Section 2. Texts for differentiation
Gweno Williams

Differentiation is an important issue for teachers, who can benefit from information about the high-quality books designed and published in English by specialist publishers for learners who experience reading challenges. Such reading resources are invaluable in the EFL classroom, for reluctant readers and for those who lack reading confidence or stamina. Stamina is defined as the will and ability to keep going, as in sport. Importantly, as well as being a very useful differentiation resource, the texts recommended here can also be enjoyed by mainstream readers. They can therefore be changed discreetly into any reading and learning situation, without creating a stigma for learners. This is vital in terms of classroom management, in order to maintain the self-esteem and motivation of young adults who may be highly sensitive about the learning challenges they are experiencing. As argued throughout this book, authentic texts are always important in the classroom as a bridge to the outside world, but sometimes scaffolding with dedicated resources is required as a preliminary. As with all texts recommended throughout, these specialist titles are well written and high quality, often directly commissioned from outstanding and best-selling authors.

Independent award-winning UK children's publisher Barrington Stoke[50] has pioneered highly readable, dyslexia-friendly, diverse illustrated fiction

---

[48] https://www.imdb.com/title/tt11333804/ and https://youtu.be/oQWI-0NE7Xg
[49] See chapter 3
[50] https://www.barringtonstoke.co.uk/

which will help **every** child to become a reader (publisher's emphasis). Dyslexia-friendly publishing features include the paper colour, a specially designed font and accessible spacing and layout. Book length is also helpfully tailored to the intended audience; Barrington Stoke's maximum word length for an older teenage novel is 17 000 words whereas standard teenage novels (see recommended examples in chapter 5) have a minimum of 40 000 words. Whilst primarily aimed at dyslexic readers, these books can also be invaluable for differentiation or more generally in the EFL classroom, particularly for learners who may have had a delayed start in English or who lack language confidence. There are numerous attractively designed Barrington Stoke titles on a wide range of themes to choose from, many written by diverse well-known prize-winning authors whose names also appear in other chapters or sections of this book. The author list includes several UK Children's Laureates such as Michael Morpurgo, Malorie Blackman and Julia Donaldson. Other prominent contemporary authors published include Alex Wheatle, David Almond and Frank Cotterell Boyce. This democratic principle offers struggling readers the same cultural access to excellent writing and exciting storylines as their more confident peers.

The most visionary and useful aspect of Barrington Stoke books for language teachers, however, is the combined Reading Age/Interest Age (RA/IA) coding system. Every book is coded according to an actual Reading Age in years, **not** school grade levels. So RA9, for example, refers to the Reading Age of a native speaker of 9 years old. Interest Age (IA) refers to the actual age of a reader who would find the topic or story interesting. The RA is invariably lower than the IA, allowing the presentation of age-appropriate, interesting content for learners who still struggle with reading, in a book which is significantly easier to read. The usefulness of this system for the classroom (and the school library) cannot be overstated. For example, Barrington Stoke currently has available well over one hundred books with a teenage Interest Age and a variably lower Reading Age, offering a wide range of choice of attractive, accessible texts to motivate young adult learners to experience reading pleasure and success. For example, highly recommended 2020 CILIP Carnegie Medal Winner *Lark* (2019) by Anthony McGowan is coded RA9/IA Teen. This means that this moving novel about young adult independence, risk and danger, a recent winner of one of the most noteworthy British children's fiction prizes, is of interest and accessible to teenage readers who have a current reading age of just 9 years old or above.

Importantly, the RA/IA code for each book is clearly displayed in the online book catalogue, but is only visible in very small print on the back cover of each book. This allows teachers to make full use of RA/IA information when selecting and ordering reading matter for learners who struggle, whilst individual readers' dignity is preserved because the codes are almost imperceptible on the books themselves. Another helpful feature of Barrington Stoke books is that both the catalogue and individual volumes list key themes of each text, to aid teacher and reader choice. So, for example, *Lark*'s themes are listed as: Brothers, Danger, Nature and Loss.

QuickReads[51] are a comparable UK Reading Agency initiative to provide appealing quality books for underconfident or reluctant adult readers of English. QuickReads are 80 to 100 pages long, with a very clear font, and look like ordinary paperbacks. New titles are published annually. Some of the most popular and best-selling UK authors are commissioned to write these very readable, well-written short novels, in a full range of genres including romance, crime, suspense, autobiography, sport and self-help. QuickReads are also subsidised to be very affordable; they are deliberately priced to cost less than a cup of coffee. Recommendations in a range of gripping genres include dramatic stories narrated by young people: *The Dare* by John Boyne (2009) and moving first-person knife crime novel *Hello Mum* (2010) by Booker Prize winner Bernadine Evaristo. Real-life personal stories include *Tackling Life* by football coach Charlie Oatway (2011), soldier Andy McNab's *Today Everything Changes* (2014), *Kung-Fu Trip* (2011) by poet and YA author Benjamin Zephaniah and *I Am Malala* (abridged) by Malala Yousafzai (2016). Romance, sometimes with a twist, includes *Girl on the Platform* by Josephine Cox (2008) and *Strangers on the 16.02* by Priya Basil (2011). Mysteries and thrillers include eerie story *The Cave* (2009) by Kate Mosse, *Hidden* by Barbara Taylor Bradford (2014) and *Blackout* by Emily Barr (2013).

QuickReads are an excellent resource for older EFL learners and have been enjoyed by some vocational learners who feel challenged by reading in English. There are over 100 titles to choose from, though some deal with more mature content which is less likely to interest younger readers, such as divorce, retirement from work or relationships with adult children.

Concerns about boys' ability and/or willingness to read are significant. American author Jon Sciezska is greatly concerned about the preponderance of boys who fall into the reluctant reader category. As the first US National Ambassador for the Arts, he created an outstanding website, GuysRead[52]. It is highly recommended for the range and appeal of the approaches and resources it presents. Sciezka's approach is to present real-life male heroes as

---

51 https://readingagency.org.uk/adults/quick-guides/quick-reads/
52 http://jsworldwide.com/guys_read.html

reading role models, and the website is full of interviews, photographs and inviting reading opportunities, all directed at a male audience. Currently, Sciezka's website lists a number of very useful themed and carefully packaged short-story collections designed to attract male readers including those who are reluctant or lack reading stamina. Other recommendations include Mike McQueen's *Getting Boys to Read* (2014), which is structured around over 100 tips for teachers, and Pieper's (2016) "Boys 'n Books" chapter (Pieper, p. 111–122).

Interconnected or themed short stories offer the option for learners to read one or more self-contained texts; they can be useful for differentiation. Short stories can offer less competent or more reluctant readers a complete and successful reading experience which matches their capabilities, to increase reading confidence and stamina. By accessing a digital repository[53] like ESL.bits learners at various competency levels can enjoy reading and listening, for free (and without advert interruptions), to a huge variety of short stories,[54] often read by the authors themselves.

Learners can also discover ways of structuring fiction through the various ways authors have chosen to organise story collections, through character, incident, time or topic, for example. For example, QuickRead *The Anniversary*, edited by Veronica Henry (2016), is a themed volume of 10 very short stories by different authors. The benefit of YA short-story collections is that they may well lead learners on to adult or more advanced crossover collections such as Arthur Conan Doyle's *Sherlock Holmes* stories.

Mexican-American writer Sandra Cisneros presents a series of moving, interconnected family vignettes in *The House on Mango Street* (1984), also discussed in chapter 8. This engaging text focuses on migration, gender, identity and opportunity. The first-person narrator is Esperanza (meaning hope in Spanish), who is acutely aware of economic and cultural pressures on her family and community. The text is apparently artlessly organised into stream-of-consciousness reflections on individual topics such as "My Name", "Laughter" and "Papa Who Wakes Up Tired in the Dark", creating a sense of intimacy with Esperanza's thoughts. She is simultaneously processing larger topics, however, such as racial injustice, poverty, opportunity and gender, as she forges her identity and considers her own potential agency to move out of the situation into a more promising future. The informal language is interspersed with songs, stories and anecdotes.[55]

---

53 See chapter 8 for a discussion of digital repositories.
54 http://esl-bits.net/ESL.English.Listening.Short.Stories/ESL.Listening.Short.Stories.html
55 See chapter 8 for digital didactic ideas for working with *The House on Mango Street*.

Out of Bounds (2001) by South African author Beverley Naidoo comprises chronologically organised stories set in comparative time periods from 1948 to 2000, with each section focusing on the changing nature of apartheid in South Africa and its impact on human lives and relationships. Naidoo unflinchingly shows the political absurdities and casual cruelties of apartheid in different periods. The collection is a powerful incentive to think about racial equality and justice; it includes a timeline presenting the legal history and implementation of apartheid. Both collections may be useful in cross-curricular work.

Complementary reading can be a particularly appropriate classroom approach for volumes of themed or linked short stories such as these. Individual stories or chapters are natural units to be shared around the class, offering learners both individual responsibility and ownership of a section of text, resulting in a shared inclusive reading experience. Learning activities could include oral or written presentations about characters or incidents, or visual or dramatic recreations of locations or events. Together, learners can create smaller presentations or units which add up to a larger overview of the text as a whole.

Section 3. Verse novels
Marthe Sofie Pande-Rolfsen and Anita Normann

The verse novel, or novel in verse, is flourishing as a genre and represents another type of texts that easily lend itself for differentiation purposes. In particular it has been reinvented in young adult (YA) fiction. Campbell (2004) suggests that verse novels' "condensed language and suggestive power […] can make a story soar beyond the possibilities of prose" (p. 616). One reason why the verse novel has recently become "one of the glories of adolescent literature" (Campbell, 2004, p. 612) relates to today's digital society, bringing readers back to oral and auditory modes, where "the voices of text have greater prominence" (Alexander, 2005, p. 270). In verse novels, readers are more likely to "experience words as sound as they read" and the informality of free verse often "accentuates the oral dimension" (Alexander, 2005, pp. 270–271).

Verse novels are accessible and can be explored by teachers like any contemporary text. Their beauty lies in the flow and the power of words; such novels are quick to read, representing a good choice for both teachers and learners. Farish (2013) notes that verse novels can be suitable for English language learners who struggle with reading, because they "promote fluency and a sense of competence in readers" (n.p.). These texts move fast and can "offer readers at any level a feeling of completion" (Farish, 2013, n.p.). Moreover, verse novels' relatively sparse but lively contemporary language and vivid storylines are attractive to reluctant readers as well as learners with reading challenges such as dyslexia. Bokelman (2018) writes that the most common reasons why verse novels are accessible to these learners are: "generous amounts of white space, economic use of language, dramatic storylines that elicit strong emotions, and an intimate narrative voice" (p. 198). Verse novels help readers to become more excited about reading, while simultaneously stimulating an interest in poetry (Abate, 2018). Listed below are some exciting examples, appropriate for learners at different levels.

The Black Flamingo
This contemporary LGBTQ+[56] young adult verse novel by British poet Dean Atta (2019) is about discovering and embracing uniqueness, as the main character grows up and explores his identity. It is written by an #ownvoices[57] mixed-race British author (a young aspiring poet), which can be important when choosing diverse texts for the classroom, as Murty and Sinar suggest above. There is also a beautiful film on YouTube (directed by Lisa Cazzato Vieyra) which can be used to accompany the novel. Through *The Black Flamingo*, learners can explore and discuss topics such as identity, gender and sexuality, as well as the culture and history of drag.

Love That Dog
This American verse novel by American author Sharon Creech (2001) features young school student Jack. Jack hates poetry, but with the help of his teacher, Miss Stretchberry, and his dog, Sky, he nonetheless manages to find his own poetic voice. This wonderfully narrated, sad yet humorous story is written as a series of free-verse poems forming Jack's short diary entries. Each diary entry constitutes one chapter, and with very little text on each page, as well as an exciting story to follow, this authentic book should be very accessible for struggling readers, as the opening chapter shows:

---

56 LGBTQ+: Lesbian, Gay, Bisexual, Transgender, Questioning/Queer and the + includes all other spectrums of sexualities and genders (such as pansexual, asexual, genderfluid, non-binary, etc.).
57 The #ownvoices movement's hashtag (introduced 2015 on Twitter by Corinne Duyvis) has been used since to search for and identify recommended texts by diverse authors about diverse characters.

SEPTEMBER 13

I don't want to
because boys
don't write poetry.

Girls do.

(Creech, 2001, p. 7)

The novel includes a number of intertextual references to famous poems; the title of the book is, in itself, a reference to a poem by National Ambassador for the Arts Walter Dean Myers: *Love That Boy* (1993). The reader discovers how Jack is inspired by, and uses, published poems as model texts in his own poetry composition. This demonstrates how learning can be scaffolded by following someone more proficient. In observing Jack's growth as a writer, readers discover how his literary style develops concurrently with a growing confidence. This can exemplify and validate writing as a process for learners. Jack's diary entry from October 4, inspired by William Carlos Williams's *The Red Wheelbarrow*, clearly shows his creative development since the first day of school.

OCTOBER 4

Do you promise
not to read it
out loud?
Do you promise
not to put it
on the board?

Okay, here it is,
but I don't like it.

> *So much depends*
> *upon*
> *a blue car*
> *splattered with mud*
> *speeding down the road.*

(Creech, 2001, p. 10)

The chapters in this free-verse novel easily lend themselves to reading out loud, for example in the form of choral reading. In class, one group could read Jack's comments to his teacher, with another group responding with Jack's own poems. See more about choral reading in chapter 2. As mentioned above, learners can also use some of the poems/diary entries as model texts for their own writing, in the same way that Jack has used Dean Meyers's poem as his inspiration. Learners could substitute things they love with "dog" and continue their own poems by following the same structure as the original and as Jack's version.

Hate That Cat
This sequel (Creech, 2008), written in the same appealing format as *Love That Dog*, returns to Jack, still mourning the death of his dog, and still coping with Miss Stretchberry's enthusiasm for poetry. The free-verse novel provides excellent opportunities for learners to familiarise themselves with well-known poets, as it includes references to poems by William Carlos Williams, T. S. Eliot, Alfred Lord Tennyson, Edgar Allan Poe and others. The teacher could for instance elicit learners' thoughts on poetry in a pre-reading stage: *What do they associate with poetry? What do they think about it? Which poems in English do they know?* Another pre-reading idea is to invite the class to discuss what this book could actually be about, by asking learners to study the front cover, and talk about what the black cat may symbolise. Both these verse novels by Creech offer rich opportunities to tap into learners' creativity in different ways. Aesthetically, they could for example create their own illustrations to some of the diary entries. Various kinaesthetic activities represent another active learning option. See active learning suggestions in chapters 2 and 4.

Further verse novel recommendations for the EFL classroom
- *Cloud Busting* (2004) by Children's Laureate and Black British author Malorie Blackman[58] is an engaging and thought-provoking short verse novel about friendship and bullying, centring on a young male protagonist. Each chapter is written in a different type of verse, teaching learners about poetic form.
- National Book Award winner *Inside Out & Back Again* (2013) by American Vietnamese author Thanhhà Lai is an autobiographically based refugee narrative following a young girl who, together with her family, is forced to move to the US due to the Vietnam War. Additional material provided includes an author interview and poetry resources useful for teaching.

---

58 Other works by Blackman, including *Noughts & Crosses*, are discussed in chapters 5 and 7.

- *Brown Girl Dreaming* (2014) by Black American author Jacqueline Woodson follows the childhood of the author until the age of ten; the novel is set at the height of the civil rights movement in the US.
- Newbery Award Winner *The Crossover* (2015), *Booked* (2016) and *Rebound* (2018) by Kwame Alexander all deal sensitively with emotions, relationships and life choices. This novel sequence focuses on young male protagonists' passion for sports (basketball and football).
- *Long Way Down* (2017) by prolific Black American author Jason Reynolds explores teenage gun violence in the US. This verse novel's total electrifying time span is 60 seconds, the time it takes an armed 15-year-old boy to descend in an elevator to meet the person who shot and killed his brother.
- Winner of the Cilip Carnegie Medal and the National Book Award *The Poet X* (2018) by Dominican American author and poet Elisabeth Acevedo is about a young girl living in Harlem who discovers slam poetry and uses it to understand the world around her. Acevedo is herself a National Poetry Slam Champion.
- *The Emperor's Babe* by Black British Booker Prize winner Bernadine Evaristo is an exciting historical first-person narrative by a Black teenage girl living in Roman Londinium (London), fighting for her own life choices in an oppressive society.

Section 4. Extensive reading
Tim Vicary

Extensive reading is recommended as an important activity for the EFL classroom. The British Council's *Teaching English* website[59] gives a concise overview of its didactic benefits, with useful practical classroom suggestions. Grabe (2009) offers an informative summary of its advantages and positive impact on L2 learner motivation (p. 311–328). Waring (2006 and 2009) goes further and argues that there is "an inescapable case" (Waring 2009) for extensive reading which "should be an indispensable part of language learning" (Waring, 2006). These studies build on Day and Bamford's (1998) pioneering evidence for the success of extensive reading as a key language-learning building block. For more about Extensive Reading, see the Extensive Reading Foundation's web page.[60]

---

59 https://www.teachingenglish.org.uk/article/extensive-reading
60 https://erfoundation.org/wordpress/

How can teachers help learners to read in English as well as they can in their native language? Learning to read in a foreign language is often described as a skill, but it should also be a pleasure, something to enjoy. The more people enjoy something, the more often they are likely to do it, and the more often they practise doing something, the better they get at doing it (Murphy 2018, p. 76). Skill and pleasure are tied closely together.

There are two broad approaches to practising reading: intensive reading and extensive reading. Intensive reading is where readers take a short text, perhaps a poem, a short story or an article a few pages long, to study and discuss intensively, in order to squeeze every last drop of meaning out of it, so that every word and sentence and every intention the author may have had is explored. This is a very useful classroom activity, but it is **not** extensive reading.

Extensive reading is the opposite. Instead of reading a few short paragraphs, learners read long passages, often whole texts. Instead of focusing on every single word, the focus is on the overall meaning. Instead of choosing a text that's challenging and difficult, readers choose something that's easy. Instead of reading for work, reading is for pleasure. Instead of reading a little, learners read a lot.

The principles of extensive reading, originally developed by Day and Bamford,[61] are straightforward:

1. **The reading material should be easy**. If learners are to read a lot, for pleasure, they shouldn't be worried too much by unknown or difficult vocabulary. It's possible to guess a few new words from the context, but too many unfamiliar words all together may put the reader off; they'll pick up a dictionary or check online once or twice, perhaps, but then they'll stop reading and look for something else. Extensive reading is not supposed to feel like work; it's supposed to be reading for pleasure.

2. **There should be a wide variety of reading material available**. Think about the individuals in any school class. Do they all like the same things? Probably not. Some will like romantic fiction. Some will like books about science or history or sport or car mechanics. See what's on the shelves in a local library or bookshop, or check out book websites. Science fiction, historical fiction, cookery, books about the migration of birds! Amazingly, there are people interested in all of these things, and more.

---

61 https://erfoundation.org/wordpress/wp-content/uploads/2013/08/Extensive-Reading-Top-10.pdf

3. **Learners should choose what they want to read, just as if they were in a bookshop or a library.** People enjoy reading what they're interested in. The more they enjoy it, the more they'll read. So let learners choose their own reading, just as you would yourself. This also means that learners should be free to stop reading something which they don't find interesting, or which is too complex, just as anyone would do if they picked up a book or a magazine which they didn't like.

4. **Learners should read as much as possible**. The whole point about extensive reading is that it is not teaching something new; it is a time to practise existing competencies. And how is reading practised? By reading. And reading. And then reading some more.

   Who do you know who is good at reading? Surely it's a person who reads a lot!

   It's simple. A person becomes a good runner by running a lot, or becomes a good swimmer by swimming a lot. Equally, becoming a good reader results from reading a lot (Waring 2011).

5. **The teacher should visibly value and encourage extensive reading**. One way is to set reading targets, maybe by asking learners to read one short book a week, 40 pages or so. This can be homework, and also a defined classroom activity. Why not have a lesson, or a special event such as a Reading Morning, where no one talks, but everyone reads? It doesn't matter what they read, as long as it's in English.

   No one talking includes YOU, the teacher, too. Have you ever tried reading when someone else is talking loudly in the same room? It's very annoying. To show learners that silent reading is valuable, the teacher must act as a role model. Sit in front of the class and read your own book. If you want to call this lesson something official, how about DEAR – Drop Everything And Read? DEAR Time – a time for reading that's really precious. Reading is intensely valuable. For an impassioned defence by ten famous writers of the value of reading, see the collection *Stop What You're Doing and Read This!* (2011).

   Imagine how great DEAR time would be. Instead of working out a lesson plan, you could just bring along the latest novel that you're enjoying, sit in front of the class, and read. And you get paid for it too. Wow! How's that for some teacher training advice?

Didactic activity suggestions

Remember that the aim is to encourage extensive reading, which means reading a lot of books, regularly, for pleasure. The sort of reading that (I hope) you yourself do as an adult, for pleasure, in your own free time. (If you don't yet, now is the very time to begin.)

The main activity that you are trying to encourage is for learners to simply read and enjoy the books, for pleasure. That could be enough in itself. However, if another activity is to be introduced, it should be the sort of thing that you could imagine doing yourself, for fun. Of course, some of these enjoyable add-on activities also help learners to develop additional basic skills required by the curriculum, specifically writing (book reviews), speaking (presentations to peers) and listening (attending presentations).

1. **Choosing which book to read next**. As outlined above, learners need plenty of choice. When they finish one book they need to be able to choose another, as if they were in a library. There may be a substantial classroom library of individual texts to choose from, or you may need to liaise with the school or local librarian. What about taking your English class on a field trip to the library, even if it's just down the corridor? Kenny Pieper (2016) makes a whole series of practical suggestions for showing and convincing learners that libraries are "an amazing adventure" (Pieper, p. 31–44). E-books are a possibility too, including searching author websites or sites such as *Goodreads*,[62] which calls itself "the world's largest community of book lovers". Crucially, however books are accessed by readers, the selection available should be diverse.

2. **Browsing and book reviews**. What is the natural thing to do when looking for a book to read? Think about your own reading; how do you choose what to read next, for pleasure? Some readers:

   a. Browse library shelves or online (E-books may be available instantly, at the click of a mouse).
   b. Look for another book by the same author, maybe by visiting the author's website.
   c. Read book reviews in print, e.g. in a newspaper, or online.
   d. Ask friends for suggestions.

---

62 https://www.goodreads.com/

These are all activities that a teacher can encourage and schedule as appropriate. Browsing author websites or book sites such as *Goodreads* online exposes the learners to more English, increasing their language practice. (Prudent teachers will want to research in advance the availability of free-of-charge E-books, e.g. from a local library.) Learners could search for reviews of the book they have just read, print them out and display them in the classroom or on a class website. They can also write their own reviews, which may agree or disagree with those they have found. Teachers can build up quite a large portfolio of these, over time, for learners to consult, or for display in the library. Learners can also upload their reviews online into a designated area.

Peer recommendation is very powerful. It can range from informal discussion to writing or delivering short persuasive recommendations: "Read this book if you like …." Completing this sentence about a book just read can be a stimulating, short, authentic writing task for learners, especially if the sentences are then displayed in the library or classroom or collated online. Teachers can also timetable sessions where learners make brief presentations about the books they have read, explaining what they liked or disliked about them. Kenny Pieper offers further valuable activity suggestions for "talking about reading" (Pieper, 2016, p. 75–85) All these feedback activities will be particularly useful when the time comes to order more books; more of the type readers enjoyed will be needed, and fewer of those they didn't.

3. **Book Clubs and Reading Circles**. In a situation where there is access to several class sets of books, there are appealing and sociable reading options. About six copies each of a few different titles will be needed for the following activities.

   Book clubs. It is natural to talk about books with friends. Many people belong to book clubs, where they all agree to read a certain book and meet to discuss it together on a scheduled date. This can be very pleasurable; readers often find that others see things in the book which they hadn't noticed. Learners can form book clubs within the class and follow through with discussion. This can feel like a sociable and mature activity, which learners will want to repeat with a different book.

   Reading circles. An interesting and more structured way of extending the book club concept is to form classroom reading circles (also called literature circles[63]). Learners form small temporary groups, and each group selects and agrees on a book to read, like a book club. They meet on a regular basis to discuss how the reading is going, and how far they have got. As they get close to the end of the text, each learner receives a different role card, outlining a task to prepare for the final discussion. Suggested roles are:

a. Discussion leader – who keeps the discussion going
b. Summariser – who summarises the main events of the story
c. Connector – who finds connections between the story and the real world
d. Word master – who finds new and interesting vocabulary
e. Passage person – who finds some of the most important passages
f. Culture collector – who compares the culture in the story to their own

Each learner, in this activity, has a specific task, but not one with a definite right or wrong answer. How they respond to the task, and perform in the discussion, depends on their own personal reaction to the book they have read, just as in real life. And with luck, if they enjoy the reading and discussion, it will encourage them to seek out new books to read, think and talk about. Which is the whole point of extensive reading, after all!

Conclusion

In conclusion, this chapter has identified a rich range of additional and specialised resources for the English classroom, together with suggestions for didactic activities. Particular attention has been given to differentiation. Various ways of realising a reading-for-everyone goal within the EFL classroom have been suggested, such as differentiation regarding topics and themes, types of texts and ways of reading, all with the aim of reaching out to and motivating all learners in the EFL classrooms. All that is left to say is: "Happy Reading!"

---

63 As discussed in chapter 7.

References

The references in this multi-authored chapter are listed in order of the sequence of chapter sections.

Inclusive texts for the classroom
Primary texts

Bell, A.A. (2010). *Diamond Eyes (Mira Chambers #1)*. Voyager.
Bell, C. (2014). *El Deafo*. Harry N. Abrams.
Dahl, R. (1975). *Danny the Champion of the World*. Jonathan Cape Publishers.
Dawson, J. (Ed.) (2019). *Proud*. Stripes.
De Le Pena, M. (2015). *Last Stop on Market Street*. G.P. Putnam's Sons Books for Young Readers.
Duffy, M. (2018). *Me Mam. Me Dad. Me*. Zephyr.
Earle, P. (2015). *Demolition Dad (Storey Street #1)*. Orion Children's Books.
Haddon, M. (2003). *The Curious Incident of the Dog in the Night-Time*. Jonathan Cape Publishers.
Ho-Yen, P. (2014). *The Boy in the Tower*. Doubleday Children's.
Hudson, C. (2006). *Dan and Diesel*. Red Fox.
Levithan, D. (2003). *Boy Meets Boy*. Alfred A. Knopf.
Mitchell, S. (Ed.) (2018). *All Out: The No-Longer-Secret Stories of Queer Teens Throughout the Ages*. Harlequin Teen.
Nova, K. (2017). *Rhythm and Poetry*. Caboodle.
Palacio, R.J. (2012). *Wonder*. Alfred A. Knopf.
Palacio, R.J. (2014). *Auggie & Me: Three Wonder Stories*. Alfred A. Knopf.
Parr, T. (2003). *The Family Book*. Little, Brown Books for Young Readers.
Parr, T. (2010). *The Earth Book*. Little, Brown Books for Young Readers.
Reeves Sturgis, B. (2017). *Still a Family*. Albert Whitman Company.
Sima, J. (2018). *Harriet Gets Carried Away*. Simon Schuster Books for Young Readers.
Stork, F. (2009). *Marcelo in the Real World*. Arthur A. Levine Books.
Thompson, M. (1996). *Andy and His Yellow Frisbee*. Woodbine House.
Toht, P. (2019). *Dress Like a Girl*. Harper Collins Publishers.
Wheatle, A. (2015). *Liccle Bit (South Crongton Trilogy #1)*. Atom.
Williamson, L. (2001). *The Art of Being Normal*. David Fickling Books.

Secondary texts

Banks, J.A., & MacGee Banks, C.A. (2010). (Eds.) *Multicultural Education: Issues and perspectives* [7th ed.]: John Wiley and Sons.
Booth, T., & Ainscow, M. (2002). *Index for Inclusion. Developing Learning and Participation in Schools*. Centre for Studies of Inclusive Education.
Brozo, W.G., Sulkunen, S., Shiel, G., Garbe, C., Pandian, A., & Valtin, R. (2014). Reading, gender, and engagement: lessons from five PISA countries. *Journal of Adolescent & Adult Literacy*, 57(7), 584–593.
Centre for Studies in Inclusion. https://www.eenet.org.uk/resources/docs/Index%20English.pdf
Dahlgren, K., & Ljunggren, J. (2010). *Klassebilder* [Images of class]. Universitetsforlaget.

Ebe, A.E. (2010). Culturally relevant texts and reading assessment for english language learners. *Reading Horizon: A Journal of Literacy and Language Arts, 50*(3). Article 5. https://scholarwords.wmich.edu/reading_horizon/vol50/Iss3/5

EmpathyLab https://www.empathylab.uk/

Gilbert, I. (Ed.). (2018). *The Working Class: Poverty, Education and Alternative Voices*. Independent Thinking Press, an imprint of Crown House Publishing.

Janks, H. (2014). *Doing Critical Literacy: Texts and Activities for Students and Teachers* (Language, Culture, and Teaching Series). Routledge.

Koopman, E.M., & Hakemulder. F. (2015). Effects of literature on empathy and self-reflection: a theoretical empirical framework. https://www.academia.edu/11386903/Effects_of_Literature_on_Empathy_and_Self-Reflection_A_Theoretical-Empirical_Framework

Kricke, M., & Neubert, S. (2017). Inclusive education as a democratic challenge – ambivalences of communities in contexts of power. *Education Sciences, 17*(1). https://doi.org/10.3390/educsci7010012

Lien, M., Lidén, H., & Vike, H. (2001). *Likhetens paradokser. Antropoligiske undersøkelser i det modern Norge* [Paradoxes of equality. Anthropological studies in modern Norway]. Universitetsforlaget.

Norwegian Directorate for Education and Training. (2019/2020). English subject curriculum (ENG01-04). https://www.udir.no/lk20/eng01-04

Reay, D. (2017). *Miseducation: Inequality, Education and the Working Classes*. Policy Press.

Rosch, M. (2014). *Developing Children's Critical Thinking Through Picturebooks*. Routledge.

Røthing, Å. (2017). Sexual orientation in Norwegian science textbooks: Heteronormativity and selective inclusion in textbooks and teaching. *Teaching and Teacher Education, 67*, October 2017, 143–151.

Seburn, T. (2017). Use of debates about LGBTQ+ in ELT materials. http://fourc.ca/debate-lgbtq/

Skarpenes, O., & Sakslind, R. (2010). Education and egalitarianism: the culture of the Norwegian middle class. *The Sociological Review, 58*(2), 219–243.

Sleeter, C.E., & Grant, G.A. (2011). Race, class, gender, and disability in current textbooks. In E. Provenzo, A. Shaver & M. Bello (Eds.). *The Textbook as Discourse: Sociocultural Dimensions of American Schoolbooks*, Routledge.

Steinland, V. (2015). *From Boundaries of Equality: Examining Inclusion and Exclusion in Textbooks for Norwegian Upper Primary School*. Unpublished MSc in Sociology, London School of Economics and Political Science.

Thornbury, S. (2013). R is for representation. http://scottthornbury.wordpress.com/2013/04/14/r-is-for-representation/

UNESCO-IBE (2016). International Bureau of Education. Reaching out to all learners: a resource pack for supporting inclusive education. http://www.ibe.unesco.org/sites/default/files/resources/ibe-crp-inclusiveeducation-2016_eng.pdf.

Texts for differentiation

Barr, E. (2013). *Blackout*. QuickReads.

Barrington Stoke. http://www.barringtonstoke.co.uk

Boyne, J. (2009). *The Dare*. QuickReads.

Cisneros, S. (1984). *The House on Mango Street*. Vintage Books.
Cox, J. (2008). *Girl on the Platform*. QuickReads.
Evaristo, B. (2010). *Hello Mum*. Penguin QuickReads.
Henry, V. (Ed.). (2016). *The Anniversary*. QuickReads.
McNab, A. (2014). *Today Everything Changes*. QuickReads.
McQueen, M. (2014). *Getting Boys to Read*. Twenty-First Century Publishing.
Mosse, K. (2009). *The Cave*. QuickReads.
Naidoo, B. (2001). *Out of Bounds: Stories of Conflict and Hope*. Puffin Books.
Oatway, C. (2011). *Tackling Life*. QuickReads.
Pieper, K. (2016). *Reading for Pleasure*. Independent Thinking Press.
Priya, B. (2011). *Strangers on the 16.02*. QuickReads.
QuickReads. https://readingagency.org.uk/adults/quick-guides/quick-reads/
Taylor Bradford, B. (2014). *Hidden*. QuickReads.
Yousafzai, M. (2016). *I Am Malala*. (Abridged) QuickReads.
Zephaniah, B. (2011). *Kung Fu Trip*. QuickReads. https://benjaminzephaniah.com/

Verse novels
Primary texts
Acevedo, E. (2018). *The Poet X*. Quill Tree Books.
Alexander, K. (2015). *The Crossover*. Andersen Press Ltd.
Alexander, K. (2016). *Booked*. Andersen Press Ltd.
Alexander, K. (2018). *Rebound*. Andersen Press Ltd.
Atta, D. (2018, April 1). *The Black Flamingo by Dean Atta, Directed by Lisa Cazzato Vieyra* [video file]. YouTube. https://www.youtube.com/watch?v=0UdejBoQ1v8
Atta, D. (2019). *The Black Flamingo*. Hodder Children's Books.
Blackman, M. (2004). *Cloud Busting*. Doubleday.
Creech, S. (2001). *Love That Dog*. HarperCollins.
Creech, S. (2008). *Hate That Cat*. HarperCollins.
Evaristo, B. (2002). *The Emperor's Babe*. Penguin.
Lai, T. (2013). *Inside Out & Back Again*. HarperCollins.
Meyers, W.D. (1993). *Brown Angels: An Album of Pictures and Verse*. HarperCollins.
Reynolds, J. (2017). *Long Way Down*. Athenium Books.
Williams, C.W. (1923). *Spring and All*. Robert McAlmon's Contact Publishing Company.
Woodson, J. (2014). *Brown Girl Dreaming*. Nancy Paulsen Books.

Secondary texts
Alexander, J. (2005). The Verse-novel: A New Genre. *Children's Literature in Education, 36*(3), 269–283.
Bokelman, M. (2018). "As Slippery and Tricky as a Wild Inky Word": Margarita Engle's *The Wild Book* and the Advantages of Verse Novels for Children with Dyslexia. *The Lion and the Unicorn, 42*(2), 198–217.
Campbell, P. (2004). The Sand in the Oyster: Vetting the Verse-Novel. *The Horn Book Magazine, 80*(5), 611–616.
Farish, T. (2013). Why Verse? *School Library Journal, 59*(11), n.p.

Extensive reading

Day, R., & Bamford, J. (1998). *Extensive Reading in the Second Language Classroom*. Cambridge University Press.

Day, R., Bassett, J., Bowler, B., Parminter, S., Bullard, N., Furr, M., … & Robb, T. (2010). *Bringing Extensive Reading into the Classroom*. Oxford University Press.

Furr, M. (Ed.). (2009). *Bookworms Club Reading Circles, Teacher's Handbook*. Oxford University Press.

Grabe, W. (2009). *Reading in a Second Language: Moving from Theory to Practice*. Cambridge University Press.

Norwegian Directorate for Education and Training. (2019/2020). Grunnleggende ferdigheter i engelsk. https://www.udir.no/lk20/eng01-04/om-faget/grunnleggende-ferdigheter.

Pieper, K. (2016). *Reading for Pleasure*. Independent Thinking Press.

Rosen, M., Callil, C., Morrison, B., Davis, J., Haddon, M., Carr, N. … & Smith, Z. (2011). *Stop What You're Doing and Read This*. Vintage Books.

The Extensive Reading Foundation (n.d.). *Promoting Extensive Reading in English as a Foreign Language*. http://erfoundation.org/wordpress/

Vicary, T. (2009). *Titanic*. Oxford Bookworms OUP.

Vicary, T. (2010). *The Everest Story*. Oxford Bookworms OUP.

Waring, R. (2006). Why extensive reading should be an indispensible part of all language programs. *The Language Teacher, 30*(7), 44–47.

Waring, R. (2009). The inescapable case for extensive reading. *Extensive Reading in English Language Teaching*, 93–111.

Waring, R. (2011). Extensive Reading in English Teaching. *Innovation and Creativity in ELT methodology*, 69–80.

7
Graphic novels in the English classroom

Hege Emma Rimmereide

Why teach graphic novels in the English as a Foreign Language (EFL) classroom? The answer is simple: it is fun, it is motivating, and it develops literacy skills (Krashen, 2004, pp. 102–103). Graphic novels employ several modalities. A mode includes the overarching systems of visual, aural and textual communication; examples of modes are the verbal and the visual modalities. Modes also refer to the use of colours, graphs, sounds and hyperlinks in multimodal texts. Emphasis on multimodal expressions is becoming increasingly important in today's society and in an educational setting (Rimmereide, 2020). To be able to decode images as well as verbal expressions is a highly relevant and important skill and is regarded as a necessary literacy skill. The definition of *reading* as a basic skill in the English curriculum includes being able to read and find information in multimodal texts (Norwegian Directorate for Education and Training, 2019/29). Another reason why graphic novels are good to introduce in the English classroom is that they enable competent readers and reluctant readers alike to engage in the reading process and become motivated to read more. For some, comprehension of texts is enhanced by visual expressions, or it may be the case that the visual expressions support reading comprehension. Moreover, graphic novels offer a wide variety of genres and stories, such as superhero stories, fantasy, comedy, historical and mythological stories and a variety of adapted versions of classic texts.

This chapter examines the relation between the visual and the verbal text, highlighting sequential storytelling. A discussion of why graphic novels should be taught and how to use graphic novels in the EFL classroom, along with tools for analysis of graphic novels, will be provided. Furthermore, some web sites will be considered, where the multimodal expression in graphic novels is explored to a fuller extent. Finally, the chapter provides suggestions for which texts could be read at what levels.

What are graphic novels?

Though "graphic novels" and "comic books" often are used interchangeably, the term *graphic novel* captures the essence of the chosen material more clearly than *comic books*. Brenner (2012) makes the distinction between the two and asserts that comics usually have about thirty pages, whereas a graphic novel could be several hundred pages long.

Richard Kyle was the first to coin the term "graphic novel" in 1964. Since then, there has been increasing interest in this art form. Will Eisner asserts the graphic novel as a unique aesthetic of sequential art and defines it as "the arrangement of pictures or images and words to narrate a story or dramatize an idea" (Eisner, 1985, p. 5), emphasising the narrative aspect of the genre. Scott McCloud's definition of graphic novels a decade later further underscores the visual aspect of the genre as well as acknowledging the recipient in his definition: "juxtaposed pictorial and other images in deliberate sequence, intended to convey information and/or to produce an aesthetic response in the viewer" (McCloud, 1994, p. 9).

Motivation

Graphic novels challenge both strong readers and reluctant readers. In his book *Power of Reading* (2004), Stephen Krashen talked about the importance of reading based on free choice, which is essential for motivation, and he underscored the significance of being exposed to reading which is motivating. Krashen found that readers exposed to comics and graphic novels not only became motivated to read, but their reading competence and comprehension were about the same as that of people who read other texts (Krashen, 2004, p. 102). Therefore, graphic novels may motivate a variety of learners and provide a wider range of literature for learners, which subsequently improves their general reading skills. Krashen (2004, p. 103) claims that reading for pleasure is important when it comes to motivation and the desire to read more. Ujiie and Krashen (1996) have found that reading for pleasure is motivational, but perhaps more importantly their research shows that pupils who read comics continue to read more books (Krashen, 2004, p. 102, 105). However, Krashen emphasises that reading comics and graphic novels does not in itself lead to advanced language development.

Even though a graphic novel has less verbal text than prose, the language is not necessarily easy (Krashen, 2004, p. 99). Yet, since comic books have less verbal text, it may not seem an overpowering challenge to read them, also because readers, and perhaps reluctant readers in particular, can benefit from the narrative support of images. Furthermore, in order to improve language and keep up motivation, the text has to be at the right level (Krashen, 2004), both in terms of language and in having the right content and being the right genre for each reader (Birketveit & Rimmereide, 2017; Birketveit, et al., 2018).

Literacy: the relationship between the visual and the verbal texts

Comics and graphic novels offer a new way of reading beyond the traditional definition of literacy, which commonly refers to written and printed text, involving reading and writing skills. Furthermore, with comics and graphic novels, as well as picturebooks (see chapter on picturebooks), *visual* literacy is also important and refers to the idea that images can be "read", and that their meaning can be communicated through a process of reading (Kress, 2003). Visual literacy means the ability to read, write and create visual images. Visual literacy is about language, communication and interaction. Seeing is not simply a process of passive reception of stimuli but also involves active construction of meaning (Janks et al., 2014). Reading texts where the verbal and the visual texts complement each other, such as comics, graphic novels and picturebooks, requires the reader to be involved in the reading process in a different way than reading prose without images, or text which is merely illustrated.

During the reading process the reader's eyes move back and forth between the verbal text and the visual text to make links between the various elements. The reading process may vary with different readers as some focus mainly on the images and read fragments of the text, others read the text and briefly look at the images, and others read the images, then the verbal text and thereafter shift back to the images. All these approaches are effective for comprehension of the story. In terms of language learning, the visuals may support the understanding of the story and may help the reader to fill the gaps that are not easily accessible through the verbal text. This way of reading is spatial, and is useful and highly relevant in today's multimodal society.

Key features of graphic novels

Graphic novels have their own vocabulary and grammar. The most important feature of the graphic novel is that the narrative is developed through images in a sequence. Central terms in comics and graphic novels are *panel*, *gutter* and *verbal text*.

Each image is referred to as a *panel*. Each panel has a "[v]isual or implied boundary, and the contents within it … tell a piece of story" (Monnin, 2010, p. 4). The panel may represent a scene in a story. Panels are often framed with a clear border whereas other panels have more blurred frames or implied boundaries and one scene moves smoothly over to the next, making links and connections (see illustrations 1–3). The panels are placed in a deliberate order, which tells about one or several events. The reading of panels on the page follows the reading pattern of regular reading, which means that one reads from top left to right, and down (illustration 6).

The second most important feature of graphic novels is the space between the panels called the *gutter*: "In this space the reader moves from one panel to the next and comes to a conclusion about what is happening" (Monnin, 2010, p. 4). The space between the panels, the gutters, may express time, tempo and movement. In this space between the panels, the readers connect two or more ideas into one idea. The gutter in graphic novels may constitute what Wolfgang Iser (Iser, 1978, pp. 165–169) calls a *gap* in the reading of a literary work of art. These gaps of indeterminacy create an account of their own, which allows the reader to fill in the gaps, or the blanks, left by the author. According to Iser (1974; 1978), all texts have these gaps, in which the text does not offer answers, or answers are not stated explicitly. Thus, the reader actively takes part in the interpretation of the action. In the gutter, in the space between each panel, the reader takes part in the creation of meaning making and active experience of a literary work (Wallner, 2019), in accordance with reader response theory, which allows the reader the opportunity of interpretation (Rosenblatt, 1995; Iser, 1974, 1978; McCloud, 1993).

The *verbal text* comes in different forms: speech bubbles, thought bubbles, text boxes and onomatopoetic representation of words (Mikkonen, 2017, p. 226). An onomatopoeic representation of a sound is often presented as part of the artwork. Another graphic novel convention is motion lines to indicate movement. An overview of basic graphic novel vocabulary to describe genre-specific features outlined by George O'Connor (2012) is listed in table 1.

Table 1. Overview of basic graphic novel vocabulary, O'Connor (2012)

Panel	The frame in which each image appears.
Gutter	The space between panels. It typically indicates a moment of transition.
Splash page	A full-page image.
Speech Bubbles	Text that indicates what characters are saying usually contained in a bubble-like shape. Also referred to as "word balloons".
Thought Balloons	Text that indicates what characters are thinking, usually contained in a balloon-like shape.
Text box	A box that contains narration, not necessarily spoken by any character
Motion or radiation lines	Lines that indicate a character's movement
Sound effects	An onomatopoeic representation of a sound, often presented as part of the artwork

This overview of basic graphic novel vocabulary (table 1) may serve as a tool for readers to identify features of the genre and for analysing comics and graphic novels. The vocabulary may also be helpful for learners in producing comics and cartoons of their own. See Stowell (2014) or online resources for helpful tools in creating own comics.

A significant and important aspect of reading graphic novels, or sequential art, is the interpretation of panels and gutters. An example from Will Eisner's *The Princess and the Frog* (1999) (illustrations 1–3) shows variation in panels and gutters and demonstrate tempo in action.

The top left panels from *The Princess and the Frog* (1999) (illustration 1) illustrate a slow tempo, because of the space between the panels. Even though the narrative, both through the diegesis (what is being told) as well as the mimesis (what is shown), presents a frustrated princess (illustration 1, top) the reader experiences slow action. Through the framing of the bottom panels of the left page, the reader understands that there is a change in action: something is happening. The action is increasingly tighter in the middle page (illustration 2). The panels are framed but there are no gutters, which speeds the action. In the spread on the right (illustration 3) the action is clearly faster; the panels are almost on top of each other, one taking over from the other and one panel blurs into the other.

McCloud's assertion that graphic novels are "sequential art in a sequence" (1994, p. 9) is highlighted through his important emphasis on *transitions* between the *panels*. McCloud proposes six panel transitions in his seminal work *Understanding Comics: The Invisible Art* (1993); below is a presentation of the various panel transitions, including examples to show the differences in panel descriptions.

Transitions between panels

The first example of transition between panels is *movement-to-movement transition*, which requires very little movement between the images. Throughout the wordless graphic novel *The Arrival*, by Shaun Tan (2006), a number of movement-to-movement panel transitions are included. The effect of the many movement-to-movement transitions and close-ups is to indicate a slow

Illustrations 1–3. Examples of panels, gutters and verbal text from Will Eisner's *The Princess and the Frog* (1999). Both boundaries and contents help to tell the story. Copyright © Will Eisner Studios, Inc. Used with permission.

development of the action, which creates an intense relationship with the characters. The slow and careful wrapping of the framed family photo from the first panel suggests the importance of the action (illustration 4).

Action-to-action transition is the most common transition of all (McCloud, 1993, p. 75), showing the progression from one panel to the next, often featuring a single subject as seen in the panels from *The Princess and the Frog* (illustration 1).

The second most common transition is the *subject-to-subject transition*, which means "staying within a scene or an idea" (McCloud, 1993, p. 71). McCloud claims that these panel descriptions require reader involvement (McCloud, 1993, p. 71). The reading requires some inference to interpret what happens (illustration 5, from *Coraline*).

The next transition between panels is the *scene-to-scene transition* "across significant distances of time and space" (McCloud, 1993, p. 71). McCloud

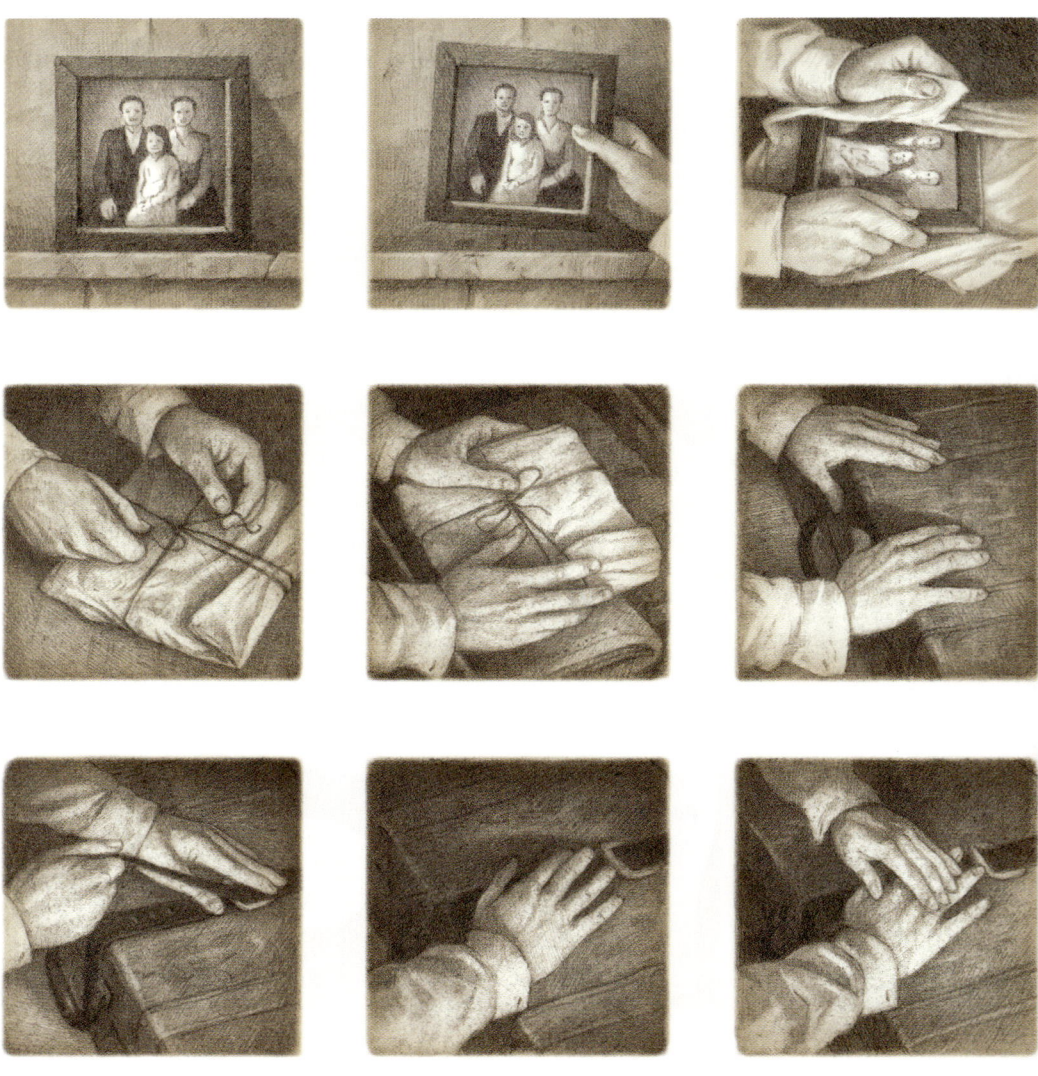

Illustration 4. *The Arrival* by Shaun Tan (2006, p. 2). Reproduced with permission from Hachette Australia.

also includes *aspect-to-aspect transitions* in his overview, in which the panels show "different aspect of a place, mood, idea" (McCloud, 1993, p. 72). Finally, McCloud mentions *non-sequiturs* where there is no obvious relation between panels (McCloud, 1993, p. 72).

The tight relation in graphic novels between the panels, and between the panels and the verbal text, is important, and this relationship affects the reading. Unlike picturebooks, where the relationship could differ more (Nikolajeva & Scott, 2001) (see chapter on picturebooks), the relationship between the verbal and visual text in graphic novels is usually complementary (Barthes, 1964, pp. 40–41). Roland Barthes' notions of *anchorage* and *relay* recognise and acknowledge how to interpret the relation between the verbal and visual text in comics and graphic novels (Barthes, 1964, pp. 40–41). Barthes' view is that anchorage is the most common relationship between verbal and visual text, where the text signifies how the image should be interpreted as the words help and guide the reader to understand the images. Relay, on the other hand, Barthes argues, is when the image and the verbal text "stand in a complementary relationship" (Barthes, 1964, pp. 40–41), such as in comics and graphic novels. Chapter 1, about picturebooks, also discusses these terms.

Narrative storytelling

The images narrate and convey the story in a different way than words alone in prose texts. The interaction between the panels, the gutters and the verbal text transcends the mutual influence between the verbal and visual text, constituting a relation between them. There are eleven types of graphic novel story panels (table 2). The different panel styles narrate the story. Eisner's definition of the graphic novel as "the arrangement of pictures or images and words to narrate a story or dramatize an idea" emphasises the *narrative*. Through both the visuals as well as the verbal, the story is narrated (Carter, 2007; Cohn, 2013). Story elements are familiar to teachers who teach literature in school, including exposition (introduction), complication (main story) and resolution (ending). In the panels, characters, setting, conflict and climax are presented and developed.

The overview of the story panels (table 2) is a helpful guide for readers and even writers of graphic novels, to create awareness of how narratives and stories are built.

Table 2. Eleven types of story panels found in graphic novels (McCloud, 1993; Monnin, 2010, 5; Monnin, 2013, pp. 1–3)

Eleven types of story panels based on the elements of story familiar to teachers when teaching traditional literature. Story panels develop or detail the story/text.	
Plot panel	Develops the graphic novel's plot, or the main set of events that unfold in the story.
Character panel	Develops individual or multiple characters.
Setting panel	Develops setting, the place(s) where the graphic novel takes place.
Conflict panel	Develops the sources of conflict in the graphic novel, the tension that motivates the story.
Rising action panel	Develops the set of events that stem from the conflict, give rise to the conflict, and lead to the climax in the graphic novel.
Climax panel	Develops the point of greatest intensity in the story.
Resolution panel	Develops the final outcome that solves the primary conflict(s) in the graphic novel.
Symbol panel	These panels usually contain images and/or words that stand for something larger than themselves.
Theme panel	Develops the main idea(s) in the graphic novel.
Foreshadowing panel	Develops the story by hinting at or alluding to what comes later.
Combination story panels	These panels use two or more of the above types.

Graphic novels in the classroom

Graphic novels offer fantastic opportunities to work with literary texts in the EFL classroom. Reading for pleasure is obviously of major importance, as allowing learners to make their own choice of text ultimately allows adapted learning to suit readers' levels and interests. Through reading graphic novels learners also have the opportunity to develop multiliteracies, especially verbal and visual literacy and becoming more aware of the images and their role and function, skills which are also transferable to other media. LK20 states, in competence aims after years 4, 7, and 10, that learners should be able both to read different types of texts and to produce multimodal texts. Furthermore, graphic novels in the EFL classroom present the opportunity to learn about narrative structures. Disparate themes and topics brought to the readers' attention invite young learners into new spaces populated by new heroes and heroines. There are several classroom activities which can be developed taking graphic novels as a starting point; this section provides suggestions for how to work with some examples in the classroom.

Dramatisation

Graphic novels offer enjoyable and useful pre- and post-reading activities. Dramatisation involves learners taking roles; there are a number of performance options, including with or without props and stage directions, using the Reader's Theatre method (Drew & Pedersen, 2012) (See chapter 2 for more about Readers' Theatre), or putting on a puppet show. Whichever is chosen, learners would clearly benefit from spending more than the minimum of one lesson on learning their lines and rehearsing. Using dialogue

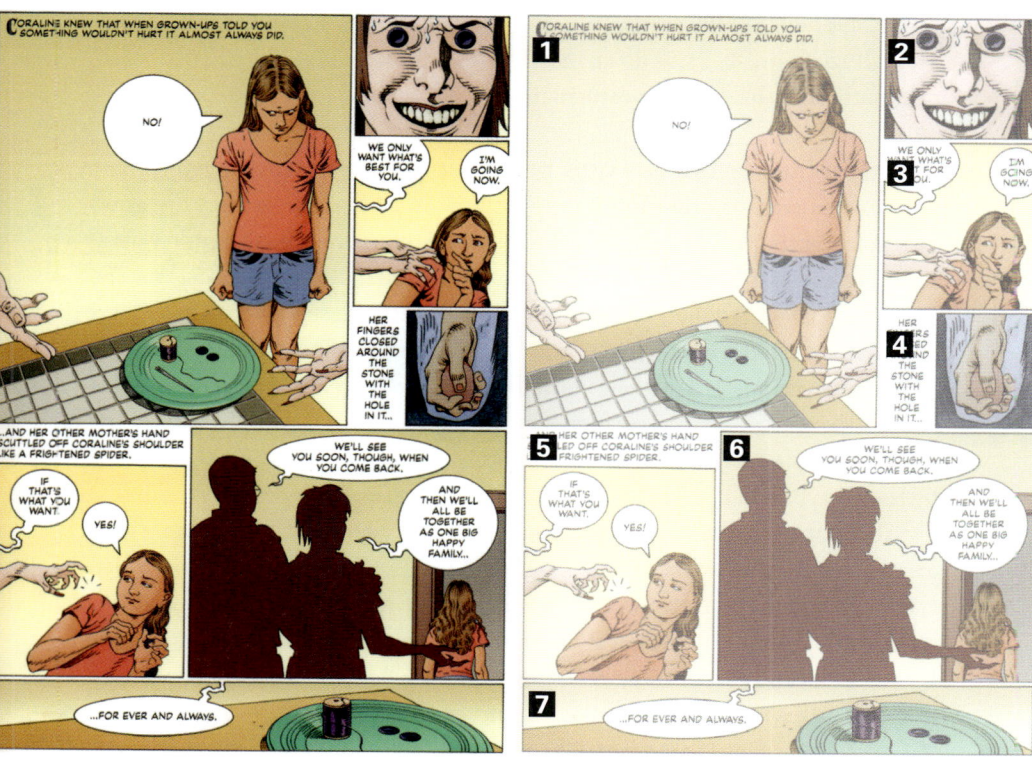

Illustration 5. *Coraline* by Neil Gaiman and Craig Russell (illustrator). Text copyright © 2002, 2008 by Neil Gaiman. Illustration copyright © 2008 by P. Craig Russel. Used by permission of HarperCollins Publishers.

Illustration 6. Reading track of panels.

from the graphic novel is a good starting point, as it can easily be adapted, either by adding lines or by deleting some of the dialogue.

Divide the class into several groups, each of which should dramatise a scene or two. It is essential for learners to prepare the dialogue in advance, preferably in writing, either by copying the dialogue from the text or by rewriting and editing the text. There are several advantages to having learners write and rewrite the text. Through writing and rewriting they make the text their own, either by adding or deleting text. In groups, learners will discuss the text orally and practise oral English. The task inevitably differentiates levels of learning, as some would be content to retype some of the text, whereas others would prefer to change the original text. What is unique in taking a graphic novel as a starting point for dramatisation is that the dialogue is already available, whilst the text itself provides learners with visual suggestions for the staging and movement of characters. Typically, fairy tales lend themselves well to dramatisation, for example Eisner's *The Princess and the Frog* (illustrations 1–3), as do any Shakespeare graphic texts which, of course, originate from dramas for performance.

Drawing (super)heroes and producing own comics

Heroes feature prominently in graphic novels. Superhero stories are good examples of the full potential of the disparate elements in a graphic novel, such as panels, splash pages and gutters. Examples include *The Avengers*, *The Spiderman*, *Black Panther*, and the unique South African superhero story *Kwezi* (illustrations 7–8), which introduces a wider audience to African aesthetics of oral storytelling tradition and mythology, and African landscape. Stories about superheroes are increasingly popular and have found their way onto the big screen, where filmmakers have predominantly kept or are vastly inspired by the storyline of the original graphic novel stories.

Alternatively, the antiheroic *Bone: Out from Boneville* by the American award-winning cartoonist Jeff Smith (2005), which is already a classic (illustration 9), could be introduced. *Bone* narrates the adventures of the sexless creature Bone and cousins on their journey to find their way back home after having been run out of their hometown, Boneville. For further examples of how to work with *Bone* in the classroom, see Crawford and Weiner (2005).

Taking *Bone* or *The Avengers* or any other hero story as a starting point offers a creative task since the model hero, or antihero, portrays an adventurous character. After having read a (super)hero story learners can be asked to create their own graphic superhero adventure story.

Illustrations 7–8. *Kwezi* by Loylson Mkize and Clyde Beech (ill.), front page and pp. 8–9. Collectors Edition 1 Issues 1–3. Cape Town: David Philip Publishers 2016.

Working with visual conventions may provide an opportunity for cross-curricular work with arts and crafts, either by emphasising drawing techniques or by producing panels digitally, for instance using a programme such as *Book Creator*, where options include comics. An enjoyable and challenging approach which highlights visual aspects considerably is for the teacher to instigate a competition for making a new hero or antihero, either in books, or allowing learners to draw on a long strip of paper draped on the walls of the classroom, including speech or thought bubbles, a textbox or a caption. This introduces more active learning activities, as it would be acceptable for learners to stand up and physically move about. Learners should additionally be taught the various graphic novel conventions of panels, frames and gutters (table 1) and what the various panels convey, such as story panels (table 2).

The requirement should be for both image and words. Everybody should make an attempt to draw a hero, or antihero, who is either engaged in a dialogue or "speaks" through a text caption in the drawing. Learners could take

Illustration 9. Jeff Smith, *Bone: Out from Boneville*, pp. 16 and 17. New York: Graphix, Scholastic

7 Graphic novels in the English classroom | 211

a scene from the text and elaborate on it, including perhaps a different point of view and seeing what happens to the storyline. Before being allowed to draw on the larger paper in the classroom, learners must make a preliminary sketch, in which they employ as many panel techniques as possible.

Aesthetic narrative approach

A way of working with literature, or any type of text, is *literature circles* (Daniels, 2002). Literature circles are collaborative, learner-centered reading strategies where each member in the group has a role during the discussions of the text. The roles are discussion director, vocabulary enricher, literary luminary and illustrator. See chapter 6 for more about reading circles.

The discussion director asks open-ended questions and solicits answers from the others in the group. "Browse through the graphic novel and look for a particularly interesting/exciting/dramatic sequence of panels. Discuss in your groups how successful you think the illustrator was in creating interest/excitement/drama, etc. Find examples of types of contrast and transitions in the text. Discuss what you think was the author's aim in using contrasts and transitions. What effect does the use of contrast and transitions have on you, as readers?"

The vocabulary enricher clarifies meanings of words and pronunciation. "Pick a sequence or a page from a graphic novel and discuss what you learn just from the words. Then discuss what you learn from only the images."

The literary luminary searches for interesting quotes and excerpts. "Find five details of how a person or object is drawn. What does each detail tell you about the characters, the place, the world?"

The illustrator creates a visual depiction of the text, by either using the visual images in the graphic novel or creating his or her own images to depict characters or scenes. "Discuss the use of colours and text fonts. How are they perceived by you, as readers?"

Graphic novel adaptations – beneficial for reluctant readers?

Adaptations intend to tell the same story as the original. However, in adaptations a certain level of remediation inevitably changes the text. Linda Hutcheon says, "the act of adaptation always involves both (re-)interpretation and then (re-)creation" (Hutcheon, 2012, p. 8). Though adaptations have several layers of interpretation, they are still works of art on their own merit. Thus, reading the adapted version of a novel can work as an independent reading experience and can simultaneously function as adapted learning in a classroom setting. Perhaps one of the major advantages of graphic novels is that they allow readers to see the whole situation, the body language and facial expressions, at the same time as reading the text. The visual support will prove helpful for many learners and may be especially beneficial for reluctant readers. It would be possible to use both an original text and a graphic novel adaptation in the classroom simultaneously, to support differentiation and to explore aspects of adaptation with learners.

Coraline (Gaiman, 2006) is a good example of a text where adaptation functions in a number of ways. Russell's use of different colours in the visuals creates distinctive moods, which is, of course, a way of interpreting the original text. This can be highlighted and may instigate a discussion among readers that will generate an awareness of the visual elements at play. In the screen animation of *Coraline*, other illustrators were involved in the process, providing a different experience which readers of both the original text and the graphic novel can enjoy. In the graphic novel adaptation of *Coraline* by the multiple award-winning British author Neil Gaiman, the visualisation enhances the textual experience. Even though the actual verbal text of the graphic novel version is virtually identical to that of the original, with only some text deleted and replaced by images, the whole reading experience is completely different. The two versions provide an opportunity to differentiate readers' preferences and engage the reader in a different way, mainly due to the visual expression. An example of this enhancement can be found on p. 51 in the graphic novel version (illustration 5). The Other Mother says nothing when Coraline refuses to have buttons sewn into her eyes, but the picture shows that she is sweating, which may be a sign of emotional distress in spite of her smile. This is, of course, an interpretation on the part of the illustrator, but may help reluctant readers, for instance, to gain an understanding of the storyline.

Another relevant contemporary graphic novel adaptation is *Noughts & Crosses* by UK Children's Laureate Malorie Blackman (2006), adapted by Ian Edginton and John Aggs (2015) (illustration 11). The original novel is part of a series of five books about reverse racism in a segregated, class-based society in a near-future dystopia.[64] In the institutionally racist society, the Crosses

---

64 See chapter 5 for more about Noughts & Crosses.

(Blacks) represent the wealthy elite and rulers, holding political positions, whereas the Noughts (whites) are poor with limited access to education and jobs. *Noughts & Crosses* has received much acclaim and is recommended by Amnesty International for teaching human rights. In addition to the graphic novel adaptation there is a stage version (Pilot Theatre 2019) and a television series (BBC, 2020).

Illustration 10. *Noughts & Crosses* by Malorie Blackman, adapted by Ian Edginton and John Aggs (2015), pp. 16–18. London: Random House.

Set in an imagined near future, *Noughts & Crosses* offers opportunities to explore the potentially difficult topic of racism in relation to historic or current events. Although no concrete reference is made to any specific location, scenes from the text recall real situations from the historically segregated Southern USA, or South Africa during the apartheid regime. However, social segregation can take place anywhere. This offers a gateway into interdiscipli-

nary discussions with Social Studies and History, and also invites discussions of the overriding themes in the curriculum (*LK20*) of Democracy and life skills (from "Overordnet del") (Norwegian Directorate for Education and Training, 2019/29). Other pertinent themes and discussion from the novel may prompt questions of empathy, moral education and citizenship (Syed et al., 2019), asking questions such as "What happens to individuals when experiencing life-changing events?"

In addition to exploring broader themes foregrounded in *Noughts & Crosses*, classroom activities can include a close reading of how the multiliteracies employed in the text underscore the themes and the build-up to the subsequent tension. For example, the reverse racism based on skin colour is accentuated by the fact that the graphic novel's aesthetics are in black and white. Illustration 10 shows scenes from the first day of school, demonstrating tension between the Noughts and the Crosses. The second panel (illustration 10, p. 17) shows Noughts protected by the police from the Crosses, as they walk across the schoolyard to enter the school. The visuals in the panel (illustration 10) indicate that the word "Blankers" is a derogatory expression, it is clearly a racist term for Noughts. Verbally abused and unwanted "Blankers" are visualised through crowded panels including onomatopoetic insults in bold letters. Although privileged Sephy (Cross) expresses the hope that Callum (Nought) will be in her class (illustration 10, p. 16), she is overwhelmed by the situation and suddenly she also shouts "Blankers". These scenes are very powerful and likely to provoke discussions and emotion among young readers. The double spread makes use of close-up panels and long shots to show the impact on the protagonists Sephy and Callum, who readers know from the introduction to be in a secret and forbidden love relationship. In these few pages, the disparate themes of segregation, racism and young love are powerfully fleshed out.

Other nonfiction graphic novels for older readers which offer interdisciplinary teaching opportunities include adaptations like David Polonsky's *Anne Frank's Diary: The Graphic Adaptation* (2018) or original works like Art Spiegelman's Pulitzer Prize winning classic *Maus* (1993), which examines Jewish experiences and history during the Second World War as well as relationships between generations. The semi-autobiographical *Persepolis* (2006) by Marjane Satrapi, which addresses the revolution in Iran, also exists as a prize-winning film (2007). This original and beautifully crafted graphic novel narrates a young girl's experiences of the Iranian revolution, which in turn promotes a discussion of historic events, particularly how politics impacts on peoples' lives. *Persepolis* is also a coming-of-age story, which young people will relate to. Jaffe's website "Using graphic novels in education: *Persepolis*"

Illustration 11. *Romeo and Juliet* in the manga version, adapted by Appignanesi and Leong (2007), pp. 42–43. London: Self Made Hero.

(2020) proposes many wonderful ways to use this text to teach issues including "Language, Literature, and Language Usage" and "Modes of Storytelling and Visual Literacy", and the website also provides "Suggested Prose Novel Pairings". The graphic novel adaptation (2011) of Khaled Hosseini's bestselling novel *The Kite Runner* deals with recent troubled political events in Afghanistan, and, most recently, Margaret Atwood's dystopian contemporary classic *The Handmaid's Tale* has been adapted into a graphic novel (2019).

Classic text adaptations

Numerous classic texts have been adapted into graphic novels, with great potential for EFL learners. Whilst major novels by Jane Austen, the Brontes and Charles Dickens are important landmarks in cultural and literary history, they can often appear disconcertingly long, complex and difficult to contemporary readers, particularly second-language learners. Yet they offer

Illustration 12. Gareth Hinds's (2013) version of Romeo and Juliet's balcony scene, pp. 48–49. © 2013 Gareth Hinds. Reproduced by permission of Walker Books Ltd, London SE11 5HJ.

invaluable cultural capital and reading pleasure through well-known characters and images, captivating stories, heart-stopping cliff-hangers and famous quotations (Chute, 2019).

Advantages of reading Shakespeare's plays in graphic novel format in the EFL classroom are many. Whether reading the play text, or watching a film or stage production, Shakespeare's language may not be easily accessible. For a young, contemporary audience a graphic version with visuals and adapted language may be more easily readable and therefore potentially better suited to the EFL classroom. The aesthetics of different graphic versions will vary as they do in different productions, thus resembling the experience of seeing the plays staged. Different graphic adaptations can be compared, exploring the impact of aesthetic choices.

One comparative way of working with a graphic version of a Shakespeare play is to take the same scene from two or more versions to compare the visual and verbal features in detail. The following examples focus on two graphic adaptations of the balcony scene (Act 2, scene 2) from *Romeo and Juliet*. The manga version of Shakespeare's *Romeo and Juliet* (adapted by Appignanesi and Leong, 2007) (illustration 11) accentuates key scenes from the play through the visuals and the use of abridged language to ensure better accessibility for younger learners. Manga, a stylised black and white visual comic book medium originating in Japan, is gaining increasing popularity with Western readers.

The manga version (illustration 11) has speech bubbles and recognisable characters. The balcony scene is vivid due to the use of panels on top of each other, lacking gutters, which gives the impression that action, thoughts and dialogue happen simultaneously. Furthermore, the close-ups place the emphasis on the characters' expressions, making the reader feel more connected to the characters' emotions.

By contrast, in Gareth Hinds' (2013, pp. 48–49) version (illustration 12), the panels demonstrate more turn-taking in the dialogue, which is fuller and has more visual prominence than in the manga version. Whilst Hinds's Juliet is strongly represented, the reader also appears to be positioned to see several of the panels from a distance, resembling the experience of an audience member watching the scene on stage.

A further rich intertextual contrast for discussion can be provided by a secret love scene from *Noughts & Crosses* (Blackman, 2006). Sephy and Callum defy the constraints that family and a segregated society place on their forbidden interracial love. Their secret meetings are extremely dangerous (illustration 13). The intertextual references to *Romeo and Juliet* in the storyline are clear; the illustrations and dialogue in the graphic novel as Callum enters via the window allude to the balcony scene and to family objections to the relationship.

Marcia Williams's graphic collections of versions of a variety of Shakespearean plays deliberately set out to highlight features of drama as a genre (illustration 14, the example shows an abridged version of *Twelfth Night*).

The characters framing the action in *Bravo, Mr. William Shakespeare!* (Williams, 2000) allude to the audience, who comment on the action. The frame also includes Shakespeare, speaking in his own words in the historic Globe theatre, which inevitably could spark discussions about the historic and cultural development of going to the theatre today and in the past.

Illustration 13. *Noughts & Crosses*, pp. 140–141, resembling Romeo and Juliet's balcony scene, where Callum secretly visits Sephy. London: Random House.

Illustration 14. Shakespeare's *Twelfth Night* from *Bravo, Mr. William Shakespeare!* by Marcia Williams (2000), pp. 21–22. © 2000 by Marcia Williams Reproduced by permission of Walker Books Ltd, London SE11 5HJ.

Graphic novels online

New media offer new opportunities for language learners interested in reading; increasing numbers of online graphic novels are available, many free of charge. Graphic novels online allow readers to go back and forth as with a book. An advantage of suitable online graphic novels is that they are instantly readily available, allowing the learner to engage in reading activity both in school and at home, where learners can read their own texts at their own pace. An increasing number of digital graphic novels are also available as apps on tablets, for instance on an iPad or a Kindle or other tablet computer. One such app is the delightful online graphic novel *The Land of the Magic Flute*, which is an interactive graphic narrative introducing new readers, viewers and listeners to the world of Mozart and opera in an astounding new way.

Another digital graphic narrative is *The Boat*, which narrates the experience of Vietnamese refugees to Australia. Currently, descendants of Vietnamese refugees represent one per cent of the Australian population. Though the narrative is somewhat sinister, the aesthetics represent the experience of both the historic and the more current experiences of being a boat refugee in a beautiful and engaging way, which enhances the reader's understanding of the experience of the Other.

With a strong female protagonist and based on research into American history, *The Dreamer Comic* runs to fifteen online volumes and associated resources where the reader can browse to find additional information about the characters. The reader clicks the "Next" button on the screen when ready to move to the next page of the chapter, for a total of ten chapters. See chapter 8 for more about digital literature.

A final suggestion for digital graphic novels is the *Classical Comics* website, where classics are available as online graphic novels.

Online graphic novels highlight the advantages of multimodality being incorporated, meaning that visual and verbal elements, together with movement and sound, create illusions like a film.

Concluding remarks

Multimodal texts such as graphic novels are fantastic to use in the classroom. They enhance multiliteracy skills, particularly visual and verbal literacy skills, they improve understanding of narrative structures and they introduce readers to new worlds. Graphic novels have the potential to develop readers' critical literacy and allow learners to be creative both through the reading process and in response to texts. Graphic novels are highly suitable for differentiation.

The tools provided for analysis in this chapter are intended to be helpful to readers and teachers alike. Readers of graphic novels can now enjoy a rich and increasing variety of texts in terms of genre and aesthetic expressions as the number of titles published grows rapidly each year, both independent texts and adaptations. Introducing graphic novels into the classroom offers a rich experience many learners will embrace as a source of language input, and, most importantly, as a way into the world of literature. Graphic novels are fabulous at telling important stories in ways that promote connection, discussion and engagement.

Graphic novel suggestions: a resource list
What to read: Which texts at what level?
Primary and lower secondary
The Absolutely True Diary of a Part-Time Indian (2009) by Sherman Alexie, illustrated by Ellen Forney
The Savage (2008) by David Almond, illustrated by Dave McKean
The Avengers (2011) by Brian Michael, illustrated by John Romita Jr
Fungus the Bogeyman (1977/2012) by Raymond Briggs
The Snowman (1978/2013) by Raymond Briggs
Spider-Man; Season One (2012) by Cullen Bunn and Neil Edwards
X-Men: Age of X (2011) Mike Carey, illustrated by Clay Mann
The Princess and the Frog by the Grimm Brothers (1995) by Will Eisner
Diary of a Wimpy Kid (2007) by Jeff Kinney
Scott Pilgrim Volume 1, Scott Pilgrim's Precious Little Life (2004) by Bryan Lee O'Malley
The Brilliant World of Tom Gates (2011) by Liz Pichon
The Invention of Hugo Cabret: A Novel in Words and Pictures (2007) by Brian Selznick
Bone: Out from Boneville (2005) by Jeff Smith
The Arrival (2006) by Shaun Tan
Romeo and Juliet (2007) by William Shakespeare, adapted by Richard Appignanesi, illustrated by Sonia Leong
Romeo and Juliet (2013) by William Shakespeare, adapted by Gareth Hinds
Point Blanc. The Graphic Novel (2007) by Anthony Horowitz and Antony Johnston, illustrated by Kanako Damerum, and Yuzuru Takasaki
Fluffy (2007) by Simone Lia
Kwezi (2016) by Loyiso Mkize and Clyde Beech
Courtney Crumrin and the Night Things (2003) by Ted Naifeh
Big Nate Goes for Broke (2012) by Lincoln Peirce

Upper secondary and Young Adult
Maus (1993) by Art Spiegelman
Persepolis: The Story of a Childhood and *Persepolis 2: The Story of a Return* (2006) by Marjane Satrapi
Noughts & Crosses: The Graphic Novel Adaptation (2015) by Malorie Blackman, adapted by Ian Edginton, illustrated John Aggs

Pride and Prejudice: A Graphic Novel (2011) by Jane Austen, adapted by Ian Edington and Robert Deas
Trickster: Native American Tales: A graphic collection (2010) by Matt Dembicki
A Contract with God: And Other Tenement Stories (1978) by Will Eisner
Hera: The Goddess and Her Glory (2011) by George O'Connor
A Taste of Chlorine (2011) by Bastien Vivès
Anne Frank's Diary: The Graphic Adaptation (2018) by David Polonsky
Bravo, Mr. William Shakespeare! (2000) by Marcia Williams
The Handmaid's Tale: The Graphic Novel (2019) by Margaret Atwood, adapted by Renée Nault
The Kite Runner Graphic Novel (2011) by Khaled Hosseini, illustrated by Fabio Celoni and Mirka Andolfo
Death on the Nile (2007) by Agatha Christie, adapted by Francois Rivière, illustrated by Solidor

References

Primary texts

Atwood, M., & Nault, R. (Ill.) (2019). *The Handmaid's Tale: The Graphic Novel*. Knopf Doubleday.
Austen, J., Deas, R. (Ill.) & Edington, I. (text adapted). (2011). *Pride and Prejudice: A Graphic Novel*. SelfMadeHero.
Bendis, M.B., & Romita, J. Jr. (Ill.). (2011). *The Avengers*. Marvel.
Blackman, M., Edginton, I. (adapted text) & Aggs, J. (Ill.). (2015). *Noughts & Crosses: The Graphic Novel Adaptation*. Random House.
Bunn, C., & Edwards N. (Ill.) (2012). *Spider-Man: Season One*. Marvel.
Carey, M., & Mann, C. (Ill.) (2011). *X-Men: Age of X*. Marvel.
Eisner, W. (1995). *The Princess and the Frog by the Grimm Brothers*. NBM.
Gaiman, N., & McKean, D. (Ill.). (2006). *Coraline*. Harper Perennial.
Gaiman, N., & Russell, C. (adapted and ill.) (2008). *Coraline*. Harper Collins.
Hosseini, K., Celoni, F., & Andolfo, M. (2011). *The Kite Runner Graphic Novel*. Riverhead Books.
Mkize, L., & Beech, C. (Ill.) (2016). *Kwezi*. Collector's edition, issues 1–3. David Philip Publishers.
Mkize, L., & Beech, C. (Ill.) (2016). *Kwezi*. Collector's edition, issues 4–6. David Philip Publishers.
Polonsky, D. (2018). *Anne Frank's Diary: The Graphic Adaptation*. Pantheon.
Satrapi, M. (2006). *Persepolis: The Story of a Childhood* and *Persepolis 2: The Story of a Return*. Jonathan Cape.
Shakespeare, W., Appignanesi, R., & Leong, S. (Ill.). (2007). *Romeo and Juliet*. SelfMadeHero.
Shakespeare, W., & Hinds, G. (2013). *Romeo and Juliet*. Candlewick.
Smith, J. (2005). *Bone: Out from Boneville*. Graphix, Scholastic.
Spiegelman, A. (1993). *Maus: A Survivor's Tale. I.* and *Maus: My Father Bleeds History. II*. Pantheon.
Tan, S. (2006). *The Arrival*. Lothian Books.
Williams, M. (2000). Shakespeare's *Twelfth Night* from *Bravo, Mr. William Shakespeare!* Candlewick.

Graphic novels online

The Magic Flute http://www.landofthemagicflute.com/#start
Chibana, N. 10 mind-blowing interactive stories that will change the way you see the world. https://visme.co/blog/10-mind-blowing-interactive-stories-that-will-change-the-way-you-see-the-world/

The Boat http://www.sbs.com.au/theboat/
The Dreamer Comic https://thedreamercomic.com/
Classical Comics http://www.classicalcomics.com/

Secondary texts

Amnesty UK. *Using Fiction to Teach Human Rights in Secondary Schools*. Amnesty International UK/Education. https://www.amnesty.org.uk/fiction-secondary-school-teach-human-rights-literature

Book Creator https://bookcreator.com/

Carter, J.B. (Ed.). (2007). *Building Literacy Connections With Graphic Novels: Page by Page, Panel by Panel*. National Council of Teachers.

Chute, H. (2019). The Graphic Novel Versions of Literary Classics Used To Seem Lowbrow. No More. https://www.nytimes.com/2019/11/12/books/review/the-iliad-a-graphic-novel-adaptation-gareth-hinds.html

Crawford, P., & Weiner, S. (2005). *Using Graphic Novels in the Classroom, Including Bone By Jeff Smith: A Guide for Teachers and Librarians*. Graphix, Scholastic. http://www.boneville.com/wp-content/uploads/2006/05/Bone_Teachers_Guide.pdf

Birketveit, A., & Rimmereide, H.E. (2017). Using Authentic Picturebooks and Illustrated Books to Improve L2 Writing Among 11-year-olds. *The Language Learning Journal, 45*(1), 100–116.

Birketveit, A., Rimmereide, H.E., Bader, M., & Fisher, L. (2018). Extensive Reading in Primary School EFL. *Acta Didactica Norge, 12*(2), Art. 9, 23 pages. https://doi.org/10.5617/adno.5643

Blackman, M. (2006). *Noughts & Crosses*. Corgi Children.

Brenner, R. (2012). WFL: Children's Room Blog. http://wflkids.blogspot.com/2012/05/graphic-novels-101-faq-by-robin-brenner.html

Cohn, N. (2013). *The Visual Language of Comics: Introduction to the Structures and Cognition of Sequential Images*. Bloomsbury.

Drew, I., & Pedersen, R.R. (2012). Reader's Theatre: A Group Reading Approach to Texts in Mainstream EFL classes. In A. Hasselgreen, I. Drew & B. Sørheim (Eds.). *The Young Language Learner: Research-Based Insights into Teaching and Learning* (pp. 71–83). Fagbokforlaget.

Eisner, W. (1990 expanded edition, reprinted 2001). *Comics & Sequential Art*. Poorhouse Press.

Hutcheon, L. (2012). *A Theory of Adaptation*. Routledge.

Iser, W. (1974). *The Act of Reading: A Theory Of Aesthetic Response*. Hopkins UP.

Iser, W. (1978). *The Implied Reader: Patterns of Communication in Prose Fiction from Bunyan to Beckett*. Johns Hopkins UP.

Jaffe, M. (2020). Using Graphic Novels in Education: *Persepolis*. http://cbldf.org/using-graphic-novels/using-graphic-novels-in-education-persepolis/

Janks, H., Dixon, K., Ferreira, A., Granville, S., & Newfield, D. (2014). *Doing Critical Literacy: Texts and Activities For Students and Teachers*. Routledge.

Krashen, S.D. (2004). *The Power of Reading: Insights from the Research* (2nd ed.). Heinemann.

Kress, G. (2003). *Literacy in the New Media Age*. Routledge.

Kyle, R. (1964). The future of "comics". http://www.thecomicbooks.com/misc/Richard%20Kyle%20The%20Future%20of%20Comics.pdf

McCloud, S. (1994). *Understanding Comic Books: The Invisible Art*. HarperPerennial.

Mikkonen, K. (2017). *The Narratology of Comic Art*. Routledge.

Monnin, K. (2010). *Teaching Graphic Novels: Practical Strategies for the ELA Classroom*. Maupin House Publishing.

Monnin, K. (2013). *Teaching Early Reader Comics and Graphic Novels*. Maupin House.

Nikolajeva, M., & Scott, C. (2001). *How Picturebooks Work*. Garland Publishing.

Norwegian Directorate for Education and Training. (2019/2020). Overordnet del. https://www.udir.no/lk20/overordnet-del

O'Connor, G. (2020). https://static.macmillan.com/static/macmillan/2020-online-resources/downloads/olympians-teachers-guide.pdf

Rimmereide, H.E. (2020). Multimodal Texts in the English Classroom. In C. Carlsen, M. Dypedahl & S.H. Iversen (Eds.), *Teaching and Learning English* (2nd ed.). Cappelen Damm Akademisk.

Rosenblatt, L. (1995). *Literature as Exploration*. Modern Language Association.

Scholastic. A Guide to Using Graphic Novels with Children and Teens. http://www.scholastic.com/teachers/lesson-plans/teaching-content/guide-using-graphic-novels-children-and-teens/

Stowell, L. (2014). *Write and Draw Your Own Comics*. Usborne Publishing.

Syed, G.K., Naylor, A., Rimmereide, H.E. Varga, Z., & Guanio-Uluru, L. (2019). Developing UK and Norwegian Undergraduate Students' Conceptions of Personal Social Issues in Young Adult Fiction Through Transnational Reflective Exchange. *English in Education*, DOI: 10.1080/04250494.2019.1676641

Ujiie, J., & Krashen, S. (1996). Comic book reading, reading enjoyment, and pleasure reading among middle class and chapter I middle school students. *Reading Improvement, 33*(1), 51–54.

Wallner, L. (2019). Gutter talk: Co-Constructing Narratives Using Comics in The Classroom. *Scandinavian Journal of Educational Research*, 63:6, 819–838, DOI: 10.1080/00313831.2018.1452290

8
Digital approaches to young adult fiction

Anita Normann

Introduction

Active engagement with well-chosen, authentic literature can contribute to instilling a life-long motivation for reading in adolescent learners, and encouraging them to connect with literary texts in combination with digital media tools may be one of several gateways to achieve this.

This chapter's purpose is to present and discuss ways of exploiting and integrating digital technology when working with literature. Digital technology is understood as various types of digital resources, equipment and applications. The general definition of digital skills in the English subject embraces aspects such as being able to use digital media and resources to strengthen language learning, meet authentic language models, interact with others and acquire relevant knowledge, and also to use digital tools for text creation. An LK20 competence aim after year 10 states, for instance, that "the pupil is expected to be able to use different digital resources and other aids in language learning, text creation and interaction" (Norwegian Directorate for Education and Training, 2019/2020). Combining the digital element with working with literature may contribute to variation in the learning process. It is, in addition, a way of tapping into learners' out-of-school practices, which may increase motivation. Active engagement with and production of own texts may additionally support learners in creating meaning from authentic literary texts. The latter refers to texts which have not been written for the purpose of language learning, and hence have a richer language than what we see in texts specifically adapted for language learners.

The teacher's role is, in this perspective, central. *The Professional Digital Competence Framework for Teachers* (Kelentric, Helland, & Arstorp, 2017) describes, on the one hand, expectations of teachers' own digital competencies and, on the other hand, how teachers can contribute to developing their pupils' digital competence. It is emphasised that children and adolescents should not be only "passive consumers of products, [...], but also active producers of content themselves" (Kelentric et al., 2017, p. 7). In line with this, it is an *action- and production-oriented approach* to working with literature (Surkamp, 2012; Vestli, 2008), in combination with using digital technology, that forms the basis for the didactic examples presented here. The examples revolve around the following keywords: interactive graphic novels, excerpts from digitised novels, digital storytelling, micro fiction, podcasting and use of digital timeline. Texts and tasks suggested are primarily aimed at secondary learners. The texts recommended in the chapter can, however, be replaced with texts suited for a younger audience, and the tasks are easily adaptable for other levels.

Digital and digitised literature

As emphasised by Thomas (2018, p. 100), digital technologies enable learners to access digital resources, collaborate online, create new material and curate existing material, all of which are highly relevant also when engaging with literature in an EFL context. Curation here refers to the process of assembling, selecting, categorising and commenting on texts by using an online content curation tool such as e.g. Scoop-it[65] or elink.[66] The personal comments added by the curator, i.e. the learner, offer added value in a curation process, making curated material more than a list of links or references. Using digital literature can make access to literary texts easier. But what do we actually mean by digital literature and how is that different to digitised literature? The next two sections aim at clarifying that question, as both terms are relevant for the English teacher who wants to draw on the possibilities offered through digital media and digital technologies when working with literature.

---

65 https://www.scoop.it/
66 https://elink.io/

Digital literature

Digital literature is defined by Rustad (2012) as literature produced by authors who exploit digital technology in the production, distribution and reception process. This type of literature must be read on screen and readers may interact with the texts in various ways. Several modalities are used to tell the story in digital literature, as e.g. written text, music, narration and animated illustrations, and because of the distinctive semiotic and aesthetic characteristics, readers are invited to a different reading experience. Rustad (2012) refers to Hayles (2007), who explains this as two types of attention, or cognitive modes. A *deep attention mode* is seen in traditional, eager readers, absorbed in their books, totally oblivious to everything going on around them. A *hyper-attention mode*, on the other hand, is characterised by readers who switch focus rapidly between different tasks, preferring multiple information streams and having a low tolerance for boredom. According to Rustad (ibid.), both types of attention are observed in the reading of digital literature. On the one hand, it invites a concentrated reading by following a fascinating story unfolding on the screen. On the other hand, the reader has to interact with the story to make it develop, such as clicking on the screen, moving the mouse, choosing between various reading paths and alternating between the various information sources. The multimodal aspect of digital literature is hence strong, and letting learners read digital literature is a way of helping them relate to the complex media and text universe of our times.

Multimodal fiction is one of several genres found in digital literature. In this type of text, there is an interplay between the various modalities being used, and the reader interacts with the text by clicking the various hyperlinks. Two very appropriate examples for secondary learners are presented further below.

Blog fiction is another type of digital literature, referring to a less formal type of writing using blogs to reach out to the readers. Additional modalities used in blog fiction are typically represented as images or sound clips. One way of presenting blog fiction is in the form of a diary, written over time, by fictional characters. Many teenagers find this to be an interesting and "doable" format of digital writing and online distribution. Blog fiction is precisely a type of out-of-school practice that a professional, digitally competent English teacher can draw on when working with literature. As a while-reading activity, learners could be asked to set up their own blogs, take on the role of a fictional character in the literary text and write this character's imaginary blog diary. A historical dimension could also be added, by letting characters in older, classic texts write their blog fiction in 2020. This is an activity that combines literature and blog fiction with creativity.

Fanfiction is another example of how to engage creatively with literature for adolescent readers. In fanfiction, writers (hence "fans") base their characters on an existing literary universe, or even move their fiction into an alternative universe. A blog platform is often exploited for sharing own stories and reading fanfiction written by other fans. Some international bestsellers, for instance the Harry Potter series by J.K. Rowling, have been subject to huge amounts of fanfiction.[67] Sauro and Sundmark (2018) looked at how blogs mediate the storytelling of classroom role-play fanfiction. Contrary to what is generally seen in this subgenre of fanfiction, the participants in their study worked collaboratively, in groups, in the physical classroom with choosing a character, finding an *empty space* (or *missing moment* (p. 6)) in the text and writing their piece of fanfiction. Only upon completion did they post their fanfiction to a blog platform. Findings from the study show that compared to extramural online fanfiction, the classroom fanfiction was less innovative, but more collective in its focus (p. 1). Moreover, allowing learners to choose their own, preferred publishing option (blog platform) and a tool they were more familiar with helped them overcome the frustration they experienced when trying to convert their stories to a given blog format. Using a familiar blog platform additionally allowed them to better exploit the affordances offered in the platform. Allowing learners some freedom in selection of digital tools and formats for engaging with literature is hence one thing we can learn from this study. Doing so may also bridge the gap between online, informal learning of English and more academic practices found in the classrooms.

Twitter fiction is a type of fiction where authors create short texts adapted to the specific format characterised by the limitation of 270 characters only (Rustad, 2012, p. 92). Twitter, launched as a micro blogging platform in 2006, has become popular for authors who want to use the platform to write and publish their short fiction texts. In Norway, the author Frode Grytten gained great popularity with his Tweet fiction short stories, published daily for one and a half years in 2011–2013. Grytten had close to 30 000 followers, and says that a good literary tweet must contain something unexpected, something which is not totally clear-cut and is a surprise.[68] These characteristics, as well as the limitations in scope, create *empty spaces* in the short Twitter texts, spaces which can later be filled by the readers, either as single- or multi-authored short texts. Fiction tweet authors must therefore rely on readers to further develop the Twitter short story in their own minds. A well-written

---

67 See for instance https://www.fanfiction.net/book/Harry-Potter/
68 https://www.ba.no/nyheter/hans-beste-pa-twitter-blir-bok/s/1-41-7373839 (May, 23, 2014)

fiction tweet, for instance presented as a daily-life experience in a nutshell, has, in other words, the potential to invite readers to continue the creation of the story, either alone or as a collaborative activity. Potential questions could be: *How does the tweet short story mirror my own experiences? Which memories come to mind? How is the story similar or different to an experience I've had? What did the story make me think of?* By using such questions as prompts, the teacher can elicit learners' reactions to and reflections on the Twitter story, and hence fill in any empty spaces. In a classroom context, this is an aspect that can and should be exploited, because it has the potential to spur secondary learners' creativity. An example of a different type of Twitter fiction is seen in American novelist Jennifer Egan's serialised science fiction short story "Black Box", from 2012. Egan used the New Yorker's Twitter account to publish her story, over a period of nine days. The story was later published in the magazine itself.[69]

Although printed texts still have a more acknowledged status as "real" literature, the examples presented above show how two well-established authors have used a social media platform to explore fictional writing. Twitter has also become a popular platform for aspiring young writers who want to share their own *flash-fiction stories*, i.e. short fiction stories of 1000 words or even less. This is also often referred to as micro fiction. Having access to a platform for sharing, a target audience and the possibilities of immediate feedback and followers may be a motivational aspect also for in-school writing. Both *Lesesenteret*[70] and *Skrivesenteret*[71] offer great resources for teachers and learners about how to work with Twitter fiction in relation to reading and writing. These resources, which can also be adapted for the EFL classroom, cover approaches for engaging with and interpreting tweet fiction, having literary conversations about tweet fiction stories, or using tweets to draw the learners' explicit attention to choices of lexis in these short (literary) texts.

The relevance of digital literature for English teachers is, arguably, twofold. It represents an alternative type of text and reading experience, which may motivate another type of readers than those deep-attention learners seen in the corners of the classrooms, with a novel between their hands, intensely engaged with the text. Digital literature can additionally be interesting as a way of integrating and using digital technology to let learners create their own content related to the literary text they are, or have been, working with. See other concrete didactic suggestions further below.

---

69 "Black Box" (Egan, 2012): https://www.newyorker.com/magazine/2012/06/04/black-box-2
70 The Norwegian Reading Centre: https://lesesenteret.uis.no/#Skole
71 The Norwegian Centre for Writing Education and Research: http://www.skrivesenteret.no/

Digitised literature

This type of literature refers to digital editions of printed texts. Choice and availability are two arguments for trying out online versions of literary texts. During the corona period of digital teaching after the lockdown of schools in 2020, many English teachers in Norway discovered the usefulness of digitised literature. More than 60 000 members (mainly teachers and student teachers) joined the Facebook group *Koronadugnad for digitale lærere*, where they shared ideas about online resources, activities, text repositories, etc. It has been said that two months of corona lockdown of schools contributed more to developing teachers' professional digital competence than the last 10–15 years. Below, some resources for online text repositories are shared, but readers are encouraged to familiarise themselves with additional online resources for accessing digitised literature.

With more than 60 000 international titles available for reading online, *Project Gutenberg*[72] holds a plethora of resources. Neither apps nor registration is necessary for reading the online texts, which are mainly older publications, since the copyright of the books has expired. Note that downloading the books may be subject to restrictions outside the U.S. More about this can be read on the project's website.

LibriVox[73] is a non-commercial, non-profit and ad-free project aimed at making all books in the public domain (i.e. not protected by copyright) available in an online audio format, at no cost. This library's catalogue of audio books can be browsed by author, title, genre and language. Listening to audio books may in general be a good alternative for learners who need special adaptation, or for everyone, when practising their listening skills. Note, however, that since the books available through LibriVox are in the public domain, they are old, and because of that, the language may strike today's adolescents as a bit antiquated. Using these recordings for reluctant readers or learners who struggle with motivation for reading may therefore not be the best of choices. The recordings may actually be more suitable as listening material for high-proficient learners who need extra challenges.

A good alternative for reluctant or struggling readers may be the excellent resource *ESL bits*,[74] where learners can both read and listen to audio narratives within a variety of genres. The fiction texts are suitable for teen and adult readers, and two listening speeds are offered. The latter element is particularly interesting in terms of adapted teaching. Allowing learners

---

72 https://www.gutenberg.org/
73 https://librivox.org/
74 http://esl-bits.net/index.htm

to decide their own listening speed may impact their overall reading of the literary text in a positive way. ESL bits is a non-profit site and contains no advertising. The texts made available here can only be read and/or listened to online, not downloaded, but the site offers many well-known and fairly recent titles of highly acclaimed young adult fiction texts, such as *Looking for Alaska* (Green, 2005), *Holes* (Sachar, 1988), *The Absolutely True Diary of a Part-Time Indian* (Alexie, 2007), *The Curious Incident of the Dog in the Night-Time* (Haddon, 2003), *The Hitchhiker's Guide to the Galaxy* (Adams, 1979/1997), *The Perks of Being a Wallflower* (Chbosky, 1999), *The Secret Life of Bees* (Kidd, 2001), *Bridge to Terabithia* (Paterson, 1977) and *The House on Mango Street* (Cisneros, 1983). A didactic example involving an excerpt from the latter audio version is presented further below.

Teachers' professional digital competence

The teacher's role is key when it comes to using technology in a way that helps learners develop basic skills and more specialised subject knowledge in English. *The Professional Digital Competence Framework for Teachers* (Kelentric et al., 2017) was published by the Norwegian Directorate for Education and Training in 2017 and consists of seven competence areas, which all contain descriptions of knowledge, skills and competence. Together, the competence areas make up a professional, digitally competent teacher. Two of the competence areas in the framework are particularly relevant in this chapter. *Subjects and basic skills* is e.g. about understanding how integration of digital resources into the learning processes can help achieve competence aims in the national curricula and address the basic skills (Kelentric et al., 2017, p. 10). A digitally competent teacher should, for instance, be able to "facilitate pupils' learning in and across subjects, based on the interplay between academic content, competence aims, digital technology, digital teaching materials and digital learning resources" (ibid.). This relates to how e.g. English teachers can make use of digital technology to achieve competence aims and help learners develop academically. It is also about utilising digital technology, in the form of both teaching material and learning resources, to support the development of other basic skills than digital skills, like reading, writing and speaking.

The second, and particularly relevant, competence area for this chapter relates to *Pedagogy and subject didactics*, which is e.g. about "Integrating digital resources into planning, organisation, implementation and evaluation of the teaching, in order to foster pupils' learning and development" (Kelentric et al., 2017, p. 13). In line with this, a digitally competent teacher should be able to develop a broad repertoire of working methods with digital teaching materials and digital learning resources. For English teachers integrating literary texts as learning resources in their classes, this could relate to having competence about how e.g. the learners, in a PWP (pre-, while- and post-) stage, could use digital technology to engage with the literature in focus. It could also relate to selecting and accessing literature, for instance knowledge about where to find literary texts online and choosing types of literary texts "outside the box", e.g. in the form of digital literature. Yet another example relates to the teacher being familiar with how the use of specific digital technology can help reluctant speakers in the classroom demonstrate their oral, productive skills,[75] for instance when presenting literary texts.

A digitally competent teacher would hence know how to manage a classroom where technology is used in a motivational way, which additionally opens up for differentiation and adaptation to learners' various needs. The Norwegian Center for ICT in Education has published a guide for technology-rich classrooms, offering advice for teachers.[76] In addition, local guidelines for netiquette, proper and safe behaviour on the Internet, are published locally, by both municipalities and schools.

Action- and production-oriented approaches to working with literature

Traditional, analytic work with literature still has a place in the language classroom, especially with upper secondary learners, but an overall perspective of this book is to present and discuss ways for EFL learners to engage more creatively and confidently with literary texts. In line with that perspective, an "action- and production-oriented literature didactics" represents an interesting and relevant approach. Surkamp (2012) explains this orientation in literature didactics as embracing two forms of learning activities:

> The active engagement with the texts means that the learners become aesthetically and artistically active, for instance by acting out the text or by transposing it into a different medium (music, image, film). In production-oriented procedures, the learners generate their own texts. In doing so, they creatively engage with a literary text by expanding, rewriting, updating and alienating it. (p. 493)

---

75 In LK06 and LK20, *basic oral skills* embrace listening, speaking and conversing, i.e. both receptive and a productive skills. This is in opposition to the *language skills* as presented in the Common European Framework of Reference for Languages (Council of Europe, 2001), where listening is seen as a separate language skill.

76 https://www.udir.no/globalassets/filer/veileder_hensiktsmessig_bruk_bm_lav.pdf

According to Vestli (2008, p. 18), learners, even in a traditional analytic approach to studying literature, are often asked to produce written and oral texts. These texts have, however, traditionally had a referential or reproductive character, as for instance asking learners to write a summary or analysis of the literary text studied in class. In an action- and production-oriented teaching of literature, the focus is rather on the learners' creative production, in a more aesthetic, artistic sense. Working with literary texts in the latter view means that the teacher decides the role of the literary text, which may be the point of departure for various activities. Action- and production-oriented methods are additionally more open to subjective and individual construction of meaning. Even excerpts from literary texts can be used to engage learners within this orientation. If, on the other hand, whole texts will be used, teachers will probably find it most efficient to read and study the text before moving on to more action- and production-oriented activities in the while- and post-reading stages. Some ideas for digital action- and production-oriented activities for working with literature are summarised below, in a table inspired by Carola Surkamp (2012).

Table 1. Action- and production-oriented, digital activities

Action-oriented digital activities	Production-oriented digital activities
Combine fiction texts with real-world stories. (See an example below, related to *The Boat*).	Create a **digital story**, with narration, images and music. (See example below, related to *My Brother's Name is Jessica*).
Make **black-out poems**,[77] based on online pages from the fiction text studied.	Produce various types of **micro fiction/flash fiction**. (See example below, related to *Simon vs the Homo-Sapiens Agenda*)
Find **digital images** that fit a given excerpt or chapter.	Create a **podcast**. (See example below, related to *The Hate U Give*).
Make a **digital storyboard** of key scenes from the book, with illustrations and written text added.	Summarise events and personal reflections in a **digital timeline**. (See example below, related to *Now Is the Time for Running*)
Transform text to any online media format, e.g. podcast, image, film …	Create a character's **imaginary blog**, where the character comments on events in the fiction story.

---

[77] Black-out poetry is when learners black out (digitally or with a black marker) words in an established fiction text until a poem is formed by the words which have not been blacked out. Learners can also search for poetry in online prose. Google *Searching for poetry in prose*, and see e.g. The New York Times's resources for allowing readers to create their own poetry based on news stories in the paper.

Action-oriented digital activities	Production-oriented digital activities
Find **background music** to fit specific scenes.	Make **audio recordings** of choral readings or Readers' Theatre performances of pivotal scenes from the text.
Use mobile phones to do **interviews** with peers in the roles of fictional characters.	
Contact authors through their webpages.	
Search for **background information** from online newspapers, authors' webpages, etc.	

In the classroom

The latter part of the chapter presents ideas for working with both whole books and excerpts, in combination with digital tools, and within an action- and production-oriented approach.

Working with the digital graphic novel
The Land of the Magic Flute

This award-winning, animated graphic novel[78] is an adaptation by Fons Schiedon[79] of Mozart's opera *The Magic Flute*. The digital novel, accessible online at no cost, creates a mysterious and captivating visual and aural experience, and can be suggested as a self-chosen text in a multi-text lower or upper secondary classroom. The English subject curriculum specifies in a competence aim after year 10 that learners should be able to "read, discuss and present content from various types of texts, including self-chosen texts" (Norwegian Directorate for Education and Training, 2019/2020). Self-chosen *digital* literature may increase many learners' motivation and is also an interesting genre in terms of adaptation for reluctant readers, who may find support in the novel's visual modes. If, on the other hand, the teacher decides to study this digital graphic novel as a single-text, teacher-decided class read with accompanying activities, some suggestions are presented below, as stages in a PWP[80]-approach.

---

[78] http://www.landofthemagicflute.com/
[79] http://www.fonsschiedon.com/
[80] Pre-, while- and post- stages

Table 2. Suggested activities for *The Land of the Magic Flute*

Pre-reading	While-reading	Post-reading
Suggestion 1: Present 5–6 screenshots from the graphic novel on the screen/Smartboard. Ask learners to talk about one or more of the questions below, and share their written answers on a joint Padlet[81] wall: • What could a story with these images be about, and why? • What could a tentative title for a novel with these images be, and why? • Which image do you like best, and why? • If you could set music to the images, what genre of music would you suggest, and why?	Go back to the joint Padlet wall, and revisit some of the questions. *What has changed in your answers, and why?*	Rewrite the novel by turning it into an online newspaper article with verbal text, hyperlinks and images.
Suggestion 2: Display the novel's six chapter titles on the board. Ask learners to share their immediate associations. *What kind of a story do you think this is?*	Freeze frame activity: Stop the reading at a pre-decided image. Ask learners to continue the story from that image. *What do you think happens next?*	Ask learners to create an interview, in the form of an audio file, with one of the characters from the novel.
Suggestion 3: Display the images (same as in Suggestion 1, above) on the Smartboard, and inform learners about the novel's title. Play excerpts from Mozart's *The Magic Flute*. Based on the images and the accompanying music; ask learners to discuss what kind of a text they think this is, and if the music contributes with any hints.	*What do the excerpts from the original opera add to the graphic novel?* First: Ask learners to think individually and add three keywords to a Menti[82] set up by the teacher in advance, in order to create a visual representation of learners' contributions. Next: Based on the word cloud created, the teacher facilitates a discussion in class around the initial question.	If students are familiar with the 1996 film adaptation of Shakespeare's *Romeo + Juliet*,[83] with modern setting and original language, ask them to compare the two adaptations, first in a group, then in a class discussion facilitated by the teacher. *Which of the two adaptations (Mozart or Shakespeare) do you like best, and why?*

---

81   www.padlet.com
82   https://www.mentimeter.com/
83   Directed by Baz Luhrmann.

The suggestions above include the use of digital tools either receptively, used by the teacher, or productively, used by the learners. There is additionally a focus on *intertextuality*, i.e. interrelationship between texts, and on *intermediality*, i.e. the interplay between different types of text and media (Thaler, 2008). The focus is on learners' active response to the text in question, and learners will use several language skills when engaging with the suggested activities. Working with a literary text in the form of a digital graphic novel may additionally tap into some learners' prior knowledge, or *schema*, which in turn may have a positive effect on their reading in English. In an interesting and highly relevant study, particularly for EFL teachers in secondary school, Brevik (2019) focused on a group of secondary (primarily vocational) learners, aged 16–17, described as outliers and characterised as poor readers in Norwegian, but good readers of English; their L2. Their reading performance in Norwegian was based on results from national tests and the participants explained their English reading proficiency by their own interest in and extensive use of technology outside school. Building on such interests by using digital novels in a classroom context may therefore be a way of bridging out-of-school learning with in-school practices, like reading and engaging with literature. The reader may additionally find it interesting that one of the profile groups identified by Brevik (ibid.) consisted of boys only. Boys, in particular, may find more motivation for reading and engaging with literature in the form of digital as compared to printed fiction.[84] An exception here may be graphic novels.[85] Added to this is the fact that online games and digital fiction share some of the same characteristics, as described in a previous section.

Combining the digital fiction story *The Boat* with real-world stories

The Boat[86] is an intense visual and auditory experience, adapted from one of the stories in *The Boat*, a collection of short stories written by the Vietnamese-Australian writer Nam Le and published in 2008. The online graphic version, adapted by Matt Huynh and published in 2015, is especially relevant today, in the current climate of refugees risking their lives to flee their country by crossing the Mediterranean in small boats, in the hope of a better future.

The Boat tells the story of a 16-year-old refugee girl sent off alone by her parents as a consequence of the Vietnam war.[87] Matching the main character

---

84 See chapter 6 for more about reluctant readers in general and boys more specifically.
85 See chapter 7 for more about graphic novels.
86 http://www.sbs.com.au/theboat/
87 See more about *The Boat* in chapter 7.

in age is one way for learners to engage with literature. In a classroom context, learners could be offered a choice between reading either *The Boat* or the print novel *Refugee Boy* (Zephaniah, 2001). The latter novel tells the story of a 14-year-old refugee boy from Ethiopia and Eritrea. The common theme for both novels would hence be refugees and migration. Another suggestion along the same thematic line is *The Bone Sparrow* (Fraillon, 2016), which is about a young refugee boy who has spent his whole life in a detention centre in Australia. As a post-reading activity when different learners study different texts around the same overall theme, learners could be asked to create a digital presentation of their own choice, aimed at peers who have read another text. Learners could additionally be asked to research online newspapers for authentic stories about young refugees, and integrate headlines from these news stories into their own presentation. Such a task can be seen in light of competence aims after both year 10 and VG1, stating that learners should be able to "read and compare different factual texts on the same topic from different sources and critically assess the reliability of the sources" (after VG1) or "read factual texts and assess the reliability of the sources" (after year 10) (Norwegian Directorate for Education and Training, 2019/2020). Combining fiction with real-world stories can also be a way of tapping into learners' intercultural awareness and their development of empathy. Thomas (2018, pp. 113–114) recommends adopting a global thinking approach and using literature to invite learners to see, learn about and interpret the world, challenge assumptions and be better informed. Furthermore, engaging learners in conversations around all aspects of intercultural awareness, including conversations related to attitudes, is described by Munden and Sandhaug (2017, p. 270), to be "among the most meaningful activities we can experience in the English classroom, if we dare to explore the issue". Working with an activity like the one suggested above could contribute to that.

Using an excerpt from the online version of *The House on Mango Street*

Mexican-American author Sandra Cisneros's award-winning Bildungsroman from 1983, *The House on Mango Street*, tells the story of 13-year-old Esperanza, growing up in the Hispanic quarter of Chicago, at the time a poor and patriarchal community. The novel deals with sensitive matters, related to puberty and to witnessing sexual harassment, domestic violence and racism. Another Esperanza is found in the YAF novel *Esperanza Rising*, set in Mexico in the 1930s (Ryan, 2000). We follow the life of 13-year-old Esperanza, who must flee to California with her mother after her dad is murdered. Their privileged life in Mexico is exchanged with the harsh life in a labour camp in California during the times of the Great Depression. Both novels are available as audiobooks, at no cost, on ESL bits.

The House on Mango Street[88] has become an influential and important coming-of-age novel. Cisneros's own narration of the novel on ESL bits makes it even more authentic and captivating to listen to, and this could be used with a competence aim after year 10, which says that learners should be able to "listen to and understand words and expressions in variants of English" (Norwegian Directorate for Education and Training, 2019/2020). One particularly interesting aspect of this novel is that it is told in a series of short vignettes, thus making it easy to work only with individual parts of the novel. The concrete didactic example presented below relates to English in vocational study programmes, and more particularly the education programme for *Design, arts and crafts*. The idea is to use the vignette *Hair*[89] (Cisneros, 1983) as an entry point for working with several language skills. *Hair* is a very short vignette in the novel, and can be used in a PWP stage as shown in the table below.

Table 3. Suggested activities for the vignette *Hair*, from *The House on Mango Street*

Pre-reading	While-reading	Post-reading
First, ask learners to work in small groups and suggest a list of words used to describe someone's hair, in general. Second, ask learners to discuss, in pairs, what their hair and hair style means to them. Fill in a Wordle[90] to create a joint word cloud. Use this as a point of departure for a class discussion. Finally, ask learners to describe, orally, a childhood memory related to someone's hair or hair style.	Learners read and listen to the vignette *Hair*, on ESL bits. How did you like the reading? What did you notice about the reading and about the text itself?	Ask learners to make a list of words used to describe hair in this vignette. Compare with their own list from the pre-reading stage. By using the vignette as an example text, or model text, learners next write their own text about hair, inspired by the vignette. They are encouraged to use vocabulary both from the first pre-reading activity and from the vignette, and to use the childhood memory as the content to be presented in the text. Finally, guide learners to the index of the book on the ESL bits site, and ask them to choose five other vignettes from the novel which they would like to listen to and/or read.

---

88 This novel is also discussed in chapter 6.
89 http://esl-bits.net/ESL.English.Learning.Audiobooks/House/02/default.html
90 For instance, by using a tool like http://www.wordle.net/

The activities suggested here show how teachers can engage learners in a variety of tasks, activating different language skills and tapping into the development of digital skills, by only using an excerpt from a novel. If learners have access to a free online book creator, such as Venngage,[91] they could additionally create their own digital infographic including their own hair story with accompanying illustrations and their list of relevant vocabulary. The infographics could be printed and displayed in the classroom, and be subject to a Gallery Walk. Alternatively, they could be submitted to the learning platform and "visited" online by peers, or shared on the classroom screen, from the computer.

Digital storytelling:
My Brother's Name is Jessica and other texts

Irish author John Boyne's young-adult fiction novel *My Brother's Name is Jessica* (Boyne, 2019) revolves around the 14-year-old main character Sam and his relationship to his transgender older brother. Potential differences in opinion about the novel, such as whether or not an author who is not himself a trans person is qualified to write about a transgender person, can be exploited to spur engagement and discussion, and hence language production. In a pre-reading stage, learners could be asked to search online for news articles or visit a discussion forum to establish a list of arguments from both sides. For EFL teachers who want to give voice to authors from the LGBTQ[92] community, *Proud* (Dawson, 2019) is an excellent choice.[93] This book is a collection of well-written short stories, poetry and art on the theme of pride. One of the stories; *I Hate Darcy Pemberley* (Lawler, 2019), contains several intertextual references to *Pride and Prejudice* (Austen, 1813/2002), which makes it an excellent object for comparison and discussion. Maybe learners could be asked to create a digital story presenting, or taking on the role of, the two very different Darcys. With a focus on gender and sexuality, a novel like *Boys Don't Cry* (Blackman, 2010/2011) may be another interesting choice for teenage readers engaged in a digital storytelling production.

Digital storytelling (DST) is a merger between the old storytelling tradition and the use of new technology. A digital story is a short story (2–3 minutes), where the spoken narrative is based on a written script developed by the storyteller, i.e. the learner. The learner's use of own voice, in combination with other modalities such as images and additional soundtrack, adds a

---

91 https://venngage.com/
92 LGBTQ: Lesbian, Gay, Bisexual, Transgender, Queer
93 This novel is also suggested in chapter 6, in the section about Inclusive texts.

personal element to the story told. When using Boyne's novel as the basis for a DST production in a post-reading stage, learners could be presented to the two following options for creating their digital story:

> *Either:* Take on the role as one of the characters in the novel. Tell a story, present an episode or share some reflections from your chosen character's point of view. Narrate your story in the first person.
>
> *Or:* Be yourself, and tell about your own reading experience from parts of or the whole novel. Use first-person narration.

These prompts are fairly general and therefore transferable to any of the literary texts mentioned above. The multi-award-winning novel *The Boy in the Striped Pyjamas* (Boyne, 2006) is another YAF novel that lends itself easily to creating digital stories, as the learners can take on the role of different characters to share their perspective on the novel's dramatic plot. That novel, along with *Wonder* (Palacio, 2012), can be recommended as potentially very interesting and engaging reading material for lower secondary EFL learners, in particular.

Creating digital stories from their own favourite reads is another relevant DST task for both primary and secondary learners. Normann (2012) tells about how a shy year 8 learner who did not feel comfortable speaking English aloud in class produced a fascinating and personal digital story about her reading of Roald Dahl's *Matilda* (Dahl, 1988). Being allowed to practise and demonstrate her oral English skills through digital storytelling became important in terms of developing self-confidence for this learner. Another example relates to year 9 learners tasked with creating a digital story about their favourite book from early childhood, or a book that had been read aloud to them. The latter was the case with one of the boys in class, who presented a digital story related to his bedtime favourite, *Good Night, Alfie Atkins*[94] (Bergström, 2008).

Digital storytelling has the potential to bring together various elements of the EFL subject, including literature, communication and language learning, with the digital element. It combines the traditional literacies of reading, writing and oral skills with the new, 21st century skills and critical literacy. As a method, it can be used by the teacher in a flipped classroom approach,

---

94 In Norwegian: "Albert Åberg", a character created by the Swedish author Gunilla Bergström.

but the most interesting use of digital storytelling is when it is used by learners, in a production and presentation role, as in the examples above. DST offers learners an alternative way of presenting both knowledge about a topic and personal reflections, and the overall learning potential of DST is always greater than the end product itself (Normann, 2011). As an alternative way of engaging with a literary text, digital storytelling is, in my experience, unrivalled. It additionally contributes to empowering learners, as DST processes are very student-active ways of working. Along the same lines, Silseth (2013) comments that media production in general, and digital storytelling more specifically, can potentially serve to expand learners' access to resources for meaning making and learning in educational practices, but that this potential must be realised in practice. The examples shared above can be helpful for teachers who want to exploit this potential for meaning making.

To learn more about the steps in a DST process, see for instance *Digital storytelling in the classroom* (Ohler, 2008) or search online for guidelines.

Micro fiction and the Twitter platform, with *Simon vs. the Homo Sapiens Agenda*

American author Becky Albertalli's much acclaimed coming-of-age novel (Albertalli, 2015) is also a well-written coming-out story, presenting a serious topic with respect, humour and wit. The novel is written as a series of emails between the protagonist Simon, a gay high-school boy, and an anonymous closeted classmate, whom he has fallen in love with. Simon is forced to come out after being blackmailed by a peer who discovers his emails.

One digital-didactic suggestion for a while- or post-reading activity with this YAF text could be to build on the use of social media and online communication, which already holds a very central role in the novel. As a way of engaging creatively with the story, learners could be asked to work in groups, focusing on one character each from the book and composing their own *tweet fiction stories* as these could have been written by the group's chosen character. The group members will need to discuss which aspects or episodes from the original text they want to present in the form of short flash-fiction stories using the Twitter platform. They additionally need to discuss how their Twitter story will be written. The limit of 280 characters forces learners to think and plan their tweets carefully, but at the same time, reading and writing such a short chunk of words may also appear as a very doable reading and writing activity for all learners. Another aspect that learners need to discuss is how to make a cohesive story, despite the fact that it will be presented as a series of single tweets. As a pre-writing activity, learners could be asked to study Grant Faulkner's entry on the New York Times blog *Going Long. Going Short* (Faulkner, 2013), and discuss the main points that Faulkner points to, related to various types of micro fiction or flash fiction. The teacher should additionally create a class hashtag, i.e. a searchable keyword for learners to use and follow, making it easy for everyone to read peer groups' tweet stories. An example of a hashtag could be #workingwithsimoninclass.

Using the Twitter platform to create *six-word stories* summarising an idea, a paragraph or a chapter is another suggestion. Six-word stories, as a genre, is probably the shortest type of flash fiction, and the following example is said to be written by Ernest Hemingway: "For sale: baby shoes, never worn". Producing such micro stories as a collaborative writing activity will both challenge learners and allow them to engage creatively with the literary text. In a pre-writing stage, learners could be encouraged to check the Twitter hashtag *sixwordstories*[95] for inspiration, or read or follow the Twitter group *sixwordstories*.[96]

As noted by e.g. Brox (2020, p. 94), learners collaborating on a piece of writing must necessarily engage in some kind of communication with each other, such as negotiating what to write and how. In Brox (ibid.), collaborative writing was related to creating webpages using a wiki as a collaborative tool. However, even for short-writing activities using the Twitter platform, interaction and communication between the writers is required. The smaller the space, the more negotiation is required and the more language is produced. Several language skills can thus be integrated into even very short digital writing activities.

The final suggestion presented in this section relates to using the Twitter platform and the specific class hashtag as a platform for a joint, written class discussion, based on the literary text studied. To get the learners started, the teacher could post a quote from the novel, followed by a question, as in these examples:

> "Sometimes it seems like everyone knows who I am, except me" (Albertalli, 2015, p. 59). *What does this quote make you think of?*
>
> "White shouldn't be the default any more than straight should be the default. There shouldn't even be a default" (Albertalli, 2015, p. 269). *Why do you agree or disagree with this quote?*

---

95 https://twitter.com/hashtag/sixwordstories
96 https://twitter.com/sixwordstories

With today's global spread of the Black Lives Matter protests, the latter quote also invites learners to go beyond the literary text, and make links to current real-world examples. Such an activity could be a way of triggering learners' critical thinking. Allowing them to use social media also for in-school purposes could help learners engage with the literary text. Teachers may experience that using Twitter as a discussion platform can change the classroom dynamic positively. It may additionally make it easier for some of the learners to take an active part in the discussion, as writing gives more time for thinking, both about the content and about the language used to express the content.

Podcasting with *The Hate U Give*

Black American author and former rapper Angie Thomas entitled her debut novel after the *THUG life*[97] concept of Tupac Shakur, the American rapper and artist better known as 2Pac. The acronym symbolises a life where you have nothing and have to go through many struggles to succeed, overcoming all obstacles to reach your aim. The story is narrated by Starr, the 16-year-old protagonist raised in a poor, predominantly Black neighbourhood, attending an elite private school in a predominantly white area of the city. Starr witnesses a white police officer shooting and killing her childhood friend Khalil, and speaks up about the shooting publicly.

Both the print version (Thomas, 2017) and the 2018 film adaption of *The Hate U Give* have received critical acclaim, and can easily be worked with in a cross-curricular topic focusing on race relations in the US. As a digital-didactic suggestion for a post-reading activity with this novel, learners may produce a podcast, in the form of an edited audio file submitted to the school's learning platform. When learners become multimedia producers of their own podcasts, opportunities open up for practising language skills, source criticism and interviewing techniques. The following guidelines for creating a short podcast can be used:

1. Intro monologue (say who you are, what you're going to talk about today, etc.): app. 30 seconds
2. Intro music jingle: max. 10 seconds
3. Context and background of today's topic: max. 1 min.
4. Introduction of today's guest(s): app. 30 seconds
5. Interview between radio host and guest(s): 2–4 min. State the aim of the interview.

---

97 THUG life: The Hate U Give Little Infants Fucks Everybody.

6. Closing remarks (thank the audience for listening, thank guests, talk briefly about the next show, etc.): max. 1 min.
7. Closing music jingle: max. 10 seconds

In groups of three, learners can be asked to choose a specific episode from the novel to focus on in their podcast, and also decide the roles to be played. Giving learners some freedom can contribute to a sense of agency and hence increased motivation for the task (Harmer, 2007/2015). In addition, it is a way of adapting the assignment to learners with different proficiency levels. Own mobile phones or tools like Audacity[98] or Garageband[99] can be used for the recording.

Producing a podcast linked to the novel can be seen as a way for learners to share a subjective literary interpretation of the text. The interpretation is, however, also coloured by how learners have been working with the novel in the pre- and while-reading stages, and hence by the teacher's role during the process. Learners' potential for developing a deeper understanding for a topic addressed in a literary text depends to a large degree on the teacher's role (Normann, forthcoming). Giving learners opportunities to work independently with digital tools as part of their engagement with a literary text does not, however, mean that the teacher becomes superfluous. A professional, digitally competent teacher (Kelentric et al., 2017) will, on the contrary, see the need of facilitating learners' learning through a variation of contextualisation.

Reading *The Hate U Give* and creating a podcast based on it also offers rich opportunities for focusing on language awareness and language noticing. A particularly interesting language aspect of this novel is, for instance, main character Starr's ability to code switch between her home and private school. Extensive use of slang adds to the portrayal of urban realities presented in the novel. Finally, attention to appropriateness, learners' attitudes to language use and forms of creative expression, as well as the difference between fluency and accuracy (Rindal, 2019), may be other relevant linguistic aspects the teacher wants to draw learners' attention to in the podcasting activity.

Digital timeline with *Now Is the Time for Running*

14-year-old Deo and his handicapped older brother, Innocent, are raised in a village in Zimbabwe, and love to play football. One day soldiers arrive, and everything changes. Deo and Innocent are the only survivors, and must flee the village. We follow the boys on their dramatic journey towards South

---

98 https://www.audacityteam.org/
99 https://www.apple.com/mac/garageband/

Africa, hoping to find safety. Hardships, hope, survival, cultural differences and xenophobia are some thematic keywords of the novel. It is told in the present tense, which creates a sense of immediacy and makes it easy for adolescent readers to follow the story and engage with the characters.

South African author Michael Williams's young adult fiction novel (Williams, 2011) builds on real-life events that happened in South Africa in 2008.[100] The book is suited, language-wise, for the oldest learners in lower secondary. Because we follow Deo for a period of about two years, it could be an interesting digital activity for the learners to use an interactive timeline[101] to work with one or more of the following tasks:

- Trace the brothers' journey and the hardship they must endure
- Present events in Deo's life
- Map out Deo's character development

These tasks can also be used as starting points for group or plenary discussions, related to some of the novel's themes. Deeper reflections from learners can be encouraged by asking them to add *descriptions* above the horizontal line and *personal reflections* below the line, as visualised below.

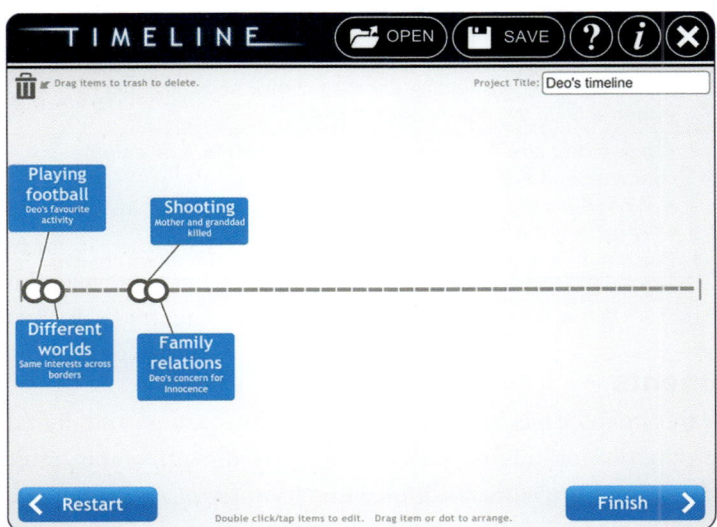

Figure 1. Interactive timeline example.

---

100 See chapter 5 for more about Now Is the Time for Running.
101 Digital timeline: http://www.readwritethink.org/files/resources/interactives/timeline_2/

Adding the latter requirement will stretch the learners further. Figure 1 shows a very basic start of building an interactive timeline with both descriptions of events and personal reflections from the reader. The comments added are shown just with headings in the figure reproduced here, but are clickable online, a feature which allows teachers and peers to see the complete contributions added by the learner. Both text and images can be added for each item, and the final timeline can be saved, printed and shared. Other more advanced timeline tools, for instance the timeline feature in Padlet,[102] support any type of digital content, including images, video, audio, documents, files, webpages or even other padlets. This invites multimodal text creation. A few additional suggestions for timeline-based activities are presented below.

Table 4. Suggestions for timeline-based activities

Activity	Short description
Fiction vs real-world	• Above the line, learners add written information related to the book or excerpt. • Below the line, they add either pictures or illustrations fitting the information above the line. Alternatively, they search online for current, real-world examples similar to the information they have shared from the novel, and add real-world headlines below the line.
Significant quotes	• Teacher distributes separate chapters to small groups of learners. • Learners discuss and decide on a few significant quotes. • Quotes are added above the line. • Below the line, learners justify each choice of quotes and its importance in the story's overall plot.

Character development	• Alone or in pairs, learners trace the development of a single character and add short items describing:
	  • What does the character do?
	  • What might this imply?
	• Presentation in plenary class or groups of all timelines created.

Final comments

The focus for this chapter has been on secondary EFL learners and digital action- and production-oriented approaches to working with young adult fiction, as an alternative to a more traditional literary analysis. An overall aim has been to show how a range of novels, whether whole texts or excerpts, can be used with various digital-didactic approaches to cover competence aims from all three core elements of the English subject in LK20: *Communication*,

---

102 Padlet: https://padlet.com/

Language learning and *Meeting with English-language text*. In the examples presented throughout this chapter, developing learners' digital skills is interwoven with other, more traditional literacy skills.

References

Adams, D. (1979/1997). *The Hitchhiker's Guide to the Galaxy*. Penguin.

Albertalli, B. (2015). *Simon vs. the Homo Sapiens Agenda*. Harper Collins.

Alexie, S. (2007). *The Absolutely True Diary of a Part-Time Indian*. Little, Brown Books for Young Readers.

Austen, J. (1813/2002). *Pride and Prejudice*. Penguin Books.

Bergström, G. (2008). *God natt, Albert Åberg*. Cappelen Damm.

Blackman, M. (2010/2011). *Boys Don't Cry*. Corgi.

Boyne, J. (2006). *The Boy in the Striped Pyjamas*. David Fickling Books.

Boyne, J. (2019). *My Brother's Name is Jessica*. Penguin Books.

Brevik, L.M. (2019). Gamers, surfers, social media users: Unpacking the role of interest in English. *Journal of Computer Assisted Learning, 35*, 595–606. doi:10.1111/jcal.12362

Brox, H. (2020). Collaborative writing with online tools. In H. Bøhn, M. Dypedahl, & G.-A. Myklevold (Eds.), *Teaching and Learning English* (pp. 92–105). Cappelen Damm Akademisk.

Chbosky, S. (1999). *The Perks of Being a Wallflower*. Simon & Schuster.

Cisneros, S. (1983). *The House on Mango Street*. Vintage.

Council of Europe. (2001). *Common European Framework of Reference for Languages: Learning, teaching, assessment (CEFR)*. Cambridge University Press.

Dahl, R. (1988). *Matilda*. Jonathan Cape.

Dawson, J. (Ed.) (2019). *PROUD*. Stripes Publishing Limited.

Faulkner, G. (2013). *Going Long. Going Short*. Retrieved from https://opinionator.blogs.nytimes.com/2013/09/30/going-long-going-short/

Fraillon, Z. (2016). *The Bone Sparrow*. Disney-Hyperion.

Green, J. (2005). *Looking for Alaska*. Dutton Juvenile.

Haddon, M. (2003). *The Curious Incident of the Dog in the Night-Time*. Jonathan Cape.

Harmer, J. (2007/2015). *The Practice of English Language Teaching*. Longman Harlow.

Kelentric, M., Helland, K., & Arstorp, A.T. (2017). *Professional Digital Competence Framework for Teachers*. The Norwegian Centre for ICT in Education.

Kidd, S.M. (2001). *The Secret Life of Bees*. Penguin Books.

Lawler, K. (2019). I Hate Darcy Pemberley. In J. Dawson (Ed.), *Proud*. Stripes Publishing Limited.

Munden, J., & Sandhaug, C. (2017). *Engelsk for Secondary School*. Gyldendal Akademisk.

Normann, A. (2011). *Digital storytelling in second language learning. A qualitative study on students' reflections on potentials for learning*. (Master's thesis), Norwegian University of Science and Technology, Trondheim.

Normann, A. (2012). «Det var en gang ei jente som ikke ville snakke engelsk». Bruken av digital storytelling i språkopplæringa. In K. Holte Haug, G. Jamissen, & C. Ohlmann (Eds.), *Digtalt fortalte historier. Refleksjon for læring*. Cappelen Damm Akademisk forlag.

Normann, A. (forthcoming). Digital storytelling og podcast; digital-didaktiske tilnærminger i arbeid med muntlige ferdigheter i engelskfaget. In M.A. Letnes, & F.M. Røkenes (Eds.), *Digital teknologi for læring og undervisning i skolen*. Universitetsforlaget.

Norwegian Directorate for Education and Training. (2019/2020). English subject curriculum (ENG01-04). Retrieved from https://www.udir.no/lk20/eng01-04

Ohler, J. (2008). *Digital Storytelling in The Classroom. New Media Pathways to Literacy, Learning and Creativity*. Corwin Press.

Palacio, R.J. (2012). *Wonder*. Alfred A. Knopf.

Paterson, K. (1977). *Bridge to Terabithia*. Thomas Y. Crowell Company.

Rindal, U. (2019). Communicative oral skills. In T. Burner, C. Carlsen, & K. Kverndokken (Eds.), *101 ways to work with communicative skills. Theoretical and practical approaches in the English classroom* (pp. 37–52). Fagbokforlaget.

Rustad, H.K. (2012). *Digital litteratur. En innføring*. Cappelen Damm Akademisk.

Ryan, P.M. (2000). *Esperanza Rising*. Scholastic.

Sachar, L. (1988). *Holes*. Farrar, Straus and Giroux.

Sauro, S., & Sundmark, B. (2018). Critically examining the use of blog-based fanfiction in the advanced language classroom. *ReCall, 31*(1), 40–55. doi: https://doi.org/10.1017/S0958344018000071

Silseth, K. (2013). Surviving the impossible: Studying students' constructions of digital stories on World War II. *Learning, Culture and Social Interaction, 2*, 155–170. doi:https://doi.org/10.1016/j.lcsi.2013.04.004

Surkamp, C. (2012). Teaching literature. In M. Middeke, T. Müller, C. Wald, & H. Zapf (Eds.), *English and American Studies. Theory and Practice* (pp. 488–495). Springer.

Thaler, E. (2008). *Teaching English Literature*. Ferdinand Schöningh.

Thomas, A. (2017). *The Hate U Give*. Harper Collins.

Thomas, P. (2018). *Approaches to Learning and Teaching Literature in English: A Toolkit for International Teachers*. Cambridge University Press.

Vestli, E.N. (2008). *Fra sokkel til klasserom: litteraturens plass i fremmedspråkundervisningen* (Vol. nr. 13 / august 2008). Fremmedspråksenteret.

Williams, M. (2011). *Now Is the Time for Running*. Little, Brown Books for Young Readers.

Zephaniah, B. (2001). *Refugee Boy*. Bloomsbury Publishing.

Table 5. Website references from chapter 8

Author	Date	Title of page	Site name	URL
	n.d.	Scoop.it!	https://www.scoop.it/	https://www.scoop.it/
	n.d.	elink	https://elink.io/	https://elink.io/
Bergensavisen	2014, May, 23	Hans beste på Twitter blir bok	www.ba.no	https://www.ba.no/nyheter/hans-beste-pa-twitter-blir-bok/s/1-41-7373839
Jennifer Egan	2012	"Black Box"	www.newyorker.com	https://www.newyorker.com/magazine/2012/06/04/black-box-2
Lesesenteret /The Norwegian Reading Centre	n.d.	Lesesenteret	https://lesesenteret.uis.no	https://lesesenteret.uis.no/#Skole
Nasjonalt senter for skriveopplæring og skriveforskning /The Norwegian Centre for Writing Education and Research	n.d.	Skrivesenteret	http://www.skrivesenteret.no/	http://www.skrivesenteret.no/
	n.d.	Project Gutenberg	https://www.gutenberg.org/	https://www.gutenberg.org/
	n.d.	LibriVox. Free public domain audiobooks.	https://librivox.org/	https://librivox.org/
	n.d.	ESL-Bits. English language learning. Listen and read	http://esl-bits.net/	http://esl-bits.net/index.htm
Senter for IKT I utdanningen	2015	Hensiktsmessig bruk av IKT I klasserommet-en veileder	www.udir.no	https://www.udir.no/globalassets/filer/veileder_hensiktsmessig_bruk_bm_lav.pdf
Fons Schiedon	n.d.	The Land of the Magic Flute	http://www.landofthemagicflute.com/	http://www.landofthemagicflute.com/
Fons Schiedon	n.d.	Fons Schiedon	http://www.fonsschiedon.com/	http://www.fonsschiedon.com/
	n.d.	Padlet	www.padlet.com	www.padlet.com
The Mentimeter Team	n.d.	Mentimeter	https://www.mentimeter.com/	https://www.mentimeter.com/
Matt Huynh	n.d.	The Boat	http://www.sbs.com.au/theboat/	http://www.sbs.com.au/theboat/
	n.d	Wordle	http://www.wordle.net/	http://www.wordle.net/
	n.d.	Venngage	https://venngage.com/	https://venngage.com/
	n.d.	#sixwordstories	twitter.com	https://twitter.com/hashtag/six-wordstories
	n.d.	Six Word Stories	twitter.com	https://twitter.com/sixwordstories
	n.d.	Audacity	https://www.audacityteam.org/	https://www.audacityteam.org/
Apple.com	n.d.	GarageBand for Mac	https://www.apple.com/mac/garageband/	https://www.apple.com/mac/garageband/
	n.d.	Timeline	www.readwritethink.org	http://www.readwritethink.org/files/resources/interactives/time-line_2/

9
Film in the English classroom

Andy Gordon

Why film?

The British Film Institute (BFI) suggests the study of film and television is important because "we live in a world **saturated** by audio-visual texts" (BFI 2000: 4, my emphasis); another commentator uses the term "bombarded" (Stafford, 2011, p. 2). This recognises that audio-visual images are a large and significant part of national and international culture – for learners of English such texts and images may constitute their most pervasive exposure to the language and its cultural products. This includes global exposure to values and behaviours encoded in these texts and images – they influence, persuade and seduce. Yet despite this bombardment, there remains a certain resistance to thinking critically about film and television; the idea of a "window on the world"[103] is a persistent one. Learners need help to learn how viewers – consumers – of this material are influenced, persuaded and seduced; how images make meaning, as well as what they mean. This chapter aims to show some ways to facilitate and encourage the move from merely passive watching to being able to analyse, understand and critique.

---

[103] "Television provides a window on the world", *Longman Dictionary of Contemporary English*. See for example Izod 1984: 6–8 for a critique of this idea.

How to study film

The focus of this chapter is on the relationship between film and literature. It is useful to consider major differences between the way a printed text communicates and the way a film text communicates. While a printed text uses either one or two methods of communication: the written word, sometimes with illustrations; a film text can use up to five overlapping methods simultaneously. John Izod (1984, p. 95), among others, points out that these are:

1. The moving visual image
2. The spoken soundtrack
3. Other recorded sounds
4. Music
5. Graphics – any *written* information shown on the screen

These may be summarised as either **visual** methods, what is seen (1 and 5), or **auditory**, what is heard (2, 3 and 4). Two further elements of viewer perception are important:

- Association (what the viewer thinks of in relation to what they see and hear)
- Putting/pulling it all together (what it might mean)

In other words, how is what is seen, heard and thought of to be interpreted by the viewer?

It is not necessary (and time usually will not allow) to show an entire film in class. A single film sequence or even a single shot can be examined to bring out significant aspects of the text. The BFI proposes eight classroom activities/teaching techniques to facilitate the study of film's distinctive features.

1. Freeze frame	Use the pause button to freeze a single frame. Review all the different elements – people, costumes, objects, etc. How are they positioned/located? What is the camera doing?
2. Sound and image	Play a short sequence hiding the screen and concentrate on what is heard. What can be inferred just from the sound (e.g., indoor or outdoor, action or mood)? Then show the same sequence with visuals – what new information can be gained?
3. "Spot the shots"	Show a film trailer (often included on a DVD, or available through YouTube). Try to work out the number of shots, where each ends, and how transitions are managed. This is the start of thinking about editing.

4. "Top and tail"	Beginnings and endings, including credits. Can viewers tell what kind of film this is going to be from its opening sequence? What about the closing sequence? Location/s may be indicated, for example. What does any music suggest? Beginnings and ends of sequences within a film can also be considered.
5. Attention seeking	How has the film been marketed? Advertisements, posters, trailers – these affect audience expectations. How do these aim to attract audiences?
6. Generic translation	Compare a passage from a printed text with the equivalent on screen – the BFI says that filmmakers must solve such problems as "first-person narrative voice or changes in point of view – how can these be rendered visually?" (2000: 17)
7. Cross-media comparison	Compare the treatment of a similar event, such as a war, a murder or a crime in newspapers and in a film – what is or is not appropriate to each form?
8. Simulation	This might be as apparently simple and basic as thinking about who could be cast as a favourite character, hero or villain – why would the actor be chosen? Alternatively, it might take a more elaborate form such as putting together a storyboard or a "pitch" for a film of a favourite story, comic or game.

The discussion that follows will draw on a number of these teaching techniques. Some will appeal more or seem more useful, depending on the particular film or genre taught. A few terms and ideas specific to film are helpful in discussing moving image texts. A minimum of specialised vocabulary might include:

Close-up, and its opposite, **long shot**, to indicate the distance between the camera (and therefore the audience) and who or what is being shown
Mise-en-scène (= "what is put in the scene") – everything (such as people, things, places; and details such as costume, colour, lighting) that appears in a particular shot or sequence of shots
Flashback and **flashforward** (recalling or anticipating what has already been or is later to be seen and/or heard)
Shot (a single image or scene[104])

---

104 The term "scene" is inconsistently used in this discussion, to refer both to a particular shot or sequence of shots, and to the "scenes" into which the DVD is (helpfully) divided, something common to many (most?) DVDs now – useful to assist navigation around a film when (as here) certain elements are to be picked out. While the DVD of *Skellig* uses the term "scene", and the DVD of *The Kite Runner* has "scene selection", the DVD of *Billy Elliot* refers to "chapters". Selecting "Disc menu" on the remote takes you straight to the section.

Didactic rationale

The following discussion of three adaptations, *Skellig*, *The Kite Runner* and *Billy Elliot*, aims to show some of the ways in which adaptations may be taught and studied, with several overall aims:

- To develop an understanding and an awareness of some of the ways in which film works, how it conveys meaning and how it may be interpreted or "read";
- To consider an adaptation as an interpretation itself, with some attention to differences between adaptation and source;
- To introduce some useful and relevant approaches, techniques and terminology to facilitate and enhance the process of reading both source and adaptation;
- To identify and draw upon a range of material, both critical and pedagogical, appropriate to the selected examples, and applicable to other examples of adaptation.

Some relevant competence aims from LK20 may be:

- After year 7, 10 and VG1, respectively: "use different digital resources and other aids in language learning, text creation and interaction".
- After VG 1, both in general and in vocational studies: "discuss and reflect on form, content and language features and literary devices in cultural forms of expression in English from different media in the English-speaking world, including music, film and gaming".

(Norwegian Directorate for Education and Training, 2019/20)

For each film, key scenes are identified, and a sample lesson plan is outlined for *Skellig*.

Recent adaptations have been chosen as examples here for three main reasons. Firstly, the sheer number of films based on books (and, more recently, books based on films). Secondly, to select high-quality texts suitable for teaching to young audiences, although each also deals with sensitive personal, social or political topics. Thirdly, the argument that the relationship between the two is a dynamic one, in which regarding (and judging) an adaptation as a more or less "faithful" version of an "original" is less productive than thinking of it as an interpretation or a reading. As Brian McFarlane says, "the critic who quibbles at failures of fidelity is really saying no more than: 'This reading of the original does not tally with mine in these and these ways'" (1996, p. 9, quoted in Stafford, 2011, p. 141), with the added implication that "my" reading is better (or right). Anyone studying a foreign language learns quickly that even where possible, a literal translation may not be the best. So, the view that adaptation (which basically means "change", as Stafford points out (2011, p. 142) is a kind of translation is fundamental to this discussion. Many commentators argue for something called "film language", to highlight this idea.[105]

Skellig (1998, 2009)

Regarded as a contemporary classic, David Almond's novel *Skellig* (1998)[106] won both the Carnegie Medal and the Whitbread Children's Book Award and was adapted as a film by A.J. Jankel (2009). In the following discussion, techniques, terminology, and approaches will be examined in detail, as a template for *The Kite Runner* and *Billy Elliot*.[107] In *Skellig*, a comparison of openings is recommended for thematic reasons. The technique of freezing the frame so that one shot or image remains on the screen for some time will allow discussion of the features of that shot/image.

Almond's novel begins with the statement, "I found him in the garage on a Sunday afternoon… That's when I saw him" (1998: 1–2). The film adaptation, however, begins with shots of birds flying, high in the sky, as the credits roll. So one difference between the two is immediately apparent: the novel puts Michael and Skellig ("I"/"him") into focus, though neither is yet named.[108] The film foregrounds the birds (see ill. 1).

Freeze the frame about ten seconds in (ill. 1). The following questions may generate initial discussion:

- What do you see in this shot?
- Where are they in relation to the camera (and therefore to us) – near or far away (that is, in close-up or in long shot)?
- What do you think of when you think of birds?
- What is the effect, what is the meaning?

---

105 One highly influential French critic, Christian Metz, gave the title *Film Language* to his 1968 book on cinema.
106 See chapter 5 for further discussion of *Skellig*.
107 All three of the texts discussed here have won multiple awards: *Billy Elliot* won a BAFTA for Best British Film in 2001; the novel *The Kite Runner* won the American Library Association Alex award in 2004, and the film was nominated for the Golden Globe: Best Foreign Film in 2007; Almond's novel *Skellig* won the Whitbread Children's Book of the Year and the Carnegie Medal in 1998; Jankel's film won the Cinekid Award in 2009, and was nominated for several Best Television awards.
108 This may be a point at which to say that first-person narration is something which it is difficult to do in film (see, e.g., Chatman, 1978, p. 9, 160, 247, for instance).

Illustration 1. This is the image to begin discussion with. It is clearer when moving. *Skellig* (2009) DVD-version. © 2009 Grace Films Ltd

Answers may be simple and straightforward: birds, the sky (there is nothing else in the *mise-en-scène*), they are far away (no close-ups), but the third question requires association, though again answers might be obvious. Perhaps flight, freedom and nature? For the final question: does the distance between the viewer and the birds suggest a distance between human beings and the natural world? What about flying? Something that human beings can't do, but have dreamed of? Jonathan Ridley claims that "humankind has always had a desire to fly" (Ridley 2019), citing the Greek myth of Daedalus and Icarus, or Leonardo da Vinci designing helicopters in the fifteenth century.

What might be the meaning of the wish to fly? Thomas Foster (2014) suggests "in general, flying is freedom, not only freedom from specific circumstances, but from those more general burdens that tie us down" (Foster 2014: 135). Flying has been a recurrent motif in British children's fiction, for example J.M. Barrie's *Peter Pan*, Roald Dahl's *The Magic Finger* or E. Nesbit's *Five Children and It* (1902), in which "it" is able to grant wishes – and the five children's first wish is for wings, although they fear they will be mistaken for angels.

To return to the opening sequence's emphasis on birds – there are over twenty-five references to birds in Almond's novel, ranging from street names

Illustration 2. Skellig (Tim Roth) with Michael (Bill Milner) during the film's spectacular flying sequence. *Skellig* (2009) DVD-version. © 2009 Grace Films Ltd

(Michael's family's new house, with its garage where Skellig is first discovered, is in Falconer Road (Almond, 1998, p. 1), the derelict house where Michael and Mina conceal Skellig is in Crow Road (Almond 1998: 39), to the blackbirds that hatch their young in the course of the story, and the owls who feed Skellig. In response to the children's repeated question, "Who/what are you?" (Almond, 1998, pp. 29, 74, 131, 158, for example), he eventually tells them:

> Something like you, something like a beast, something like a bird, something like an angel. (Almond 1998, p. 158)

The equivalent self-description comes almost at the end of the film, when Mina and Michael see Skellig for the last time. But it takes the form of a dialogue:

> *Skellig:* I'm something like you – something like a bird.
> *Michael:* Something like an angel?
> *Skellig:* Yeah. Something like that.[109]

---

109 DVD Scene 12, approximately 3½ minutes into the scene.

The motif of birds is pursued and developed in the film in somewhat different ways. As well as the birds at the beginning, small details such as birds on the wallpaper in the Falconer Road house (emphasised with a close-up – one of the functions of the close-up) are included, along with the owls who feed Skellig.

The opening film shot of birds flying is followed immediately by a short sequence showing Michael at the top of the tower, about to jump. This is an example of *flash-forward*, anticipation of something to be shown later in the film. It provokes the question of why he intends to jump, something which will not be explained until the spectacular flying sequence mentioned above. Michael jumps to make Skellig prove that he can fly – but in Skellig saving Michael's life as well as the baby's there is reciprocity and mutual aid. This is perhaps more subtly dealt with in the book, where Skellig eventually thanks Michael and Mina for "giving me my life again" (Almond, 1998, p. 158).

The opening sequence is followed by shots of the shed (a garage in the book), inviting the viewer to wonder what the connection is between the derelict building and the action that is to come (The entire opening sequence discussed here lasts only a few minutes, but can generate substantial discussion relevant to the story that follows.)

Illustration 3. Skellig (Tim Roth) with Michael's baby sister – Michael's mother comments, "[T]here was such tenderness in his eyes... I knew it would be alright" (Almond 1998: 150). *Skellig* (2009) DVD-version. © 2009 Grace Films Ltd

The idea and the theme of flight can be followed up further – Michael's mother's dream in the novel of Skellig coming to the baby in the hospital (Almond, 1998, pp. 149–150) is actually shown (as fact?) in the film;[110] Michael and Mina first experiencing flight with Skellig, much less spectacular in the book, than in the film (Almond, 1998, pp. 110–11), or the three feathers left by Skellig for the children (Almond, 1998, pp. 162), a detail omitted from the film.

> ### SUGGESTED LESSON PLAN BASED ON THE ABOVE
> (Timings are approximate: if an activity is going well, the time can be extended. It may be found that there is enough material here for two lessons rather than one).
>
> ### MATERIALS
> - *Skellig* DVD;
> - Either duplicated copies or screen slides of
>   - the five methods of meaning;
>   - A.J. Jankel's comments on the flying sequence;
>   - Perhaps Benioff's words "the central story";
> - Duplicated copies of the opening paragraph ("I found him in the garage… worrying about the baby" (Almond, 1988, pp. 1–2), and of Michael's mother's account of her dream (149–151, "Another dream… I smiled and nodded").
>
> **5 minutes** Introduce the idea of *adaptation*, perhaps bringing out two key points
> - an adaptation will always differ from its source and is best thought of as an *interpretation* of that source;
> - the five methods of signification detailed above.
>
> **5 minutes** Consider the opening of the novel (first paragraph (6 lines) – stress the reference to Dr Death and concerns for the baby) to illustrate one point of difference between a printed text and a film text – first-person narration. For discussion – how might the opening be filmed?
>
> **5 minutes** Show the opening sequence – all three sections: the birds; Michael at the top of the tower; the shed. Do the three coming together suggest possible connections? The term *flash-forward* can be introduced in connection with the second section.

---

110 DVD Scene 11, about 7 minutes, 10 seconds into the scene (it lasts for about three minutes). It is useful here to consider the effect of the music, identified earlier as one of the means by which film can communicate meaning – music is used sparingly in this film, so it is worth thinking about what it adds (in terms, say, of mood) to this particular scene.

5 minutes Some details about the text (story); these can be minimal, such as
- Michael's discovery of Skellig in the shed/garage;
- The baby's illness, and its severity.

5–10 minutes Freeze frame on the birds (the BFI suggests that the objective is to demonstrate that 'everything that is seen and heard is chosen deliberately… in order to signify specific things' (2000:16). The image is shown above (ill. 1).

What are the associations of birds and flying? It might be useful to show some of the cover images of different editions (reproduced below).

5–10 minutes The main flying sequence (DVD scene 11, about 5:30 into the scene) – why does the film make this so spectacular?

Comment by A.J. Jankel, director:
There are a lot of things in the book that were just alluded to, that I felt really needed to be properly illustrated on film… the main one being that you never really get to see Skellig fly in the book… and so that was one of the major things that we had to address… We don't exactly know what Skellig is, but he's not that winged white wishy-feathered angel, if you like, he's not that character.

5–10 minutes The sequence showing Skellig with the baby in the hospital – also discussed above (also scene 11, about 7.10 from the start of the scene) to compare with the extract from the novel.

5 minutes Conclusions?
- Skellig as (some kind of) angel;
- Skellig saving the life of the baby.

If time allows, the session could end with a brief look at the short sequence where the schoolchildren are singing Robbie Williams' "Angels" (1997) (DVD Scene 2), and introduce the term *salvation* if unfamiliar.

Reproduced by permission of Hodder Children's Books, an imprint of Hachette Children's Group, Carmelite House, 50 Victoria Embankment, London, EC4Y 0DZ

Illustration 4. The cover of the Hodder paperback edition of *Skellig*. It is clear here that it represents an angel.

Several other topics can be discussed in *Skellig*, such as schooling. Mina is home-schooled; in the novel she has a number of disparaging comments to make about mainstream education, citing poet William Blake's "How can a bird that is born for joy/Sit in a cage and sing" to support her views.[111]

Home-schooling remains a somewhat controversial issue – though legal in Austria, Australia, Canada, Denmark, Finland, France, Ireland, Norway, the UK and the USA, it is illegal in Germany, the Netherlands and Spain, while in Sweden it is governed by such stringent regulations as effectively to constitute a ban. Discussion may generate reflections on what education in general, and schools in particular, are actually *for*. Mina and her mother seem to subscribe to the view trenchantly expressed by John Taylor Gatto:

> Public schooling serves no other tangible purpose than state-sponsored babysitting of people from age 6 to age 18 for homogenization, indoctrination and conditioning. (Gatto, 2017, p. 53)[112]

The topic of education can for instance be linked to a competence aim after year 10, stating that learners will "explore and describe ways of living, ways of thinking, communication patterns and diversity in the English-speaking world" (Norwegian Directorate of Education and Training, 2019). The same topic is imaginatively and creatively explored also in *Skellig*'s companion novel, *My Name Is Mina*.

Ideas of flight and flying also connect *Skellig* with the second text to be discussed here – Khaled Hosseini's *The Kite Runner*, where it is the kite of the title that exemplifies the motif of flight, and a number of issues identified so far, such as freedom, are also relevant. In representing a main character who is unlike us, and who is probably not even human, *Skellig* is concerned with difference, with what theorists have termed *otherness*.

---

111 Blake, William (1794), "The School Boy", *Songs of Innocence and of Experience*. Earlier in the poem, Blake, writing from the child's point of view, has expressed a deep dissatisfaction with institutionalised education:
"… [T]o go to school in a summer morn,
O! It drives all joy away;
Under a cruel eye outworn,
The little ones spend the day
In sighing and dismay."

112 Interestingly, here Gatto's remark seems to chime with the thinking of Louis Althusser, who identifies education as one example of an *ideological state apparatus* (ISA), a means for the dissemination of ideology in a concealed and symbolic fashion. Althusser's thinking may be linked in turn to an influential approach to film known as screen theory, associated with the early 1970s British journal *Screen*, which proposed that film images are mirrors in which viewers accede to subjectivity, hence conformity. For screen theorists, film is also an ideological state apparatus.

To much of the Western world, Afghanistan has seemed both *other*, and also a problem to be solved – Hosseini's novel gives a voice to otherness, exploring internal, social and political difference.

The Kite Runner (2003, 2007)

Here, discussion starts with an examination of the poster used in marketing the film (illustration 5), which relates most directly to the BFI's category 5, 'attention-seeking', but is also a statement in itself, designed as a comment on *The Kite Runner*. The poster functions as an interpretation of the source text, offering something like a shorthand version of the story it is promoting, while at the same time inviting curiosity: the promoters want you to want to see this film, to discover the connections that the poster has tantalisingly suggested.

A starting-point might be the following questions:

Why do you think this image has been chosen?	How might it make people want to see the film?
	What do you think it tells us about the story?
What can you see here?	What has been included in the picture? The poster has been constructed to say something specific.

Since this discussion is concerned with visual texts and how we read them, we might begin by considering the way the eye is drawn into the image and then encouraged to move around it. For instance, we read from top to bottom, left to right. The poster presents us with the title (an example of graphics). But *before* that – occupying the same space and dominating the image – is a kite, set against the white clouds and blue sky. A viewer's eye is usually drawn towards the lightest area of a picture – the kite, small as it is in comparison with other elements of the poster, is clearly emphasised in this way, indicating its importance alongside the title. But the kite is linked by its string to the ground – and the poster itself is grounded by the two human figures we will come to know as Amir and Hassan, embracing in boyhood friendship, united by another kite.

So what might all this *mean*? The sun is breaking through the clouds – as well as making this the lightest area, it suggests something *positive*. An idea of hope? The message inserted between the sky and the ground – 'There is a way to be good again' – adds to this. Redemption? Does the sky evoke ideas of heaven? What is the connection between the grounded boys (we might notice how *dark* they are in contrast to the rest of the image), the kite and the sky?

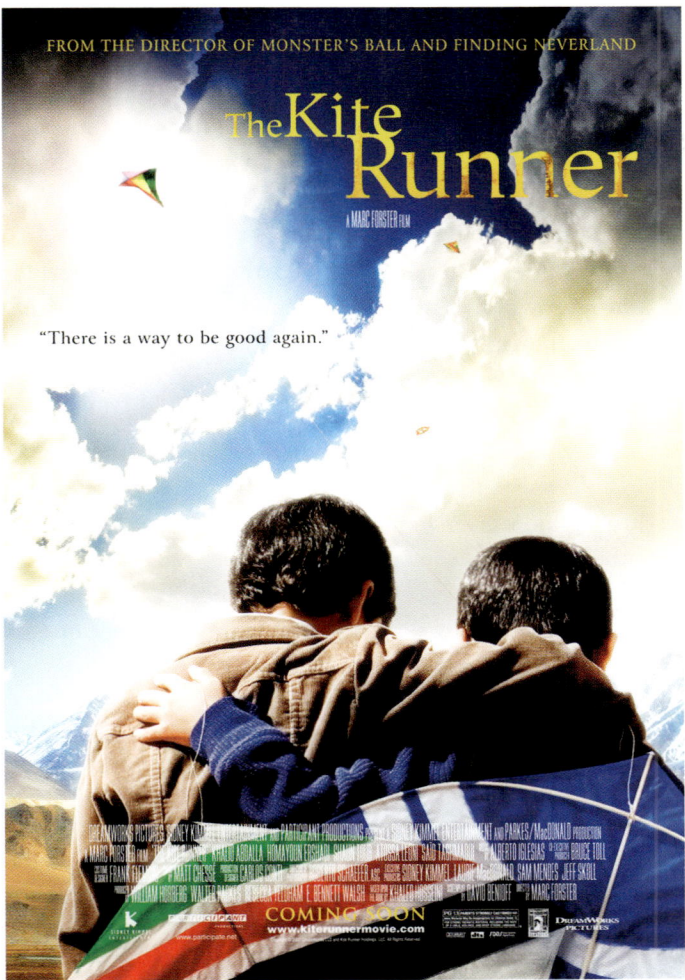

Illustration 5.
Foto: © Dream-Works/courtesy Everett Collection/NTB

- Why should what turns out to be a story about Afghanistan have this particular title? Not just kites, but *running* – escape? To freedom?[113]
- A related question (once something about the story is known) might be, "Who is the Kite Runner of the title?" Not Amir – he is the Kite *Flyer*, but Hassan.

Prominent in the poster and in the marketing campaign as a whole is one particular line from Hosseini's text – "There is a way to be good again" (Hosseini,

---

[113] A little background on Afghanistan might be helpful here – the distinction between the majority Pashtun and the Hazara. Hassan and his father are Hazara.

2003, pp. 168, 270). As well as looking at the poster, it may be useful to look at the film trailer – another promotional device – which emphasises the kites, the boys and their friendship (though the film trailer, unlike the poster, emphasises the backdrop of a country torn by war, with images of military vehicles and soldiers[114]), and that particular line. Its meaning is worth dwelling on – "again" tells us that once someone was good, implies that then they were not good, and asserts that goodness may be recovered. Reviewers of Hosseini's novel referred to it as "a passionate story of betrayal and redemption" (*Kirkus Reviews*), and one "where a search for a child [i.e., Sohrab] finally makes a coward into a man" (*The Observer*). There are clues to the themes in these reviews – most notably, "betrayal and redemption".

The screenwriter of *The Kite Runner*, David Benioff, identifies perhaps the most important interpretative decision made by adaptors as the identification of "the central story" (interview with Rebecca Murray for About.com Guide). Such a task is also one which is undertaken in marketing the film, and accounts for differences between the film and its source. But identifying "the central story" is a useful guide to the selection of key scenes for examination and discussion.

One particular scene immediately suggests itself for analysis, because its significance to the overall story, in both the novel and the film, is so great. The novel's opening lines signal this importance:

> I became what I am today at the age of twelve, on a frigid overcast day in the winter of 1975. I remember the precise moment, crouching beneath a crumbling mud wall, peeking into the alley near the frozen creek... (Hosseini, 2003: 1)
>
> ... I crept close to the mouth of the alley. Held my breath. Peeked around the corner (Hosseini, 2003, p. 62).

In the novel, six chapters separate these two references – one reason would be suspense. But can the film replicate this suspenseful delay? How? And in any case, should it? Does it?

What Amir witnesses is the most controversial scene of the novel, which proved every bit as controversial when it was filmed (see for example, Milvy 2007). His friend, Hassan, "the Kite Runner", apparently the son of Amir's father's servant (though later revealed to be the illegitimate son of Amir's father himself), has gone to retrieve the kite with which Amir, "the Kite

---

114 Included on the DVD, but also available on YouTube.

Flyer", has just won the kite-flying competition. Hassan encounters the local bully, Assef, and two of his fellows, who demand the kite. Out of loyalty to Amir, Hassan refuses. What follows is male rape, witnessed by Amir who is too afraid to intervene:

> I had one last chance to make a decision. One final opportunity to decide who I was going to be. I could step into that alley, stand up for Hassan – the way he'd stood up for me all those times in the past – and accept whatever would happen to me. Or I could run. In the end, I ran (Hosseini, 2003, p. 68).

For years, Amir is haunted by guilt for his inaction.

This scene is paralleled by a much later scene which amounts to Amir's expiation. Amir has returned to Afghanistan to look for Hassan's son, Sohrab. Hassan and his wife have been executed by the Taliban, and Amir has learned that the child is in an orphanage. The orphanage director informs him that the boy has been taken by a Taliban leader, who visits the orphanage regularly, usually to take a girl – "[b]ut not always" (Hosseini, 2003, p. 224). Tracking down the Talib – and witnessing a brutal stoning to death – Amir discovers that he is the bully Assef, who may now have raped Sohrab. This possibility is strongly suggested in the novel, where Sohrab says, "I'm so dirty and full of sin … The bad man and the other two … did things to me" (Hosseini, 2003, p. 278).

The film makes this more explicit – Sohrab tells Amir, "He [Assef] used to come get me in the morning before prayers. I didn't want him to get me any more … I'm so dirty."

However, Amir's atonement for not having intervened in that crucial rape incident comes as a brutal beating by Assef, which in the novel leaves him hospitalised with major injuries. He is told by the doctor that he could have died (Hosseini, 2003, p. 259). The film shows the violence of the beating, but omits the hospitalisation, perhaps because the filmmakers felt that the visual representation of violence – Amir is left badly, and visibly, bruised and bloodied by the assault – was enough. Both book and film include the way the attack ends – the vicious Assef is shot in the eye with a stone by Sohrab, who has inherited his father's talent with the catapult.

Clearly, the rape scene is crucial – it is the defining moment of the central character's life. When the novel is taught in the United States, many teachers find it necessary to warn parents about this scene. It was perhaps inevitable that the film version would cause controversy – the film as well as the book was banned in Afghanistan, and the three child actors had to relocate to the United Arab Emirates. In her *Salon* interview with Hosseini, Erika Milvy describes:

some Afghans' outrage at the movie, which includes a 30-second scene depicting the rape of a boy, played by a 12-year-old Afghan, Ahmad Khan Mahmidzada. (Mahmidzada's parents said they had no knowledge of this plot point when they agreed to let their son act in the movie.) Word of the rape scene has triggered threats of violence against the three Afghan child actors who appear in the film, demands that the scene be cut, articles about Hollywood exploitation – and an ensuing P.R. disaster for Paramount, which agreed to delay the film's release until the kids were safely out of Afghanistan. [Eventually] the studio announced that the children and their guardians had been relocated to an unnamed city in the United Arab Emirates, clearing the way for the film's release (Milvy 2007).

Nonetheless, according to the film's producer Rebecca Yeldham, this scene was far less shocking than had been the original intention. There is no nudity, and the actor playing Hassan did not remove his trousers. The scene lasts for only about half a minute, and all that is shown is a boy unfastening his trousers and a shot of trousers being slightly pulled down. A body double was used for both these shots. Indeed, the only visually graphic detail is a shot of droplets of blood on the snow – the novel includes Amir noticing "those tiny drops that fell from between [Hassan's] legs and stained the snow black" (Hosseini, 2003, pp. 69, 270). Since it preys upon Amir's mind for over a quarter of a century, this scene was clearly too important to be missed – the necessity of atoning for his non-intervention is signalled by the words spoken by his father's old friend, Rahim Khan, that prompt Amir's return to Afghanistan to seek out Sohrab.

SUGGESTED KEY SCENES (relating to the idea of being good again, identified as (part of) "the central story")		
SCENE	SIGNIFICANCE	THEMES
The rape scene (DVD scene 5, about 4 minutes long; novel 66-9)	Makes Amir what he is, and therefore motivates the entire story AMIR AS COWARD	Crime/sin BETRAYAL
Amir's beating (DVD scene 14, begins about 11 minutes into the scene, lasting about 3 minutes; novel 251-5)	Demonstrates (a) the physical brutality of Assef; (b) Amir paying back for not intervening in the rape; (c) a degree of revenge against Assef AMIR AS PENITENT	Expiation/atonement REDEMPTION (stage 1)
The closing scene (DVD scene 16, the kite-flying begins after about 3 minutes and the scene lasts about 4 minutes, to the credits; novel 320-4)	Repayment to Sohrab of the debt Amir can't repay Hassan – Sohrab's desire to go to San Francisco (Hosseini 2003: 281-2, 297) and Amir's promise (Hosseini 2003: 297) AMIR'S FULFILMENT	Happy ending REDEMPTION (stage 2)

Billy Elliot (2000, 2001)

Skellig and *The Kite Runner* were novels before being adapted to film. What happens when this process is reversed – when the film is the source, and the adaptation is a novel – or "novelisation" (sometimes the preferred term)? The 2000 film *Billy Elliot*, directed by Stephen Daldry, screenplay by Lee Hall, was published as a novel in 2001, written by Melvin Burgess. Burgess closely followed the film and screenplay but also made his own significant changes. The most important of these is multiple first-person narration. Burgess gives each of the main characters the opportunity to tell the story from his own point of view; the majority of the novel is narrated by Billy, with substantial sections told by his father; sections are narrated by Billy's older brother; one chapter by Billy's friend Michael. A section is even told by the pawnbroker to whom Billy's father takes his dead wife's jewellery, desperate for money to take Billy to London for his audition at the Royal Ballet School. This method of narration gives access to the thoughts and feelings of numerous characters, something that is difficult for film to do. So, while Bragg's novelisation begins with Billy himself, it is his father, Jackie, who closes the text, proudly witnessing his son's performance in the famous ballet *Swan Lake* at London's Covent Garden Opera House.

- What is the difference between the multiple narration of Burgess' novel, and (say) first-person narration (as has been the case in both the other novels discussed here)?

This method of multiple narration distributes readers' sympathies amongst the range of characters, and reminds us that this is not just Billy's story, whereas the film focuses the viewer's attention on Billy's own experiences, played out against the background of the 1984–1985 real life British miners' strike.

Once again, discussion will proceed from a single image, though the entire closing section of the film could usefully be shown.

As before, the opening question is simply "What do you see?" asking for a focus on the *mise-en-scène*, and again leading to some straightforward and simple responses. In the light of the discussion so far, two possible answers – performing the role of a swan suggests a human being flying, and some of the ideas associated with flying have been referred to throughout. The fact that the image is of a male dancer might lead to considerations of ballet as gendered feminine/female. But the image requires some contextualising – it might be helpful to provide some basic information about *Swan Lake*, possibly in the form of a very brief synopsis of the story (Billy's inspirational teacher, Mrs

Illustration 6. Billy (played by Adam Cooper) in the final sequence of the film. Billy Eliot (2000) DVD-version. © 2000 Tiger Aspect Pictures (Billy Boy) Limited.

Wilkinson, gives her version of this in DVD chapter 8, "A ghost story"; the equivalent section in the novel is 79–80) plus some further information about the particular performance that is referred to – the actor taking the role of Billy here is not Jamie Bell, who plays the part throughout the rest of the film, but Adam Cooper, who took the lead role in Matthew Bourne's all-male 1995 production of *Swan Lake* at Sadler's Wells Theatre in London, an interpretation of Tchaikovsky's 1877 ballet which went on to become the longest running ballet in London's West End and on Broadway. It is this particular production that the film refers to – it is available on DVD through Amazon, if there is interest. The significance of this performance in itself might be worth pursuing – and is easy to research through Wikipedia, Amazon, IMDb, and so forth.

Bourne's production raises several interesting and relevant questions about adaptation. Like a play, a ballet such as *Swan Lake* is only actualised in the interpretation that producers, directors, dancers have made of it – one might say it only *exists* as/in those interpretations.

Bourne chooses to re-tell the story as one in which a human male falls in love with a male swan. In Tchaikovsky, which can obviously be seen as the source, though he himself took the story from a number of other sources, mainly German and Russian, the ending sees the two swans die and ascend to heaven, forever united in love. A happy ending or a tragic ending? What difference does it make if it becomes a gay love story – perhaps it is only in heaven that two such lovers could find a happy ending?

Watching this performance, Billy's father Jackie shows his emotions very clearly in the film; in the novel these must be expressed in words:

> [H]e jumped like a bloody star. I thought he was going to hang forever in the air. It's marvellous the way they look just for a second as if they're never going to come down and no one – no one, no one, no one – does it as well as our Billy (Burgess, 2001, p. 155).

Issues of gender resonate throughout the film. Amnaa Mohdin, interviewing director Stephen Baldry in 2017, proposes four broad areas of interest that motivate the selection of scenes for possible examination and discussion:

- Dancing;
- Labour rights;
- Gender and sexuality;
- Social class.

But the particular image and scene described above lead back to what Mohdin identifies as "the film's most memorable scene"; Billy's audition at the Royal Ballet School. This can be found at the DVD's chapter 15, "The Interview". It lasts for only approximately five minutes, so is short enough to show in the classroom. Some ways into consideration of this scene might include the following:

How are Billy and his father's feelings of inferiority shown?	There are a number of possible answers to this; the most obvious is probably the looks of unease exchanged by Billy and his father, but also important is the fact that visually they are dominated by their surroundings – freezing the frame on a selected shot from the previous DVD chapter, "The Audition" might demonstrate this even more clearly. It relates to the overall concern with social class.
How might Billy's responses to the panel's questions be described?	Broadly, as inarticulate – the number of times he begins his answer with, "Dunno", for example. But his answer to the final question, just before he and his father leave, is markedly different.
Does this scene prepare for what is to follow? How?	In a way, it does not – the exchange of glances between the panellists, the looks that suggest they are disappointed by his answers make the audience think that Billy has failed the interview. His subsequent success is a surprise.

Here is Mohdin's comment on that final question:

> Just as Billy and his father are about to leave the room, one of the judges on the panel asks Billy: "What does it feel like when you're dancing?" Billy pauses before saying, "dunno". Two judges on the panel, including the one who asked the question, look disappointed.
>
> Billy eventually answers and in just over a minute, his broken sentences and raw description makes a powerful statement on how expression through art can set you free. Billy… says: "… It sort of feels good. It's sort of safe and that… But, once I get going, I sort of forget everything. I sort of disappear. I can feel a change in my whole body. I'm just there… I have this fire in my whole body. I'm flying… like a bird. Like electricity… Yeah, like electricity."

Stephen Daldry explains, "Billy is struggling to articulate something that he has never had to articulate [before]" (Mohdin 2017). He adds that Billy's response is "very honest and very emotional" but it's not just about Billy: "it's about the dad as well. He has never heard his son express what he feels like." This point goes back to the earlier question about multiple narration – this is not only Billy's story. Burgess chooses to tell it from the father's point of view:

> [Billy] said "Dunno" – which was what he'd said to every other bloody question they'd asked him. But then he had a little think and he said something about it feeling like flying. "It starts off sort of stiff," he said, "but once I get going I forget what's going on and I sort of disappear. Like there's fire in me whole body. Like a bird. Like electricity," he said. "Yeah, like electricity." (Burgess, 2001, p. 143)

Billy's whole story is played out against the backdrop of the 1984–1985 miners' strike, so a final important element to consider would be the film and the novel's representation of this. The miners' strike, widely described as "the most bitter industrial dispute in British history" (e.g., BBC News website "On this Day 1950–2000" for 12 March), is, like *Swan Lake*, a simple matter to research – here, discussion will be confined to the observation that while Billy's personal story moves towards a happy ending, the story of the miners' strike follows an entirely opposite trajectory. One sequence from the film brings together the issues raised: as Billy's teacher, Miss Wilkinson, drives through a monumentally industrial landscape, she tells Billy her version of the story of the ballet, while the music playing throughout the sequence is *Swan Lake* itself (DVD chapter 8, "A Ghost Story"). The notion of a ghost story, here expressed as Billy's dismissal of *Swan Lake*, seems appropriate for the setting, about to be rendered ghostly at the hands of UK Prime Minister Margaret Thatcher's government. As Billy's father puts it towards the end of Burgess's adaptation:

We lost our future, didn't we?... We lost that future – but we won another future – for Billy. And that's something, isn't it? (Burgess, 2001, p. 147)

Summary: Suggestions for *Billy Eliot*		
Scene	**Significance**	**Themes**
The final sequence (DVD chapter 14, novel 153–155)	Demonstrates (a) the fulfilment of Billy's personal dream; (b) a public and historic milestone; (c) the unity of the family – George: "I never thought I'd see Jackie and Tony come together over ballet dancing, I'll tell you that for nothing!" (Burgess, 2001, p. 129)	Dancing (as flying); masculinity (gender/sexuality); success/achievement
The audition and the interview (DVD chapters 14–15; novel 130–147, with narration split between Billy and his father	Billy's difficulties of expression – but at least these people are taking him seriously – and final articulation of his feelings when dancing.	Social class; dancing (compared by Billy to flying)
Any scene demonstrating the background of industrial unrest, but possibly DVD chapter 8, "A Ghost Story" (novel 79–80)	Though Billy's story (personal) may have a happy ending (upward trajectory), the miners' story (political) will not (downward trajectory)	Labour rights; historical background; the relationship between text and context

Further suggestions

Most of the following suggestions[115] come from Tim Stafford (2011, pp. 164–165).[116]

For younger learners	
Book	**Film**
Roald Dahl, *The Witches* (London: Jonathan Cape, 1983)	*The Witches* (Jim Henson Pictures, 1990)
Roald Dahl, *James and the Giant Peach* (London: Penguin Classics, 2011, originally 1961)	*James and The Giant Peach* (Walt Disney Pictures, 1996)

---

115 The three texts discussed in this chapter have been added to Stafford's list. Narinder Dhami, *Bend It Like Beckham* (2002), Cornelia Funke, *Inkheart* (2003), Patrick Ness, *A Monster Calls* (2012), R.J. Palacio, *Wonder* (2012) and Angie Thomas, *The Hate U Give* (2017) have also been added, plus the later Harry Potter books and films.

116 A number of these texts are also discussed in chapter 5 and chapter 7

Roald Dahl, *Matilda* (London: Jonathan Cape, 1988)	*Matilda* (TriStar Pictures, 1996)
Roald Dahl, *Fantastic Mr Fox* (London: George Allen & Unwin, 1970)	*Fantastic Mr Fox* (Twentieth Century Fox, 2009)
Dr Seuss, *How the Grinch Stole Christmas* (New York: Random House, 1957)	*The Grinch* (Universal Pictures, 2000)
Dr Seuss, *The Cat in the Hat* (New York: Random House, 1957)	*The Cat in The Hat* (Universal Pictures, 2003)
Maurice Sendak, *Where the Wild Things Are* (New York: Harper & Row, 1963)	*Where the Wild Things Are* (Warner Brothers, 2009)
For older learners	
Book	**Film**
Chris Van Allsburg, *Jumanji* (New York: Houghton Mifflin, 1981)	*Jumanji* (TriStar Pictures, 1995)
David Almond, *Skellig* (London: Hodder Children's Books, 1998)	*Skellig* (Grace Films Limited, 2009)
Melvin Burgess, *Billy Elliot* (Frome: Chicken House, 2001)	*Billy Elliot* (Working Title Films and BBC Films in association with the Arts Council of England, 2000)
Lewis Carroll, *Alice's Adventures in Wonderland and Through the Looking-glass* (1865, 1871)	*Alice in Wonderland* (Walt Disney Pictures, 2010)
Narinder Dhami (novelisation) *Bend It Like Beckham* (2002)	*Bend It Like Beckham* (Redbus Film Distribution/Warner Home Video, 2002)
Charles Dickens, *A Christmas Carol* (London: Chapman & Hall, 1843)	*A Christmas Carol* (Walt Disney Pictures, 2009)
Tony DiTerlizzi and Holly Black, *The Spiderwick Chronicles* (New York: Simon & Schuster, 2003–2009)	*The Spiderwick Chronicles* (Nickelodeon Movies, 2008)
Jeanne DuPrau, *The City of Ember* (New York: Random House, 2003)	*City of Ember* (Walden Media, 2008)
Cornelia Funke, *Inkheart* (London and New York: Scholastic, 2003)	*Inkheart* (New Line Cinema, 2008)
Neil Gaiman, *Coraline* (London: Bloomsbury and Harper Collins, 2002)	*Coraline* (Universal, 2009)
Khaled Hosseini, *The Kite Runner* (New York: Riverhead Books, 2003)	*The Kite Runner* (Sidney Kimmel Entertainment, 2007)
Dick King-Smith, *The Sheep-Pig* (London: Gollancz, 1983)	*Babe* (Universal, 1995)
C.S. Lewis, *The Lion, the Witch and the Wardrobe* (London: Geoffrey Bles, 1950)	*The Lion, the Witch and the Wardrobe* (Walt Disney Pictures, 2005)

C.S. Lewis, *Prince Caspian* (London: Geoffrey Bles, 1951)	*Prince Caspian* (Walt Disney Pictures, 2008)
Patrick Ness, *A Monster Calls* (London: Walker Books, 2012)	*A Monster Calls* (Entertainment One UK Limited, 2017)
R.J. Palacio, *Wonder* (London: Random House, 2012)	*Wonder* (Lionsgate, 2017)
Philip Pullman, *Northern Lights* (*His Dark Materials*, Vol. 1) (London: Scholastic, 1995)	*The Golden Compass* (New Line Cinema, 2007)
J.K. Rowling, *Harry Potter and the Philosopher's Stone* (London: Bloomsbury, 1997)	*Harry Potter and the Philosopher's Stone* (Warner Brothers, 2001)
J.K. Rowling, *Harry Potter and the Chamber of Secrets* (London: Bloomsbury, 1998)	*Harry Potter and the Chamber of Secrets* (Warner Brothers, 2002)
J.K. Rowling, *Harry Potter and the Prisoner of Azkaban* (London: Bloomsbury, 1999)	*Harry Potter and the Prisoner of Azkaban* (Warner Brothers, 2004)
J.K. Rowling, *Harry Potter and the Goblet of Fire* (London: Bloomsbury, 2000)	*Harry Potter and the Goblet of Fire* (Warner Brothers, 2005)
J.K. Rowling, *Harry Potter and the Order of the Phoenix* (London: Bloomsbury, 2003)	*Harry Potter and the Order of the Phoenix* (Warner Brothers, 2007)
J.K. Rowling, *Harry Potter and the Half-Blood Prince* (London: Bloomsbury, 2005)	*Harry Potter and the Half-Blood Prince* (Warner Brothers, 2009)
J.K. Rowling, *Harry Potter and the Deathly Hallows* (London: Bloomsbury, 2007)	*Harry Potter and the Deathly Hallows* (Part 1) (Warner Brothers, 2010)
	Harry Potter and the Deathly Hallows (Part 2) (Warner Brothers, 2011)
Angie Thomas, *The Hate U Give* (London: Walker Books, 2017)	*The Hate U Give* (Twentieth Century Fox, 2018)

Conclusion

The approach outlined here, of taking key scenes from both versions of the text, is always useful, and works to support interpretation. One final caution has been implicit in this discussion from the outset – because of their differences, and because of the interpretative choices made by the adaptor, a film version of a printed text, or a printed text version of a film, is never a *substitute* for the source, and the two must not be confused. It is important that the adaptation is seen as a reading or interpretation of its source, and as something that productively leads back to that source – whichever might finally be preferred.

References

Almond, D. (1998). *Skellig*. Hodder Children's Books.

Althusser, L. (2001, originally 1970). Ideology and ideological state apparatuses. In *Lenin and Philosophy and Other Essays.* Monthly Review Press.

Benioff, D. (2005). *The Kite Runner: A Portrait of the Marc Forster Film*. Newmarket Press.

BFI (2000). *Moving Images in the Classroom: A Secondary Teacher's Guide to Using Film and Television*. British Film Institute.

Brennan, G. (1999). Skellig the Heights; Briefing; People; Places; Profile; David Almond. 12 February 1999 tes.com. Available at: https://www.tes.com/news/skellig-heightsbriefingpeopleprofiledavid-almond

Burgess, M. (2001). *Billy Elliot*. Chicken House.

Chatman, S. (1978). *Story and Discourse: Narrative Structure in Fiction and Film*. Cornell University Press.

Daldry, S. (dir.) (2000). *Billy Elliot*.[DVD]. Co-production between BBC Films, Tiger Aspect Pictures and Working Title Films.

Forster, M. (dir.) (2007). *The Kite Runner*.[DVD]. Sidney Kimmel Entertainment.

Foster, T.C. (2014). *How to Read Literature like a Professor*. Harper Perennial.

Gatto, J.T. (2017). *The Underground History of American Education: A Schoolteacher's Intimate Investigation into the Problem of Modern Schooling*. Valor Academy.

Hosseini, K. (2003). *The Kite Runner*. Riverhead Books.

Izod, J. (1984). *Reading the Screen: an Introduction to Film Studies*. Longman.

Jankel, A.J. (dir.) (2009). *Skellig*.[DVD]. Grace Films Limited.

McFarlane, B. (1996). *Novel to Film*. Oxford University Press.

Milvy, E. (2007). *The Kite Runner* controversy. Available at: https://www.salon.com/2007/12/09/hosseini/#:~:text=In%20the%20film%20of%20%22The,been%20threats%20against%20the%20actors.

Mohdin, A. (2017). *Billy Eliot*'s director explains the true meaning behind the film's most memorable scene. *Quartz*, 6 October 2017. Available at: https://qz.com/1096401/director-stephen-daldry-on-billy-elliot-the-meaning-and-message-behind-the-films-most-memorable-scene/

Nel, P., & Paul, L. (2011). (Eds.), *Keywords for Children's Literature*. New York University Press.

Norwegian Directorate for Education and Training. (2019/2020). English subject curriculum (ENG01-04). https://www.udir.no/lk20/eng01-04

Ridley, J. (2019). Leonardo da Vinci's Helicopter. *The Conversation.com*, 3 May 2019.

Stafford, T. (2011). *Teaching Visual Literature in the Primary Classroom*. Routledge.

10

Drama in the English classroom

Gweno Williams

Introduction

This chapter aims to encourage and inspire intending and current teachers to use drama creatively in EFL teaching for the wide range of pedagogic rewards it can offer. Teacher under-confidence or unrealistic resource perceptions sometimes raise questions about whether and how drama can be used successfully in the language classroom. However, the relative organisational and pedagogic challenge can be rewarded by rich benefits, advancing pupil speaking confidence and oral expression very fast.

Sometimes overlooked in discussions of children's literature, drama is one of the major English literary genres which should not be ignored in EFL teaching. Numerous starting points and useful resources for teachers are presented, including online materials, to suggest that using drama in the classroom is neither difficult nor problematic. Competence aims in the LK20 English subject curriculum state that learners should read "various types of texts" (Norwegian Directorate for Education and Training, 2019/20) and bringing drama into the English classroom is one way of obtaining this.

The chapter aims to equip teachers with the ability and confidence to use drama and performance concepts and activities effectively. The focus is on methodology and approaches rather than solely recommending content. When engaging learners in performance, teachers should not worry about accuracy or errors; the power of the activity is in liberating learners' confidence and language production. Fluency of response and engagement are more important than accuracy, as drama generates a live creative language situation through an empowering kinaesthetic learning process. Drama is a social, collective, collaborative activity, employing live language in real time. An affirmative interactive learning experience, drama uses three of the five main language skills: speaking, listening and reading.

> Facilitators have pointed out that drama activities are the integration of several language skills. (Nordin et al., 2012, p. 199)

The level of attention, engagement and concentration required in drama is profoundly active and creates a dynamic environment. Drama allows different learning styles to flourish, including improvisation, and does not privilege traditional academic skills, so all learners can be successful.

> Multiliteracies pedagogy suggests that overlaying these different modes for students to express their ideas and understanding better equips the language learners for life outside the classroom. Drama tasks in this course provided a meaningful basis for the use of multiple modes of meaning-making (Ntelioglou, 2011, p. 606).

Educators from societies as diverse as Canada, Taiwan, Malaysia and Iran concur that drama brings multiple benefits to EFL learners in addition to strengthening language learning (Gorjian et al., 2010; Nordin et al., 2012; Cheng & Wilson, 2011; Ntelioglou, 2011). Drama activities naturally use the cycle of repetition, rehearsal and reiteration which is intrinsic to successful language learning. Drama generates motivation and confidence, liberating language use.

> Being engaged in active drama, language learners can imagine themselves living in the world of the play, and this could increase their motivation (Gorjian et al., 2010, p. 9).

The Drama Network's cross-cultural DICE project (**D**rama **I**mproves Lisbon **K**ey **C**ompetencies in **E**ducation) demonstrates how incorporating drama into education benefits learners not only in language competence but also confidence, social skills and wellbeing. Their 2014 online publication *Making a World of Difference* is available via Taylor and Francis online. The full project report is available online[117] and will be of interest to teachers keen to incor-

---

117 http://www.dramanetwork.eu/file/Policy%20Paper%20long.pdf

porate drama into their classes. It includes key findings of the research project as well as short case studies demonstrating how drama can increase key skills such as cultural awareness, interpersonal skills and language skills. The report also includes practical suggestions for the classroom, demonstrating how teachers can begin to incorporate drama into their classes and develop their own style of educational drama appropriate for their particular teaching context.

The UK-based *National Association for the Teaching of Drama* website[118] offers resources for drama at all educational levels, including international news and resources and annual UK conferences for teachers. It hosts the *Journal for Drama in Education*, which publishes reflective accounts of practical drama teaching and theoretical articles.

The pedagogic value and demands of drama

In order to bring drama successfully into the language classroom, the teacher needs to shift into the co-ordinating role of producer/director or facilitator in order to allow the learners as much ownership of the activity as possible. This role change requires imaginative flexibility on all sides. It also readily opens up the space for creativity, improvisation and spontaneity, where English becomes the medium rather than the focus. Learners can become more motivated to actively use the target language, as suggested by Nordin et al.:

> Based on observations, drama activities seemed to motivate the students to actively communicate in the target language with each other, for example during the group discussions, the rehearsal and the performance. English has become the medium of communication in all the drama activities. Observations on the drama activities implemented indicated that these activities provide more opportunities for students to use and practice the target language actively." (Nordin et al., 2012, p. 200).

Drama is essentially participatory, active rather than passive, thereby distracting attention from mechanistic aspects of language learning, and creating a powerful context-based need for communication. Drama encourages language creation as part of improvisation, putting language learning into an authentic situation. The gains of drama work are much greater than any risks as the collective and communal experience of drama builds trust, relationships, confidence.

---

118 http://www.natd.eu

> When students are given opportunities to practice their English language and perform it in front of an audience, the chances for them to acquire their ESL skills are higher. This is because through all the drama activities conducted, the students were given opportunities to speak their language, listen to the language as well as read and write the language. Thus, such opportunities could enhance their English language skills, as well as improve their English language proficiency (Nordin et al., 2012, p. 201).

Where language teaching needs to embed vocabulary or constructions through repetition, it is important to note that drama offers rich and apparently natural opportunities for learning through repetition in the form of rehearsals. Drama also offers prime opportunities to showcase language learning as *performance* before an *audience* of fellow pupils, peers or family. Ample associated writing and speaking extension activities for publicity, analysis and reflection are possible. These might include posters, tickets, programmes, advertisements or reviews. Importantly, songs and music interwoven into the drama are appropriate and productive ways of delivering and extending group language, as well as including hesitant or reluctant speakers by using choral activities to break down initial barriers. Drama can create a sense of pride, achievement, affirmation and shared pleasure.

This chapter encourages teachers to engage with drama as producers, within their own classroom environments, with learners as actors, speaking English authentically for the sake of the performance rather than for the sake of the lesson:

> The teaching style in the drama classroom, where learners are assigned roles to perform, makes classroom activities an enjoyable experience … focusing more on the dramatic performance rather than on the text itself. Learning literature in this approach is basically an active process inducing students to produce necessary content in action instead of mere memorisation (Gorjian et al., 2010, p. 9).

Drama approaches for the primary classroom

Pedagogically, drama can be one of the primary teacher's most dynamic and flexible tools. Surprisingly, there is no automatic need for a play text in the primary classroom. Instead, new vocabulary, including in the form of nursery rhymes, songs or poems, can be very easily scaffolded as *dialogue* around a very simple *plot* involving as many *characters* as are needed for everyone in the class to be involved. Drama is particularly suitable for differentiation at all levels as individual language requirements in roles can be tailored to learner language ability or speaking confidence, with larger roles for more able language learners, including narrators and speakers who can offer words of welcome to the audience and thanks for attending and performance. However, this does not mean that learners are restricted by their current language ability when engaging in drama activities. Indeed, Ntelioglou found that drama helped learners to improve their vocabulary and comprehension: "They [learners] explained that the drama tasks helped them to understand difficult vocabulary as they were trying to embody the written text and that 'words make more sense when you act them out'" (Ntelioglou, 2011, p. 609). Finally, the presence of an invited audience can increase the sense of an authentic experience as well as the pride, pleasure and confidence resulting from successful performance.

UK Children's Laureate Julia Donaldson focused on drama as an important genre for schools. She introduced the concept of picturebook plays whereby teachers and learners together can turn favourite picturebooks into flexible plays without the need for a script. So many children's books involve a journey which includes a series of meetings and dialogues. For example, *The Gruffalo* by Julia Donaldson, *I Want My Hat Back* by Jon Scieszka and *Handa's Surprise* by Eileen Browne are all plotted around a journey involving meetings or interactions with a series of creatures. The beauty of this very simple plotline is that it can be creatively extended to include as many meetings and speakers as there are potential actors. The model is simple, consistent and inclusive. The Scottish Book Trust has outstanding online free-of-charge resources about quick preparatory drama activities for picturebook plays[119] and detailed guidelines[120] for devising plays from *Jack and the Beanstalk* by Richard Walker, *LullabyHullabaloo* by Mick Inkpen and *Monkey Puzzle* by Julia Donaldson.

Julia Donaldson has also published three whole class plays for performance, all of which are very suitable for cross-curricular work with History. These are *Bombs and Blackberries*, *Chariots and Champions* and *Persephone* (which is published in *Play Time*, an edited collection of 11 short plays for ages 7+).

Performing poetry

One of the most satisfying ways to begin drama activities in the EFL classroom is through poetry performance. See chapter 2 for several performance suggestions. An easy and appealing drama continuum runs from reading or

---

[119] https://www.scottishbooktrust.com/learning-resources/picture-book-drama-activities
[120] https://www.scottishbooktrust.com/learning-resources/how-to-turn-picture-books-into-plays

speaking poems aloud, to dividing them into questions and answers or dialogues or chorus and response, to creating characters with different accents and mannerisms, to using simple costume and props, to full scale performance. Advancing along this performance continuum can build motivation and enjoyment for learners and teachers. Classroom poetry performances can be very flexible with regard to time required. They can be quick and informal, perhaps used as ice-breakers, or they can be practised and polished into a more rehearsed elaborate delivery. Two recent poetry anthologies provide wonderful material for poetry performance. Julia Donaldson's edited collection *Poems to Perform* (2013) includes conversations like Clare Bevan's "The Treasures" or John Agard's "What a Shame You Lost Your Tail"; proliferating stories like Roger McGough's "The Sound Collector" or Brian Patten's "The Trouble With My Brother" and choral extravaganzas like John Foster's "The Dinosaur Rap" or Gervase Phinn's "Today, I Feel". There are humorous, sad and thought-provoking poems on a wide range of topics, suitable for all grade levels. There is a very useful appendix of performance suggestions.

Award-winning British performance poet Joseph Coelho's collection of 20 of his own poems *Poems Aloud: Poems are for reading out loud!* (2020) is designed to teach children 20 different ways to perform poetry. Aimed at both shy and confident performers, the volume includes tongue twisters, comic verse, poems to project to a whole class and poems to whisper in someone's ear.

Finally, as a performance poet, Benjamin Zephaniah is in a league of his own. His poems are often funny and also frequently serious, politically challenging and angry. Learners will enjoy his inspiring performances on his website https://benjaminzephaniah.com/, above all the much loved classic poem for children "Talking Turkeys" in Jamaican patois,[121] from the volume of the same name, which opens with: "Be nice to yu turkeys dis Christmas…"

Pedagogic case study: "The Owl and the Pussy-cat"

This case study is suitable for all ages and can involve up to 40 learners. It demonstrates how drama can generate active language used in realistic interactions and create pleasure in learning. The target language becomes subsidiary or incidental to the creative activity of producing and performing a play so that language learning becomes fuller and deeper. As Gorjian et al. suggest, "Through dramatization, the content is presented in the form of lan-

---

121 Patois or Patwa is a co-official language of Jamaica, sometimes also called Jamaican Creole.

guage in action and, hence, the learners' motivation is heightened" (Gorjian et al., 2010: 10).

This example sets out to demonstrate that no more than an ordinary classroom is needed for a production which can be developed in one hour. A play text is not even required, as Victorian poet Edward Lear's (1812–1888) popular and well-known nonsense poem "The Owl and the Pussy-cat" can be adapted into a highly successful drama. It could be staged as a love story, an adventure drama or a musical, with extra songs included.

Linguistically, this widely anthologised poem has many of the characteristics of the nursery rhymes introduced in Grade 1 in Norway. "The Owl and the Pussy-cat" uses repetition, non-sequitur or illogic and invented language (e.g. "runcible", "Bong-tree"). These nonsense words, together with the archaic "tarried", give learners the useful experience of encountering new vocabulary which is understood entirely contextually.

Here is a detailed account of how this poem can be successfully used to generate a drama lesson with minimal resources. All learners begin with a printed copy of the poem which they read together with the teacher who explains that this will be the basis of a collective play performance. Learners are asked to identify and take on obvious acting parts, e.g. Owl, Pussy-cat, Pig, Turkey, Narrators. Typically, class numbers will create the need for further acting roles which can include, for example, Bong-trees, piglets, waves of the sea, wedding guests, bridesmaids, etc. The only limit here is the imagination of the learners and teacher/producer. The next step is a walk-through/read-through where the lines are appropriately divided up. For this, all learners need to be on their feet with desks, chairs and bags placed out of the way. It soon becomes clear that sound effects as well as words are required, including animal sounds for the characters and appropriate noises for the trees and the sea. At its simplest, this is "show and tell" theatre. By this point it is likely that a sense of warmth and community will have been created in the classroom through collective laughter and surprise. Clearly this will be "laughing with" and not "laughing at" individuals. Next, the teacher/producer can explain that the performance is actually going to be a musical, which will include at least three songs. Even the youngest Norwegian learners are in the happy position of being able to sing a large number of songs in English. Learners can be canvassed for suggestions. Appropriate choices might include "Twinkle, Twinkle Little Star", "Row, Row, Row Your Boat" and a wedding song (e.g. "Congratulations", "Blue Moon", "All You Need Is Love"), to be included at suitable points throughout the performance. Again, learners can make suggestions here. Importantly, the inclusion of songs means that all participants will use the target language in the course of the activity. They will also have read and listened with attention, and some will have necessarily created language.

The teacher needs to come provided with a bag of props (properties) related to the poem, including a honey jar, an old-fashioned five-pound note, rings, a coin and a small guitar or ukulele. Once the musical has been rehearsed in its long form, complete with sound effects and songs, the concept of group direction can be introduced. Group direction is a drama activity whereby all participants have an equal responsibility for watching the action critically and making suggestions for improvement. Once the group direction suggestions have been incorporated, it will be time for the dress rehearsal. Through repetition and rehearsal, learners will become increasingly familiar with their own allocated passages of language. Some may even be able to dispense with the poem or script. The teacher/producer's responsibility is to keep the pace fast and cheerful to maintain learners engagement and aid classroom control. Group direction can be briefly reintroduced after the dress rehearsal when the final performance is close to ready. If it is possible to include an audience, learner attention will be more focused, as will pride in the communal achievement. The play should conclude with a dance in classic comic mode. A simple freeze-frame ending can be very effective. The performance should end with a round of collective applause celebrating the pleasure and success of the activity. It is useful to conclude the activity with a de-briefing, asking what learners have most enjoyed about the activity and the experience. Typical answers will probably include contribution, creativity, inclusivity and laughter. Above all, the learners focus will be on the pleasure of the activity rather than consciously on language learned and used.

There are at least three moments in "The Owl and the Pussy-cat" when additional language needs to be created. Firstly, a Narrator's welcome to the audience and thanks for watching the play are required. Secondly, in the wedding, performed by the Turkey, the language of the marriage ceremony needs to be generated, and conversations with the wedding guests, if included. Finally, comedy can be created by extending the dialogue between Owl, Pussy-cat and Pig when they are bargaining for the wedding ring. For example, piglets can be introduced who argue vociferously with the Pig over the agreement to sell the ring for as little as one shilling (5 pence in UK currency or 1 krone in Norwegian). This is one of the points in the play where a dramatic decision about tone needs to be made. Is this an easy exchange or a hard-won sales pitch? The other is the Owl's response to the Pussy-cat's ardent proposal. Is the Owl enthusiastic, shocked or diffident, for example? In each case, there can be a class discussion about motives and reactions. Each scene can be played and replayed in different ways according to dramatic choices made.

This is a very simple example of a classroom production which can be created from start to finish in one hour. It can also, of course, be extended as a much more elaborate rehearsed and costumed activity, for full performance with an audience.

Further pedagogic example: a Christmas nativity play

One of the most traditional drama activities in British primary schools is the production of a Christmas nativity play about the birth of Baby Jesus, offering opportunities for welcome and important community engagement. This strong popular cultural tradition may derive originally from medieval mystery plays, short Biblical dramas performed annually on wagons in the open air, telling the story of the world from Creation to the Last Judgement, with the nativity story as central. (See, for example, the *York Mystery Plays* www.yorkmysteryplays.org.) British primary schools produce this core narrative as an inclusive Christmas drama, often performed by the youngest children. A short model text appears in *Twinkle Twinkle* (Munden and Myhre, 2011, pp. 163–167), including additional classroom theme work. The play can be flexibly adapted to include as many performers as required, in the same manner as "The Owl and the Pussy-cat". As suggested by Munden and Myhre, putting on such a play offers an opportunity for strong cultural connection with the English-speaking world. The cultural power of nativity plays and the great affection they are held in is reflected in the way they often feature as comic inter-texts in other works, such as Frank Cotterell Boyce's novel *Millions* or the playtext and television production *The Flint Street Nativity* (Mortimer, 1999).

Lower secondary upwards: playscripts and drama adaptations

For older learners, it may well be more useful and appropriate to work with a play text, involving more sophisticated reading comprehension. When introducing learners to the distinctive features of drama, Mick Wallis's *Studying Plays* (1998) offers a particularly clear explication of the key generic conventions and elements of dramatic texts: plot, characters, dialogue, conflict. Drama is multi-voiced, open to directorial emphasis, filtered through audience perception and response, potentially open-ended. Drama is immediate, always now, a process in which the audience are implicated and experience with the characters, a process which, at best, evokes profound emotional engagement and sympathy, leading to catharsis.

Plays for young people often deal with themes relevant to teenagers, who may value the freedom of speaking someone else's words on a challenging topic, rather than their own. Staging drama is essentially a problem-solving activity, which may also focus on a text with a problem at its core, such as *Dear Nobody* (1998, playtext) by Berlie Doherty, or *Miss Yesterday* by Alan Ayckbourn (2004). Group direction (explained above) is an equalising communication strategy, generating respect for and trust in the views of others. When the teacher's role is less authoritative, learners begin to act as decision-makers and directors.

In addition to play texts, novels are frequently adapted for the stage, allowing learners access to these narratives in another genre, both as performers and as potential audiences. Examples of texts mentioned in other chapters which are also adapted as play texts or stage productions include *The Arrival* by Shaun Tan, *Lionboy* by Zizou Corder, *Dear Nobody* by Berlie Doherty, *Skellig* by David Almond, *War Horse* and *Private Peaceful* by Michael Morpurgo, *Face* and *Refugee Boy* by Benjamin Zephaniah and *The Curious Incident of the Dog in the Night-Time* by Mark Haddon. These stage adaptations offer shorter, more interactive versions of the text for reading and hopefully small-scale performance. For example, *The Arrival* was adapted as a play in 2013 by Kristine Landon-Smith and Sita Brahmachari. One classroom strategy would be to teach the picturebook and compare it with the multiple voices of the immigrants of different nationalities which feature in the short scenes of the play. The play text includes an interview with Shaun Tan and also indicates that the migrant nationalities in the play are open to adaptation, so the play text could be a very rich starting point for improvisation of performance or writing tasks, relating to the picturebook.

Drama is a profoundly social and collaborative activity, particularly appropriate for this age range. Drama can enhance social skills and citizenship. Distinguished British playwright David Edgar wrote: "A recent Europe-wide study of 5 000 13- to 16-year-olds found that drama in schools significantly increases teenagers' capacity to communicate and to learn, to relate to each other and to tolerate minorities, as well as making them more likely to vote (by contrast, those who didn't do drama were likelier to watch television and play computer games)." ("Why should we fund the arts?": *The Guardian* 05/01/12) DICE (Drama Improves Key Competences in Education).[122]

---

122 Reference: www.dramanetwork.eu

Teachers should also take whatever local opportunities present themselves to take learners on theatre visits or welcome actors or Theatre in Education groups into their schools where possible. Learners need to understand and enjoy the experience of being an audience member, with a sense of what to look for in live performance. Increasingly, live theatre performances are available screened or streamed, allowing much wider access. The more engagement learners are offered with drama, the more readily they will acquire language and confidence and enjoyment through this genre.

Theatre for Young Audiences is the UK branch of the international organisation *Theatre for Children and Young People*.[123] It offers information on current productions, events and drama trends both in the UK and worldwide, with a focus on supporting and promoting inclusivity through drama.

Introducing Shakespeare at secondary level

The pre-eminence of Shakespeare in world theatre and in English-speaking culture means it is particularly important for English learners to have some knowledge of his plays, read as universal in their themes and concerns. Experience of Shakespeare's plays offers access to cultural capital and shared knowledge and understanding, since the privileged cultural position of Shakespeare is unequalled. EFL learners need a degree of familiarity with Shakespeare to be able to engage with the culture and language they are learning.

However, the language can seem, or can indeed be, an initial barrier for learners. EFL teachers need ways of bypassing the language at first, and foregrounding the stories of the plays, with all their immediacy. Shakespeare is the only author named in the UK School National Curriculum; British schools often introduce the plays through the *Shakespeare Story* series, by Andrew Matthews, illustrated by Tony Ross, or through similar texts. These attractive, short, easy to read illustrated volumes summarise the story of each play, with a few key original quotations, and provide an excellent basis for learners to explore and improvise the action, in contemporary language. The key quotations can then be a springboard to engaging with Shakespeare's language, and ultimately owning it.

Famously, Shakespeare contributed over 3000 new words to the English language, as the first author to write them down in his plays. He expanded the stylistic range of English and is the most frequently quoted writer in the language (RSC Education Resources).

---

123 http://tya-uk.org

> Educational drama in general, and Shakespeare in particular, can provide rich resources to address some of the linguistic and socio-cultural shortcomings of existing ESL (English as a Second Language) teaching (Cheng and Wilson, 2011, p. 542).

Sean McEvoy's *Shakespeare: The Basics* offers a useful overview of Shakespeare's language, the plays as performance texts, and different dramatic genres. Whilst is it important to introduce learners to Shakespeare, it may seem daunting to attempt to teach an entire Shakespeare play during the time available within the EFL curriculum. The option of choosing one element from an accessible play and exploring it with EFL learners in a variety of media is an opportunity to create interest in and a taste for Shakespeare's plays to be pursued later. Arguably, the teacher's responsibility is to introduce learners to Shakespeare and to create an enthusiastic appetite for his work as the basis for further encounters. In her essay *"All the colours of the wind": Shakespeare and the Primary Student* (Burdett in Miller, 2003, pp. 44–55), Canadian teacher Lois Burdett offers a revelatory account of introducing grade 1 and 2 learners to elements of all of Shakespeare's plays. Burdett teaches in Stratford, Ontario, the site of an annual Shakespeare festival, and introduces her learners to a relevant detail of whichever play is to be performed in a compelling, even transformatory, manner. She suggests that the study of Shakespeare is a means to an end specifically in the areas of language development and the enhancement of communication skills.

EFL teachers should not ignore or bypass Shakespeare, nor do they have to take on the onerous responsibility of teaching entire plays. Rather, it is sufficient to introduce learners selectively to aspects of Shakespeare's plays. Indeed, Naomi Miller's inspiring collection, *Reimagining Shakespeare for Children and Young Adults*, includes numerous case studies and examples of successful introduction of Shakespeare in different learning situations, of which Burdett's example is only one. The crucial aim is to introduce the plays as performance texts, open to interpretation and subject to multiple meanings. Reading Shakespeare's plays will not be sufficient. It is crucial to give learners the experience of speaking, listening and performing the text to engage with it. Rich resources are available to support investigation of Shakespeare's plays as performance texts.

For example, *Sounding Shakespeare* (Pande-Rolfsen & Heide, 2019) is a recent active imaginative interdisciplinary English and Music project aiming to build confidence about teaching Shakespeare in Norwegian teacher trainees and "decrease the fear factor of using Shakespeare in the classroom" (p. 92). The project team, Marthe Sofie Pande-Rolfsen and Anne-Lise Heide, argue convincingly that positive experiences of studying Shakespeare must begin with teachers. "If pupils are to encounter Shakespeare in school, then student teachers should experience ways of working with Shakespeare during their teacher training" (p. 87). The project explores how creative cross-curricular approaches in English and music, which culminate in performance, can contribute to meaningful experiences of Shakespeare's text, in this case *A Midsummer Night's Dream*. The project demonstrates how both teacher-led and free play with language and sound can enthuse and empower learners to appreciate, own and perform Shakespeare's language successfully.

The British Royal Shakespeare Company website[124] provides a wealth of educational resources ranging from videos of workshops to research on how Shakespeare is taught around the world. This website will be valuable for teachers wishing to introduce their learners to Shakespeare's plays in performance.

It is also interesting and useful to spend a little time talking about the cultural world of the London theatres. This is made very much easier by the recent excavation and re-building of the Globe Theatre on London's South Bank. Images of the theatre and its status as a place of communal entertainment can give young learners a sense of actuality about Shakespeare's theatre and performances of the plays; well-illustrated texts such as Peter Crisp's *A Look Inside A Shakespearean Theatre* (1998) will be useful here. Shakespeare's Globe Theatre website provides information about current and past productions as well as educational resources for teachers and educational tours for classes of all ages; the website offers a virtual tour that can help to provide a tangible context when discussing the history and culture of Shakespeare's theatre.[125]

The adult experience of Shakespeare is an iterative one; enthusiasts and theatre-goers are likely to encounter many productions, versions and adaptations of the same text in their lifetimes. It is not a case that one version or one production will suffice; the pleasure lies in re-encountering Shakespeare, or as his first editors John Heminge and Henry Condell said, "Read him again and again" (Shakespeare, First Folio, 1623).

How to read Shakespeare – key moments or extracts

Since the recommended aim is introduction rather than complete coverage, it is appropriate to choose Shakespeare plays with themes and plots likely to appeal to the relevant learner age group. *Romeo and Juliet* is widely studied at

---

124 http://www.rsc.org.uk
125 www.shakespearesglobe.com

secondary level. *Macbeth*, *The Merchant of Venice*, *Twelfth Night* and *The Taming of the Shrew* are suggested as alternatives likely to be of interest and appeal to young people. For these plays, one way to approach the plot is to explore the choices that are made by the characters and discuss the advantages and disadvantages of the actions undertaken. Is Macbeth right to arrange for Banquo to be killed? Is it fair for Jessica to run away from her father Shylock (with his money too)? Is it wise for Romeo and Juliet to trust Friar Lawrence's plan and advice?

Whilst *Romeo and Juliet* is a love tragedy, offering opportunities to explore the romantic plot as well as the tragic conflict between the young lovers and their world, *Macbeth* offers a darker picture of ambition and conflict with exciting and unanticipated supernatural dramatic elements, which may appeal particularly to boys or reluctant readers. *The Merchant of Venice*, by contrast, offers a love plot, a consideration of gender roles and restrictions through cross-dressing and stark ethical dilemmas, involving racial and religious prejudice. The comedies *The Taming of the Shrew* and *Twelfth Night* have been freely adapted into American romances with contemporary settings in the films *Ten Things I Hate About You* (1999) and *She's the Man* (2006). The contrast in versions and adaptations of *Romeo and Juliet* is extreme and therefore very interesting. They range from Franco Zeffirelli's (1968) lavish period Italianate film production to Baz Luhrmann's (1996) action movie-style interpretation brought sharply up to date in America, to *West Side Story* (1961) in stage and screen versions, through to Malorie Blackman's teen series *Noughts & Crosses* (2001). See chapters 5 and 7 for further discussions on some of the titles mentioned above.

Pedagogic case study: *Macbeth*

EFL teachers are encouraged to explore *Macbeth*, which depicts profound personal dilemmas and choices, allowing young learners to engage with the emotions and responses of the characters. Macbeth is recommended as a play likely to appeal to boys due to its emphasis on action, war and the supernatural. The language of *Macbeth* is so powerful and immediate that short passages can be taken and used as a stimulus for a range of drama and language activities. Cheng and Wilson present powerful arguments for different approaches to *Macbeth* in the EFL classroom to motivate learners and energise usage of the target language.

> A social and playful learning process such as this, then, recognises students as resourceful language users and acknowledges their creativity in approaching new knowledge (Cheng and Wilson, 2011, p. 552).

Suggested starting points for working with *Macbeth* as a live performance text in the EFL classroom can include the following:

Moral debates

One powerful way to explore *Macbeth* through discussion or "hot-seating" is to focus on the moral status of actions. How acceptable is it, morally, to kill an armed soldier in battle? How acceptable to execute a rebel? How acceptable to kill a sleeping guest and kinsman? To have a friend and his child murdered? To arrange for women and children to be murdered in the absence of male protection? In debating the ethical status of each action, learners can be encouraged to read, dispute and appreciate the relevant passages from *Macbeth* as part of their debate, as well as understanding the plot progression. Enabling learners to focus on and explore each separate dilemma rather than getting entangled in the language is one of the most memorable ways to engage learners actively with key moments in the play.

Comparative productions of key scenes

Film can be one of the most effective resources for introducing learners to Shakespeare since the visual elements support and explicate the language and allow learners to engage strongly with incidents and events. Multiple film versions of *Macbeth* exist, and the recommendation would be to choose favourite passages from the play, work on the language in class giving learners full opportunity to explore situations in their own words, and then view and evaluate the scenes in key film productions (Polanski, 1971; Gold, 1983).

Multiple versions

There is also the option of using multiple versions of the texts in the classrooms. The graphic novel version of *Macbeth* (Oval projects 1982), which uses the full text, is so visually absorbing that students have been known to sit and read in class and be unwilling to stop. Equally, retellings such as Tony Bradman's *Macbeth* (2007), divided into five acts, or the prose version *Macbeth: A Shakespeare Story* by Andrew Matthews and Tony Ross (with notes on themes and Shakespeare's Globe at the end) are short and simply written. A different approach is to explore the engaging *I, Shakespeare* texts by actor and director Tim Crouch. These are well-known Shakespeare plays, re-told in monologues for young audiences by minor characters. *I, Banquo* begins with an electric guitar and Banquo's first-person memory of his friendship with and ultimate fear of Macbeth, who eventually arranges his murder. Banquo's teenage son, Fleance, provides the electric guitar accompaniment throughout and speaks his few lines from the play. The *I, Shakespeare* scripts are short, vivid, true to the play and contemporary in their tone.

Conclusion

The wealth of publications and resources dealing with Shakespeare are such that this can only be a starting point. Once teachers have experimented successfully with the activities suggested above, they are encouraged to investigate the wide and growing range of resources available.

Teachers are sometimes anxious about using drama or dramatic methods in the classroom, fearing loss of control, confusion or lack of learning. These examples have been set out to show that EFL teachers who are willing to take the relative risk of working with drama in the classroom can generate powerful, memorable and enjoyable language learning in a realistic, interactive context.

References

Adams, R. (Ed.). (1985). *Teaching Shakespeare: Essays on Approaches to Shakespeare in Schools and Colleges*. Robert Royce.
Aers, L., & Wheale, N. (Eds.). (1991). *Shakespeare in the Changing Curriculum*. Routledge.
Blackman, M. (2001). *Noughts & Crosses*. Corgi Books.
Bradman, T. (2007). *Macbeth*. A&C Black Publishers.
Carpenter, H. (1994). *Shakespeare Without the Boring Bits*. Viking.
Cheng, A.Y., & Winston, J. (2011). Shakespeare as a second language: Playfulness, power and pedagogy in the ESL Classroom. *RiDE: The Journal of Applied Theatre and Performance, 16*(4), 541–556.
Chrisp, P. (1998). *A Look Inside a Shakespearean Theatre*. Hodder Wayland.
Coles, J. (2009). Testing Shakespeare to the Limit: Teaching Macbeth in a Year 9 Classroom. *English in Education, 43*(1), 32–49.
Complicite UK. (2013). *Lionboy* [Play] *Corder Z* (Original author) http://www.complicite.org/
Crouch, T. (2011). *I, Shakespeare*. Oberon Books.
Cziboly, A. (2015). DICE – The impact of educational drama and theatre on key competences. *p-e-r-f-o-r-m-a-n-c-e, 2*(1–2). http://www.p-e-r-f-o-r-m-a-n-c-e.org/?p=2003
Doherty, B. (Author)., & O'Neill, R. (Script editor). (1998). *Dear Nobody*. [Play]. Collins.
Donaldson, J. (2000). *Monkey Puzzle*. Macmillan Children's Books.
Donaldson, J. (2006). *Play Time*. Macmillan Children's Books.
Donaldson, J. (2018). *Bombs and Blackberries*. Hodder Children's Books.
Donaldson, J. (2020). *Chariots and Champions*. Hodder Children's Books.
Eriksson, A.S., Heggstad, K.M., Heggstad K., & Cziboly Á. (2014). "Rolling the DICE". Introduction to the international research project Drama Improves Lisbon Key Competences in Education, Research in Drama Education: *The Journal of Applied Theatre and Performance, 19*(4), 403–408.

Fickman, A. (Director). (2006). *She's the Man*. [Motion Picture]. USA: Dreamworks SKG.

Firth, T. (2009). *The Flint Street Nativity*. [Playscript]. Samuel French.

Gold, J. (1983). *Macbeth*. [Television Series]. UK: British Broadcasting Corporation.

Gorjian B., Moosavinia S.R., & Jabripour, A. (2010). Dramatic Performance in Teaching Drama in EFL Contexts. *The Electronic Journal for English as a Second Language, 13*(4). http://www.tesl-ej.org/wordpress/issues/volume13/ej52/ej52a4/

Greenhalgh, S. (2009). Drama. In J. Maybin & N.J. Watson (Eds)., *Children's Literature: Approaches and Territories*. Palgrave Macmillan.

Haddon, M. (Writer), & Stephens, S. (Script editor). (2012). *The Curious Incident of the Dog in the Night-Time*. [Play]. Bloomsbury Methuen Drama.

Inkpen, M. (1993). *LullabyHullabaloo*. Hodder Children's Books.

Irish, T. (2011). Would you risk it for Shakespeare? A case study of using active approaches in the English classroom. *English In Education, 45*(1). doi: 10.1111/j.1754–8845.2010.01081.x

Junger, G. (Director). (1999). *10 Things I Hate About You*. USA: Buena Vista.

Kupfer, D.C. (2009). The Merchant of Venice: Schools, Libraries, and Censors. *Library Philosophy and Practice*. Paper 234. http://digitalcommons.unl.edu/libphilprac/234.

Landon Smith, K. (Director), Brahmachari, S. (Script editor), & Tan, S. (Original author). (2013). *The Arrival*. [Play]. Bloomsbury Methuen Drama.

Lear, E. (1871). The Owl and the Pussy-cat. In A. Sage (1995). *The Hutchinson Treasury of Children's Literature* (pp. 238–239). Random House.

Lurman, B. (1996). *Romeo + Juliet*. [Motion Picture]. USA: Twentieth Century Fox Film Corporation.

Matthews, A. (2003). *Macbeth: A Shakespeare Story*. Orchard Books.

Mcevoy, S. (2006). *Shakespeare: The Basics* (2nd ed.). Routledge.

Miller, N.J. (2003). *Reimagining Shakespeare For Children and Young Adults*. Routledge.

Mortimer, M. (Director). (1999). *The Flint Street Nativity*. [DVD]. IMC Vision.

Munden, J., & Myhre, A. (2011). *Twinkle Twinkle*. (2nd ed.). HøyskoleForlaget.

Nordin, N.A., Sharif, N.M., Fong, N.S., Mansor, W., & Zakaria, M.H. (2012). Fulfilling the tasks of reading, writing, speaking and listening through drama workshop. *Procedia – Social and Behavioral Sciences*. 66. http://dx.doi.org/10.1016/j.sbspro.2012.11.261

Norwegian Directorate for Education and Training. (2019/2020). English subject curriculum (ENG01-04). https://www.udir.no/lk20/eng01-04

Ntelioglou, B.Y. (2011). "But why do I have to take this class?" The mandatory Drama-ESL Class and Multiliteracies Pedagogy. *Ride: The Journal Of Applied Theatre And Performance, 16*(4), 595–615.

Pande-Rolfsen, M.S., & Heide, A-L. (2019). Sounding Shakespeare: An interdisciplinary educational design project in music and English. *Early Modern Culture Online, 7*(1), 87–104.

Polanski, R. (1971). *Macbeth*. [Motion Picture]. USA: Columbia Pictures.

Robbins, J., & Wise, R. (Directors). (1961). *West Side Story*. [Motion Picture]. USA: United Artists.

Rose, H. (Ed.). (2000). *Plays for Children*: Faber & Faber.

Rosen, M. (2007). *What's so special about Shakespeare?* Walker Books.

Shakespeare, W. (Author)., & Von (Illustrator). (1982). *Macbeth*. [Graphic novel]. Oval.

Shakespeare, W. (Author)., & Hinman, C. (Ed.). (1996). *First Folio of Shakespeare: The Norton Facsimile*. First published 1623. W. W. Norton & Company Inc.

The National Centre for Early Music. (2010). *York Mystery Plays*. Retrieved from http://www.yorkmysteryplays.org/

Walker, R. (1999). *Jack and the Beanstalk*. Barefoot Books.

Wallis, M., & Shepherd, S. (1998). *Studying Plays*. Arnold.

Whaley, A. (2011). 'I could teach you how to choose right': Using Holocaust memoir to teach Shakespeare's *The Merchant of Venice*. *Changing English: Studies in Culture and Education, 18*(4) 361–369.

Zeffirelli, F. (Director). (1968). *Romeo and Juliet*. [Motion Picture]. USA: Paramount Pictures.

Index

A

Aboriginal
   language 46
   way of life 38
action- and production-oriented 236, 237, 238
adaptation(s) 105, 150, 154, 156, 161, 212, 213, 216, 218, 225, 234, 236, 238, 239, 258, 259, 263, 271, 272, 274, 277, 287, 288, 291, 292
   as interpretation 277
   of novels 197
adapted learning 206, 213
adjectives 23, 48, 49, 50, 51, 76, 79, 130, 132
adventure page 28
anchorage 28
animal rights 156
archetypes 121
attitude 93, 96
audience 282, 287
authentic texts 9, 11, 17, 52, 59, 62, 99, 178
authors' websites 146, 190

B

Bildungsroman 148
black history 151
Black Lives Matter 247
black-out poetry 237

Book Clubs 190
book creator 209, 243
bullying 151

C

characters 31
Children's Laureate 146, 283
children's literature 31
children's literature awards 145
choice 17, 198
choosing texts 142
   select appropriate texts 98
choral reading 68, 185
Christmas nativity play 287
citizenship 91, 112, 143, 170, 288
classroom reading activities 160, 187, 189
climate change 150
climax of the story 27
close-up(s) 29, 51, 202, 219, 257, 259, 260, 262
   panels 216
co-authoring 25
codes of conduct 121
code-switching 107, 110
collaborative writing 246
collocations 50
colours 18, 27, 38, 39, 48, 55, 100, 101, 197, 212, 213, 290
comedy 120, 197

comics 22, 198
comic-strip features 39
competence aim 106, 162, 265
competent readers 197
counterpoint 22
coursebook 23
cover 18, 27
creative skills 51
creative writing 154
creativity 281
critical literacy 172, 244
critical thinking 172, 247
cross-curricular 18, 51, 130, 135, 142,
    182, 209, 247, 283
    perspective 27
    project between English and physical
        education 135
    teaching 164
cultural capital 289
culture capsule 100, 101, 103
curation 230

D
democracy 170, 216
didactic ideas 48
differentiation 13, 17, 83, 142, 145, 162,
    169, 178, 179, 181, 182, 191, 193, 213,
    236, 282
different learning styles 280
digital 229
    graphic novel 238
    literature 231
    media 229, 230
    media tools 229
    repository 181
    skills 229
    storytelling 230, 243
    technology 229
    text repositories 144
    timeline 230, 248

digitised literature 234
disability 106, 107, 159, 164, 175
disabled 97
Disney films 128
diverse 178
    abilities 170, 175
    texts 91, 92, 97, 112
diversity 169
double spread 19
drama 279, 282, 288
    benefits to learners 280
    group direction 286
dual address 23
dybdelæring 142
dyslexia 179

E
ecological message 38
EFL
    learner 22, 23
element of wonder 120
ELF 96
empathy 63, 141, 148, 164, 169, 172,
    174, 216, 241
empty space 232
endpapers 27
English and arts 18, 51
English in vocational study programmes
    242
enhancing interaction 34
equality 144, 164, 170, 176
    racial equality 182
ESL bits 234
exaggerated illustrations 34
extensive reading 12, 13, 23, 52, 144,
    165, 170, 186, 187, 188, 189, 191, 195
extracts of stories 18

F

fairness 178
fairy tale 22, 119
   as archetypes 126
   as texts for foreign language learning 129
   created by identifiable authors 121
   functions of 123
   gender patterns 128
   genre, structural functions and laws 120
   in the classroom 130
   literary 120
   modern 127
   narrative code 124
   oral form 120
   patterns 123
   reversed traditional 34
fantasy 197
fear factor 290
female roles 22
feminist fairy tales 128
fiction 232
   blog fiction 231
   fan fiction 232
   micro fiction 230, 245
   multimodal fiction 231
   Twitter fiction 232
fidelity 258
film 45
   adaption 14, 66, 128, 129, 259
first-person
   narration 271
   narrative 147
   narrator 31
flashback 257
flash-forward 262, 263
folk tale 121, 123
   epic laws 123
fonts 18, 27, 28, 39, 45
food 101, 107, 117
foreign language learning 22
format 27, 28
frame 28
free-verse poems 183
freezing the frame 259, 273
frequency 22

G

The Gambia 107, 111, 116
gaps 19, 199
gender 155, 183
gender roles 151
genre 22
Ghana 107
global citizenship 169
Global Englishes 10, 11, 13, 91, 94, 96, 98
graphic novel 197, 198, 199, 200, 202, 205, 206, 207, 208, 209, 212, 213, 217, 218, 219, 224, 225, 230
   adaptation 160, 212, 213, 214, 217
   vocabulary 201
graphics 256
gutter 200, 201, 205, 208, 209, 219

H

happy ending 120
hermeneutic circle 18
high-frequency adjectives 23
historic and mythological stories 197
humour 18, 34
hypotext 34

I

iconotext 19, 28
identity 183
illustrated books 19
illustrations 18, 27
incidents 120

inclusive 74, 112, 169, 170, 171, 172, 174, 182, 192, 283, 287
   learning 97, 112
inclusivity 138, 289
in-depth learning 142
India 95, 99, 101, 102, 105, 106, 113, 116, 117
Indian English 92, 95, 96, 107
intercultural
   awareness 241
   competence 11, 13, 61, 62, 91, 92, 93, 94
   learning 46
   understanding 46
interpretation 29, 58, 93, 173, 200, 201, 212, 213, 248, 258, 263, 272, 290, 292
intertextual 34, 39, 49, 219, 243
   competence 34
   references 184
intertextuality 31, 240
irony 22, 34

J
Jamaican patois 284

K
key scenes 219, 237, 258, 268, 277, 293

L
language
   awareness 91, 248
   input 23
   learning 199
layout 18
leitmotifs 24
LGBTQ 97, 174, 175, 183, 193, 243
library partnership 144
LibriVox 234
literacies 244
literacy 28, 51, 72, 224, 251
   relation between the visual and the verbal texts 199
   skill 197
   the new 28
literary awards 145
literary quality 144
literature circle 191, 212
LK20 9, 10, 11, 12, 13, 23, 46, 50, 92, 94, 96, 99, 111, 112, 141, 142, 146, 148, 169, 170, 172, 174, 206, 216
   competence aims 11, 12, 92, 99, 129, 135, 136, 141, 144, 172, 206, 229, 235, 238, 241, 242, 250, 258, 279
   Democracy and Citizenship 13, 94, 112, 148, 159, 163, 172
   Health and Life Skills 94, 146, 163
   interdisciplinary work 142
long shots 29, 51, 216, 257, 259
low-frequency adjectives 23

M
magic 120
meaning-making 17, 19
media 142, 143, 145, 152, 156, 158, 163, 164, 206, 224, 231, 237, 240, 245, 257, 258, 290
medium shots 29
mental health 147
meta-fiction 154
metafictive layers 39
metamorphosis 120
methods of communication 256
migration 46, 163
mimesis 201
mirrors 92, 121, 265
mise-en-scène 257, 260, 271
mode
   deep attention mode 231
   hyper-attention mode 231
model texts 76, 184, 185

moods 38, 213
motif 27, 120
motivation 27, 198, 280
movement 31
multi-cultural
　education 171
　picturebooks 46
multilingual 13, 62, 92, 111
multiliteracies 206, 280
multi-modal 62, 73, 142, 197, 198, 199, 206, 231, 250
multimodality 224
multi-modal versions 145
multiperspectivity 94
multi-text classroom 144, 162, 163
Myanmar 100, 101
Mystery Plays/York Mystery Plays 287

N

narration 19, 201, 231, 237, 242, 271, 274, 275
　first-person 244, 259, 263, 271
narrative 22, 23, 25, 27, 28, 48, 51, 52, 61, 72, 123, 124, 143, 145, 149, 150, 152, 154, 155, 156, 157, 158, 161, 162, 164, 178, 183, 185, 186, 198, 199, 200, 201, 205, 206, 212, 224, 234, 243, 257, 287, 288, 293
　desire 18
　skills 23
　voice 31
narrator 29, 34
natural environment 38
negative space 28
newspapers 22
Nigeria 95, 118
Nigerian English 95
nonsense 22
novelisation 271
nursery rhymes 22

O

oral tradition of storytelling 119
oral approaches 68
orienteering 135
original tales 120
outdoor learning 130
#ownvoices 99, 172, 175, 176, 177, 178, 183

P

panel(s) 203, 204, 205, 206, 208, 209, 212, 216
panoramic view 29
paper 27
paratext 27
passion for reading 143
peer recommendation 190
performance 72, 279, 282
perspective(s) 31, 34
picturebook 17, 19
　definition of 20
　learners making their own 51
　teaching potential 48
　the EFL potential 17
pictures 17, 31
picture-text interaction 18
playscripts 287
plot 31
plurivocal 94
podcasting 230, 247
poetry 59, 60
　and language learning 60
　anthologies 63, 64, 284
　as literature and art 61
　as song 75
　benefits 59, 63, 68, 72
　classic versus contemporary 65
　performance 62, 64, 72, 73, 74, 283
　walk 76, 78
　wall 65, 81

ways of reading 68
websites 67
writing 67, 76, 78
point of view 31
politics of representation 138
pop-up books 22
postmodern book 39
prejudice 148, 157, 158, 159, 164
pre-reading 185
professional digital competence 235
    Professional Digital Competence Framework for Teachers 235
Project Gutenberg 234
prompts 233, 244
Protestant work-ethic values 121

Q
quotes 250

R
racial difference 159
racial injustice 181
racism 150
reader expectations 18, 27
reader response theory 19
Reader's theatre 72, 238
    method 207
reading 169
    comprehension 197
    experience 213
    for pleasure 187, 198
    process 199, 224
    role models 181
Reading Age/Interest Age 179
Reading Circles 190
refugee 158
relay 28
reluctant readers 17, 156, 169, 197, 198
    reluctant adult readers 180
repetition 22

rise of the middle class 125
Romanticism 121

S
schema 240
seasons 38
setting 29
sexuality 155
Shakespeare 289
    how to read Shakespeare 291
    Macbeth 292
six-word stories 246
skills 244
slam poetry 74
sliding doors 111
social
    class 48, 171, 176, 273, 275
    media 110, 233, 245, 247
    positions 34
specific vocabulary 22
spoken word 74
stage adaptations 288
stereotypical characters 119
stories 119
student-active ways of working 245
subversive rhymes 128
superheroes 197
sustainability 94
symbol 27

T
teenage 152
teenage readers 143, 146
    ages 11–13 148
    features of teen fiction 147
telling tales 122
texts, how to choose 144, 145
themes of the tales 125
title 27
title page 18, 27

traditional tales 120
transport 101

U
U-shaped plot 120

V
verbal and visual modalities 197
verbal text 17, 31
verse novels 13, 170, 182, 185, 194
visual impact 45
visual literacy 94, 199, 217
vocabulary 22, 23, 48, 49, 50, 55, 61, 91, 103, 116, 117, 119, 130, 131, 132, 134, 135, 137, 187, 191, 200, 212, 243, 257, 282, 283, 285

vocational 142, 143, 180, 258
   English 169
   learners 162, 240

W
ways of reading 160, 191
whole stories 18
windows 92, 93, 101
working class 28, 34, 97, 177
writing
   frame 78, 79
   prompts 78